D0933649

For Sandra —
With warm wishes —
Jerry Porthub
June 6, 2005

An Adventure in Education

An Adventure in Education

The College of Wooster

from

Howard Lowry

to the

Twenty-First Century

JERROLD K. FOOTLICK

The Kent State University Press

KENT, OHIO

The photograph on the front of the dust jacket is by Matt Dilyard, official photographer of The College of Wooster. In the two eight-page photo inserts, Dilyard also made the photos of Ray McCall, Ted Williams, Gordon Tait, Steve Moore, Maria Sexton, Mark Wilson, David Gedalecia, Hayden Schilling, Flo and Stan Gault, and all of the photos except for the one of Kauke Arch. Some of the other photos appeared in issues of the *Index* or *Voice*, which are in Special Collections, but the photographers, who may have been students, cannot be determined. Others of the earlier photos were almost certainly made by Rod Williams and Art Murray for the College and by Bert Bond for the *Daily Record*.

To the memory of Art Murray, whose love for Wooster was unbounded,
and whose many beneficences, often unsung, were immeasurable

And to the "Readers," Bob Tignor, Gene Bay, Mary Neagoy,
who contributed so much to the College once again,
as they have for their adult lives

And to Ceil,
Always

Contents

Preface

To be invited by my colleagues on the Board of Trustees to write the modern history of The College of Wooster is an honor. The author of two earlier volumes, Lucy Lillian Notestein, was a distinguished graduate of the College, whose father was a member of its first graduating class in 1873 and of its faculty for fifty-five years. Perhaps no better distinction exists between the modest Wooster she described in its earlier days and the aspirational College of today than the titles of the three volumes. The first two were both called *Wooster of the Middle West.* We do not call this volume Wooster of the World, but it would hardly be inappropriate.

My connections are more modest than Notestein's, but I am not bereft. When my family moved to Wooster in 1942, four faculty families were our neighbors, less than two blocks from campus. My father, a pharmacist, organized and supplied the pharmacy for the Navy V-5 unit during World War II (one benefit was tickets to the Tommy Dorsey Spotlight Bands concert). As a boy walking up Bever Street to watch football or baseball practice on campus, I was greeted by Prexy Wishart from his retirement front yard. I knew Howard Lowry first while I was a teenager, then as a Wooster student, and afterward he was a friend. I believe I can fairly call each of his successors as president—Garber Drushal, Henry Copeland, Stan Hales, and Grant Cornwell—a friend. I have been a trustee of the College since 1978 (with one short break) and am now an emeritus life trustee. I could not begin to name my warm ties to other alumni, trustee colleagues, and faculty; suffice it to say that on research trips to Wooster, I regularly visited Lowry Center, where a group of retired faculty gathers every morning for coffee and gossip.

This volume can be distinguished from Notestein's in a number of other ways, beginning with perspective. Notestein wrote that as she was still working on the manuscript for the second volume in the 1960s, Lowry, her friend, insisted that the book end in 1944, without any discussion of his presidency; the volume should allow for historical perspective. My marching orders from the Board of Trustees were to bring the history as closely up to date as reasonable; we agreed to end with the spring 2012 dedication of the Scot Center. Some would say, to paraphrase a Truman Capote complaint about another writer's work, that writing about events this close to the present is not history, it's just journalism. So be it. In a similar vein, I occasionally use quotes without attribution, as I promised the speakers I would. This fits my mantra for the book: it is intended to tell a story, as fairly and accurately as possible, even when the information is unpleasant; this is not, after all, a coffee-table picture book. But neither The College of Wooster nor anyone associated with it should be embarrassed.

We worked to make the book both informative and readable (even, it might be hoped, sometimes entertaining). One way to confirm this goal is that readers, certainly including loyal alumni, say to themselves or others a number of times, "Gee, I didn't know that." I made some other decisions in consultation with my first readers. One concerns names. Thus, it is Stan Gault, not Stanley C. Gault; Ted Williams, not Theodore Roosevelt Williams; Carol Dix, not Carolyn Dix or Mrs. Raymond E. Dix, as she was identified in catalogs. I conducted scores of formal interviews and scores more fruitful informal conversations, and I spent uncountable hours in Special Collections (the College archives). I use footnotes sparingly. In the endnotes, I do not list the source for every fact or quotation; rather, I provide the general sources for all the facts and quotations in each chapter. Anyone who wants to pursue them can do so—and this is important: All of the research material, including transcripts of the interviews, can be found in Special Collections.

Among the earliest interviewees were three people I considered vital to the story: Clare Adel Schreiber, wife of the chairman of the Department of German, close friend of Lowry's, longtime director of the College nursery school; Bill Kieffer, among the most eminent chemists in Wooster's chemistry department; Vi Startzman Robertson, beloved both as director of the College health service and within the city of Wooster, where the Viola Startzman Free Clinic stands in tribute. All of them, now gone, were in their nineties when I interviewed them, all of them mentally alert. Al Van Wie, dedicated alumnus, basketball coach, athletic director, campaigned hard to make this project happen. Al died a few weeks before the manuscript was completed; he is the person I regret most not seeing the finished product.

A note about organization: One obvious pattern would have been to trace the College history chronologically from 1944 to 2012. Yet, so many important topics range through nearly the entire period that to drop them into each chapter would be to minimize their impact. These include religion and religious studies, issues of race, the role of female faculty, buildings, sports. So the book first covers the Lowry years chronologically, follows with topical chapters, then returns to chronology for later years. This might guide those with particular interest in certain topics or certain years.

It hardly needs saying how much advice and cooperation the author of a history like this needs. Obviously, those who gave their time and thought to the formal interviews were critically important, and many others offered helpful information. Not everyone who contributed can be mentioned here, but a few must be, beginning with my friends and colleagues on the Board of Trustees, led by its chairman Jim Wilson, who brought me to the project, and his supportive successor, Dave Gunning. Sally Whitman currently holds the title executive assistant for presidential events, but having served in the president's office since 1985, she could be more accurately described as its institutional memory; she smoothed my task in innumerable ways. On the matter of support, thanks must go to Ken Bogucki, general manager of the Wooster Inn, and the Inn's guest services manager, Kathy Kruse, whose generosity made my frequent visits comfortable and pleasant.

The publisher of this third volume of Wooster's history—as with the first two volumes—is the Kent State University Press. The professionalism of its staff, guided by Director Will Underwood, eased an always difficult task. I thank the managing editor, Mary Young. And I thank especially Erin Holman for her dedicated and thoughtful, even witty, editing.

It simply would not have been possible to produce this book without Special Collections at the College. Denise Monbarren, its skilled and extremely well-organized director, and her associates responded to every need and request with care, patience, and good humor. For most of my research time, Denise's deputy, Elaine Smith Snyder, also provided unfailing aid. Denise chooses and trains a group of careful, hardworking interns; among the several I worked with, I must mention Kelsey Williams, class of 2014, and Dan Grantham and Katie Morton, class of 2013. The interns also searched the archives for photographs; in this area I thank Tammy Troup, who prepared the photos for publication, and offer very special thanks to Matt Dilyard, the College photographer since 1994, who pored through his own voluminous and valuable files.

Now to my first readers. We agreed at the start that the book needed additional eyes and judgments from trustees with extraordinary knowledge, background, and dedication to the College. I cannot imagine how the three people I asked could have been more supportive or more generous. They spent many hours studying draft chapters. They made numerous comments and suggestions—combining warmth and authority. All are alumni and trustees (two now emeritus). In order of seniority (and with only brief mention of their many accomplishments), they are Bob Tignor, Rosengarten Professor of Modern and Contemporary History, Emeritus, at Princeton University, and for fifteen years chairman of its Department of History. Gene Bay, retired pastor and head of staff at the Bryn Mawr Presbyterian Church and retired president of the Colgate Rochester Crozer Divinity School. Mary Neagoy, former vice president of corporate communications at NBC and senior vice president of communications for MTV Networks; she is a former president of the Wooster Alumni Association and a current trustee. I cannot thank them enough.

The readers actually were second in line to see the various iterations of this manuscript. Ceil Cleveland, my wife, sees everything first. Ceil, a graduate of a liberal arts college, has been a university professor, founding editor of an Ivy League university magazine, vice president of a research university, and author of both textbooks and novels. I bow to her skills and devotion to writing and editing. And I thank her for her contributions here.

Jerrold K. Footlick
Durham, North Carolina

PART 1

The Lowry Years

CHAPTER 1

A Visionary Arrives

We have never assumed here that a senior with a diploma is an educated
man. Who, indeed, ever is? He is a potentially educated man, who knows
how to continue his education to the very end of his life.

HOWARD LOWRY

Baccalaureate, June 4, 1967

This story begins with Howard Lowry—how could it not begin with Howard Lowry, who brought to The College of Wooster the academic standard
that for nearly three-quarters of a century has distinguished it from other
outstanding liberal arts colleges; the scholar admired and honored on
both sides of the Atlantic; the orator with a baritone so mellifluous that
his lectures sounded operatic; the nineteenth-century Romantic who
cherished the company of attractive young women yet somehow could
not bring himself to marry one; the stalwart campus leader who, as his
intellect and very life ebbed in the mid-1960s, appeared perplexed by
a new generation of students unappreciative of the stability offered by
Wooster's religious history and traditional calm.

Let us start with the story of how Lowry was almost accidentally offered the presidency of the College, third choice of a frustrated Board of
Trustees to follow Prexy Wishart's twenty-five year reign.

Charles F. Wishart, a Presbyterian minister from Chicago who came
to The College of Wooster as president in 1919 and led it through the
Roaring Twenties and the Great Depression and into World War II, had

announced that he would give up his position on July 1, 1944. Small in stature and cherubic in mien, Wishart had earned the fond soubriquet "Prexy," but he was no soft touch. In 1923, barely into his presidency, this unheralded leader of a small college in Ohio stood as the progressive candidate for moderator of the Presbyterian Church USA and defeated the fundamentalist legend William Jennings Bryan in the most bitterly contested election the church had ever known.

Now he was going, but the committee charged with choosing his successor, led by the chief justice of the Supreme Court of Ohio, Wooster alumnus Carl V. Weygandt, felt confident about its task. It was as if a puff of white smoke had floated instantly through the ceiling of the meeting room; committee members had only to turn to their own leader, the chairman of the College's Board of Trustees, for a new president. He was Arthur Holly Compton, a scion of the most notable family Wooster had ever produced. Compton's father, Elias, had been a professor of philosophy and dean of the College for thirty-two years and his mother, Otelia, its de facto First Lady, presiding from their modest frame Victorian on College Avenue, a gathering place for faculty and students and every important person who ever came to Wooster. One Compton son would go on to become president of the Massachusetts Institute of Technology; another would become president of Washington State University, and the only daughter, "the smartest of the bunch," a family member said, would marry a university president.

Arthur Compton was then a professor of physics at the University of Chicago. But he was already internationally renowned, winner of the 1927 Nobel Prize in Physics, at the age of thirty-five, for his demonstration of the particle concept of electromagnetic radiation, what is known to this day as the Compton effect. Who better to lead his alma mater? Yet when his friend Carl Weygandt approached him, Compton seemed oddly reluctant. He was flattered and honored, but it was not a good time; he was working on a project that could not be interrupted.

What Compton could not tell the Wooster suitors—just as he could not even tell Robert Maynard Hutchins, the president of his own university—was that this was an element of the Manhattan Project. In a row of onetime squash courts, under the grandstand of Stagg Field, essentially abandoned since the university abandoned intercollegiate football, Compton and his closest colleague, the Italian immigrant physicist Enrico Fermi, had created a plutonium chain reaction that could trigger an atomic bomb, which, if their experiment had gone awry, might have destroyed not only the Hyde Park campus but most of the South Side of Chicago. When the reaction was touched off and proved successful, Compton could call chemist James Bryant Conant, president of Harvard University and chairman of a secret committee designated to explore the possibilities of wartime use of nuclear fission, and inform him, in the famous coded words, "Our Italian navigator has just landed in the new world." Conant would reply, "Were the natives friendly?" and Compton: "Everyone landed safe and happy." This accomplishment led to the hurried construction of Oak Ridge, an entire new city in the Cumberland mountains of East Tennessee, to house a production facility that Compton left Chicago to oversee.

None of that would be known to the world, however, until August 6, 1945, and the Wooster trustees had to look elsewhere. After sorting through nearly a hundred possibilities, they soon settled on a second choice, John Bruere, a Presbyterian minister who had been the activist, quick-witted dean of men at the College for six years. Now, fairly near Wishart's retirement date, word leaked that Bruere was the choice, and several faculty leaders confronted trustee chairman Compton at the family home on College Avenue. If Bruere were to become president, they suggested, he could be met by a faculty rebellion. The trustees agonized, finally backed off—and Bruere, learning the harsh news, instantly resigned. (He soon accepted a pastorate in inner-city Cleveland, where he served admirably for more than two decades.)

Having swung and missed twice, the trustees were cautious. One question particularly troubled them. The College of Wooster was owned by the Presbyterian Church, and each of its six presidents had been a Presbyterian clergyman. Wishart thought his successor should be as well, a spiritual leader and fund-raiser for the campus, leaving to a dean the primary academic responsibilities. That's how Wishart was remembered by one of his admirers, Bill Kieffer, the eminent chemist who taught at Wooster for nearly four decades. As an undergraduate, Kieffer had been, in his own word, a "handyman" for the Wishart family, raking leaves, serving dinner, standing as a butler at social events. "Prexy Wishart was primarily a pastor," Kieffer said. "He was great at preaching sermons and was really a wonderful fellow. But he was just not an academic." Several board members, including some clergymen, also questioned Wishart's view of the presidency.

During the discussion, Lowry, a former faculty member at Wooster who had become a trustee when he left to join the English department at Princeton University, offered his opinion: "My leaning would be an educator. What I distrust is the feeling that the only spiritual leadership in this country comes from the ministry; for there is a type of person rising on the university campus who, in his quite simple but genuine religious feeling, is going to impress students more than a preacher."

In fact, Lowry, something of a golden boy at Wooster, had long been thought of as a presidential possibility. As a student, he roomed with the Elias Compton family and was appointed to the English faculty immediately upon his graduation in 1923. In describing a group of young faculty who joined the College during the 1920s, chronicler Lucy Lillian Notestein said: "Of all the others, Howard Lowry was the most brilliant, with a mind that flashed like a lighthouse in the darkness yet with the difference that one couldn't predict just when or where it would suddenly illumine the mind's landscape with a phrase or an interpretation; one knew only that moment would come. His classes were an experience to be long remembered."

While remaining on the Wooster faculty, Lowry earned a PhD at Yale University and built a career as a Matthew Arnold scholar; in 1934 he was appointed general editor of the American arm of the Oxford University Press. Although this opportunity led Lowry to commute frequently by Pennsylvania Railroad between Wooster and New York—the train made regular stops at a now-razed station at the east end of Liberty Street—and occasionally to spend a week or more in the city, the College thought him too valuable to complain about the schedule. In his productive stint with the press, Lowry shepherded scores of manuscripts, among them *The Oxford Companion to American Literature* and the book he said he would most liked to have written, Samuel Eliot Morison and Henry Steele Commager's classic text, *The Growth of the American Republic*. Finally, in 1940, the lure of the East became too strong, and he left Wooster for Princeton.

Although still closely connected to Wooster as a trustee, Lowry had not been formally considered for the presidency, but with the position still open, several professors who were former colleagues weighed in on his side; so did the board chairman, Compton, who was a close personal friend. At a May 12, 1944, Board of Trustees meeting, Weygandt, with perhaps something less than enthusiasm, announced Lowry's nomination for president.

Howard Foster Lowry was that day two months short of his forty-third birthday. He was tall, dark, and handsome, possessed of a commanding manner and a voice that spellbound audiences old and young. Cosmopolitan, European-traveled, charming in any circle, he was comfortable with men and catnip to women. A lifelong bachelor, Lowry had come close to marrying more than once; his closest romantic relationships may have ended for different reasons, but there appeared to be one constant: his widowed mother, Daisy Lowry, who lived with him in Princeton and moved with him to the president's home in Wooster, where she remained until her death in 1960.

The campus Howard Lowry took charge of in 1944 was unlike it had ever been in its seventy-eight year history. It was a small college in a small town in the midst of a world war. Less than three months after D-Day, American soldiers had broken free of the hedgerows of Normandy and marched triumphantly down the Champs-Élysées, while Marines had died by the hundreds on blood-soaked sand and terrifying cliffs to wrest Guam back from the Japanese. The College's enrollment, more than 1,000 before the war, had dwindled to about 550, civilians, that is—of whom 466 were girls.[1] The few boys were either seventeen-year-olds squeezing in a year of college before military service (Stan Gault, Wooster High School Class of 1943, was among them) or those designated 4-F, rejected by the military for physical reasons, often an embarrassment in those keenly patriotic days.

But upwards of six hundred other students dominated the campus during the 1943–44 academic year, cadets in what was officially known as the Naval Flight Preparatory School, or more popularly, the Navy V-5 program. At the start of the war, the savvy Wishart understood the potential risk to the College's enrollment and finances; just after Pearl Harbor, he wrote government authorities offering Wooster as a military training site, then went to Washington to lobby the navy. The first V-5 cadets arrived in January 1943, and the navy all but took over the campus in those war years. To provide housing for the cadets, freshmen boys were moved out of Douglas Hall and freshman girls out of Hoover Cottage; other cadets lived and ate in Kenarden Lodge. V-5 used Kauke, Scovel, Taylor, and Severance halls for classes, marching between them in formation, and Severance

1. At this time, college students were *girls* and *boys*, and they will be addressed as such, until in the 1960s, when they evolved into *women* and *men*.

Gymnasium for exercises. Most of the instructors were Wooster faculty members who retrained to teach outside their field of expertise: among them, geologist Charley Moke in mathematics; biologist Warren Spencer in physics; and an eclectic array of teachers in navigation, including two coaches, L. C. Boles and Johnny Swigart, as well as economist Kingman Eberhart, George Bradford from English, even Dan Parmelee, director of the Wooster Symphony. To further the war effort, a few College faculty members stepped even further outside their fields of expertise: after his classroom day ended, Willy Schreiber, longtime chairman of the German department, went to work at the Bauer Ladder Company; his wife, Clare Adel, remembered that their small sons weren't impressed with a college professor father but were very proud of their dad working in a war plant.

The navy, of course, paid for what it used, which benefited not only the College but also the city of Wooster, largely through a contract that allowed the College to buy supplies, including food, from local merchants and farmers. (The city contributed to the war effort in a variety of ways: one of its leading industries, Gerstenslager's, manufactured shell casings for artillery rounds.) But just as important, since this was the closest most of the townsfolk got to participating in the war effort, citizens reveled in events small and large, navy officers playing slow-pitch softball against Wooster businessmen, or the famous Tommy Dorsey performing as part of the nationally broadcast Coca-Cola Spotlight Bands series. Students lined up for hours waiting for the band bus to arrive, then they and a few fortunate townspeople packed Severance Gym into a fire marshal's nightmare.

V-5 was fundamentally a serious business, young men training to fly Wildcats and Hellcats off aircraft carrier decks. But they were more than ready to have fun during brief hours of liberty. The cadets organized dances in Douglas and the gym—there was usually a major dance as each battalion finished its tour at Wooster—to which they invited girls from the community as well as the campus, and College girls entertained the cadets at dances and mixers. The social events were well chaperoned, to be sure, by officers' wives and College families, since these boys were not seventeen or 4-F; mostly college age, they were smart enough and sturdy enough to pass stringent recruiting tests and sported the swagger common to fighter pilots. Small wonder that College girls faced parietal restrictions unknown even in older, darker ages on campus—some of which were not removed until years later.

These were bright young kids, though, and they did not always follow rules as strictly as their elders might have liked or even known about. Girls who were on campus then remembered (even some seven decades later) open windows in the back of Holden Hall out of which a few of their number fled for clandestine dates—late-night toboggan rides in winter, strolls near Miller Lake or on the golf course. Although each battalion of V-5 cadets was on campus only for three months, a number of marriages—lasting marriages—grew from these wartime romances. Vivian Douglas, who grew up thirteen miles from Wooster, in the village of Dalton, met a cadet from Iowa named Dave Smith in the fall of 1944; they wrote to each other nearly every day but didn't see each other again until the next spring. Their marriage, begun not long after war's end, lasted more than sixty years.

To be clear, the V-5 presence was only part of Wooster students' experiences during World War II. The class of 1947 lived through some of the most remarkable experiences imaginable. These students spent their last year in high school during the trying early stage of the war, then their first year in college (Lowry's first year as president) as the tide turned. Each Wednesday morning during the war, at precisely 10:25, the Chapel bell would toll for one full minute, while students paused between classes in respect to Wooster men serving overseas. One of them, leaving for the Marine Corps, wrote in a girl friend's *Index* (school yearbook): "If those white buildings are still gleaming in the sunshine on the Hill (I guess you don't realize that they do gleam until you leave), if those beautiful Elms are still standing on the quadrangle . . . I'll somehow be assured that a good life still awaits me there. . . . Keep pumping the plasma into Wooster. When this thing is over I want to come back to a place that is alive!" The girls did their part for the war effort. They volunteered with the Red Cross and at the local hospital. They made and altered their own clothes and were known to sew a classmate into a gown for a dance, then cut her out of it afterward. Deprived of silk stockings and nylons, they painted their legs tan with liquid cosmetics. They also gained equality, after a fashion: in 1944 the College designated smoking rooms in girls' dormitories, just like the boys' dorms.

At the same time, the 1944–45 student handbook informed the girls that "quiet hours" were in force from 8 P.M. until 6 A.M. Sunday through Friday, that they were to be in their dorms by 10 P.M. on weekdays, 10:30 P.M. on Fridays, and 11:30 P.M. on Saturdays. Further, it ordered, "There

shall be no motoring whatsoever outside the city limits without permission from the Dean of Women" and stated, "Bumming [hitch-hiking] is
forbidden." A few coed rules were also noted: "In social affairs, young
men are expected to conform to the regulations adopted by the Women's
Self-Government Association," and "It has been the custom of the student
body since 1916 to have no dates at football games." President Lowry's
handbook greeting began, "Inasmuch as you and I are both new at
Wooster this fall, I feel a special bond between us." It could be assumed,
however, that he was not subject to the list of "Freshman Rules" contained
in the handbook: "Freshmen shall wear their Freshman caps [beanies]
until Christmas vacation unless they outpoint the Sophomores in the
annual Bag-Rush held the first Saturday of the school year, in which case
the caps are discarded at Thanksgiving time. . . . Freshmen men must tip
their caps to all women on the campus. . . . Freshmen must not walk on
the grass of the campus. . . . Freshmen are required to gather wood for
the bon-fires during football season. . . . Freshmen are expected to visit
upperclassmen as soon as possible and to make friends with them."

The navy notified the College in the spring of 1944 that it was winding
down its flight preparatory program, and by the time the last battalion
graduated in October 1944, an estimated four thousand cadets had attended the small college. But in July Wooster became the site for a new
preflight program, the Naval Academic Refresher Unit. These cadets
were not raw recruits but rather seasoned men from the fleet, plus some
Marines and Coast Guardsmen, who were to train as combat pilots. Although its numbers were smaller, the naval presence at the College did
not end until February 1946, by which time the trainees were mixing with
the earliest batch of returning GIs, newly minted civilians. The College
celebrated its military contribution with a Testimonial Dinner at Babcock
Hall on February 4, 1946, at which the dozens of faculty members who
had taught cadets were honored.

In the meantime, there was a college to attend to. Lowry had spent
part of the summer winding down his Princeton affairs while actively setting a team in place. He recruited his old friend Bill Taeusch, an English
professor at Western Reserve University, to succeed the retired William
Westhafer as dean of the college. Myron Peyton arrived in Spanish and
Bill Craig in speech, and Fran Guille, a graduate of the College who had
taught off and on, became acting dean of women. (The *Index* observed

that she was one of the best-dressed women on campus and made most of her own clothes.) The year was to have its unpleasantness. The football team, where the roster changed every week as V-5 cadets moved in and out, lost all of its five games, finishing the only nonwinning season in Wooster's history. More seriously, Bill Syrios, who owned the Shack, the snack bar across Pine Street from the campus, suffered a stroke, before slowly recovering. Saddest of all, Otelia Compton, widow of the College's first dean and Lowry's hostess when he was a student, died on December 15, 1944, at the age of eighty-six.

Still, Lowry began his first academic year September 1, 1944 with the war winding down and aspirations rising. In his October 1944 inaugural address, he glowed with pride. "A college is the corner of men's hearts where hope has not died," he began. "The art of a college is the shaping of human life, under benefit of fact, in terms of what we hope." Lowry promised that within a year the College would publish a document outlining its academic plans. Then he hinted at some possible elements: "Personally, I want to see here a carefully integrated pattern of education, with some organic life of its own, culminating in independent work during junior and senior years." Later in his speech, he returned to the theme: "As the crown of [a student's] work—and it is the crown—he offers a senior thesis. . . . This is not a program for honors students alone. It is a challenge to every man and woman to come to his best, according to his capacity." Such education "represents an aristocratic education on democratic principles. . . . The student ceases to be the passive recipient of information; he participates in his own education, and develops habits that look forward to his continuing his liberal studies to the end of his life."

True to the new president's promise, in December 1945 the College published a pamphlet titled "Wooster: Adventure in Education." It was nothing short of a manifesto—describing in considerable detail what a Wooster education was and what it was intended to become. No author was credited, but judging from its vision and its sophisticated language (as well as its several references to the College's president, who was never named), this could only have been Lowry. Not every element from that essay remains a rule of the College, but its most important elements do—in particular, the most important intellectual exercise the College has ever known—and so much of Lowry's thinking retains contemporary influence that it deserves lengthy quotation.

We believe our new program is so fundamental, so squarely based on the deep, quiet things of the human spirit and on whatever has silently civilized men and given them true pleasure through the years, that it will cause no particular commotion except in the student who follows it. . . .

We believe, moreover, that all liberal education is a continuing education. It offers increase and renewal till the very end of life. . . . A liberal education, with such a content and a method, is clearly a vocational asset. We have too long apologized for its so-called impracticality, and it is high time we stopped doing so.

As part of its program, the College inaugurates a special plan of upperclass study. . . . The term "independent study" is an attempt to suggest the heart of the upperclass program and the human adventure it encourages. . . . What Wooster seeks, at least, is a four-year program in which there is constant progression and a degree of culmination, with the student more and more participating in his own education.

. . . The crown of independent study is the senior essay or problem. . . . *Independent study is not reserved for the intellectually elite alone,* for foreordained members of Phi Beta Kappa. . . . The new program is democratic and aristocratic at once—aristocratic in that it challenges a student to come to his own best; democratic, in that it offers the opportunity and challenge to everyone. It is not a program limited to honors students alone. Every man and woman is potentially an honors candidate, allowed the chance to find himself even after a possibly slow start. . . . His final hard-won laurels often come as a shock to him and to his friends. But this shock is a wonderful thing to watch when it happens. It can be one of the honest triumphs in education. And the one to whom it happens will feel its force for the rest of his natural life. . . . Independent study gives to the main business of college the element of participation that through the years has given meaning to athletics, dramatics, and other "activities." It makes study itself an "activity." . . .

The direction of independent work must not, of course, load a faculty simply with an extra chore. Otherwise the whole plan becomes a farce or takes from the teacher an unwise amount of time and energy. . . . All this demands a larger faculty than otherwise would be required; but it is our belief that no money spent for higher education could be better spent.

It is also our thought that this program is particularly appropriate for a Christian college. The very essence of Christianity is its stress on the importance of the individual life. . . . At the heart of Wooster's adventure is the Christian religion. The evangelical Christian faith brought the college into being as a Presbyterian institution under the care of the Synod of Ohio. . . . Although the spirit of its own denomination prevails at Wooster, the college attracts many students of other religious groups, who do not find the campus "appallingly Presbyterian." . . . In short, the living spirit of evangelical Christianity, under the auspices of a great Church that has always loved learning, is the heart of Wooster. . . . [2]

To aid the faculty in its own adventure, the College has inaugurated a new program of research and sabbatical leaves that we believe to be one of the most generous in the country. Any professor wishing to engage in research or writing will, upon proper application, be permitted a year's leave of absence every fifth year with full salary. . . . On the other hand, Wooster does not hold for a narrow definition of "research," or that research must invariably issue in successful publication. The College will never judge its teachers by the weight of their annual bibliographies nor honor the mere proliferation of triviality.

There, Lowry offered a vision that in many respects still guides the College. Perhaps not the strenuous emphasis on the "Christian college of liberal arts and sciences," an assurance offered quite consciously by a deeply religious man who was also its first president not to be an ordained Presbyterian minister. And the College has grown to double the size Lowry thought ideal. But his fierce argument for the lifelong value of a liberal arts education—and, indeed, its practicality in the marketplace—continues to stand true. And most of all, this introduction of Independent Study for every student—"And the one to whom it happens will feel its force for the rest of his natural life"—plus a remarkably generous small-college research leave program for faculty remain true.

Now, nearly seven decades later, as anyone ever associated with The

2. According to Presbyterian clergy who have examined this text, Lowry is here using the term "evangelical Christianity" in its traditional sense, to indicate a tradition in keeping with the life and teaching of Jesus, not as Christian social conservatives later came to appropriate the term.

College of Wooster knows—for that matter, anyone cognizant of American higher education knows, for this is a nationally admired plan—Independent Study continues to be the hallmark of a Wooster education. It is the single intellectual element that distinguishes Wooster from dozens of other quality liberal arts institutions; Howard Lowry would be proud of its lasting impact. Indeed, one might identify Lowry as the most influential single figure in the College's history, more than Louis Holden, who as president led its rebirth after the catastrophic fire of 1902; more than Elias Compton, who served as dean for more than three decades and fathered Wooster's First Family; more than anyone else.

Still, in many respects Wooster in the twenty-first century would be almost unrecognizable to Lowry. The College of Wooster has never been a revolutionary kind of place. But since 1944 it has evolved—has it ever!—in so many ways. As this devoted and devout Presbyterian wrote in his first "Adventure in Education": "At the heart of Wooster's adventure is the Christian religion. The evangelical Christian faith brought the college into being as a Presbyterian institution." It is fair to observe that evangelical Christianity is now far from the heart of campus life, academically or socially.

In Lowry's era, a singular group of female scholars, nearly all of them hired by Prexy Wishart, at salaries lower than the men were receiving—these women couldn't, after all, get jobs at the major universities that had awarded them PhDs, and almost all of them were single—were towering figures on campus: Dunham, Thayer, Johnson, Coyle, Guille, Ihrig, and others. When this cadre retired, the roster of female scholars diminished to a stalwart few, only to return in full bloom as new generations of women, equally well prepared—but, significantly, mostly married, with children, usually outspoken feminists—took their places at the College's highest levels.

The College's finances, its endowment essentially managed during the early days by a covey of local businessmen from a corner drugstore booth and its revenue almost unable to dent the operating budget, let alone build the endowment, were a frequent concern for trustees, although perhaps not Lowry, who didn't much worry about those things. He was known to refer occasionally to a deus ex machina check in his pocket, although no one else was ever sure about such a check or its authorizer. Today, an endowment in the hundreds of millions is carefully structured by a group of dedicated professionals.

Academically, Wooster has eliminated a year of required Bible-based courses and added a host of new majors, from archaeology to women's, gender, and sexuality studies, from biochemistry to computer science. It has changed the calendar from semesters to quarters and back again. As something of a companion to I.S., it has instituted a freshman program to serve as an introduction to scholarly life, which itself has been revised several times over the years. It doesn't even have "freshmen" anymore; these students are "first-years."

In sports, it has advanced from five intercollegiate teams, all male, to twenty-one, eleven of them female. And the athletic department that once consisted of five men, its roster unchanged since the 1920s, took a surprising turn in 1949 when Wooster hired as its football coach an unknown high school teacher from Defiance, Ohio, who spent his spare time writing poetry and painting on barn siding. Admittedly, Wooster's football team is not likely to tie Ohio State as it did in 1924, but its golf team won a national championship and its baseball and basketball teams are regularly national championship contenders.

No student is known to want "smoking privileges" in dormitories—rather, "residence halls"—anymore. Men and women live in the same buildings. Students (twenty-one or older, of course) can buy beer on campus; the president entertains trustees at cocktail parties. There is no Color Day, no May queen, no Homecoming queen. There are no rules requiring women to wear skirts to class or specifying what they may wear while sunbathing on campus. Much of this change was forced upon the College by generations of students responding to the outcries among their peers nationwide. They rallied in support of black civil rights and coed housing. They marched against the Vietnam War. They posed for yearbook pictures, women and men alike longhaired, in sweatshirts and towels.

In Lowry's time, what is now known as "diversity" barely existed. Wooster enrolled almost no black students, and international students mainly meant children of missionaries shipped home by their parents for sound Presbyterian educations, living together in a church-supported dorm. Now upward of a quarter of the student body consists of African Americans, Latinos, and natives not only of China and Japan but also of countries that didn't even exist in the 1940s, like Kenya and Vietnam. In Lowry's time, the faculty consisted of evangelical Christians—prospective teachers were required to acknowledge their religious allegiance on the application form. No Roman

Catholics, no Jews, no Muslims, no Hindus. The dates that much of this changed cannot be determined precisely, but it is fairly clear that the first African American faculty member did not arrive until 1959 and the first Jewish faculty appointment did not come until 1971.

If Howard Lowry was the nationally recognized scholar who put Wooster on the intellectual map, his successors have also proved themselves valuable to the College. Just as Lowry was a third choice, each of the following four encountered some resistance. J. Garber Drushal (1967–77), flung into the presidency upon Lowry's death, was not the scholar his predecessor was, but his grace and leadership skills piloted the College through a financial crisis and a decade of campus unrest. Over and over again, Drushal's contemporaries cited him as "the right man in the right place at the right time."

Henry J. Copeland (1977–95), as a young dean of forty-one, an unexpected choice, led Wooster to spectacular strength in the twin pillars of any institution—academic quality and financial stability. During his eighteen-year term, Wooster added a dozen majors, polished its hiring practices, built a worthy balance between teaching and research—and increased its endowment an astonishing tenfold. R. Stanton Hales (1995–2007), faced with an unnerved faculty and student body after a failed presidential search, calmed the campus, knew everyone from junior faculty to student leaders to custodians by name, and presided over the largest financial campaign in the school's history and a renovation and building effort rivaled perhaps only by Louis Holden. Grant Cornwell (2007–), the first president since 1919 without previous connection to the College, was viewed cautiously by some faculty at the start, but he has applied his fresh opportunity in a panoply of ways, extending Wooster's global reach, stabilizing enrollment, widening student choices, stimulating faculty, and reconstituting the administrative structure, the net of which is to inspire confidence in its future.

Today, diversity is assumed to encompass racial and ethnic groups, but only a year or two into Howard Lowry's presidency, the College encountered an influx of students more diverse than it had ever known. In this case, they were primarily young white men, hardened young men, veterans of World War II who had given years of their lives to defending their country and were eager to reap the promised rewards for their struggle. So that is where we pick up the story of nearly three-quarters of a century of evolution at The College of Wooster.

CHAPTER 2

The Vets Arrive—and I.S., Too!

About once a century, the U.S. Congress passes a law of monumental importance to education. In the eighteenth century, under the Articles of Confederation it approved the Land Ordinance of 1785, which, among other things, led to the creation of the states of Ohio, Indiana, Michigan, Illinois, and Wisconsin and barred slavery in those mostly unsettled western lands. At the same time, the ordinance acknowledged the importance of educating the young; it also required that a portion of each township in those territories be set aside "for the maintenance of public schools." In the nineteenth century, while the Civil War raged, Congress passed the Morrill Act, which supported the creation of land-grant universities, whose initial purpose was to teach agriculture and the mechanical arts and to make higher education available to people of all social classes. The historian Henry Steele Commager proclaimed the Morrill Act, "with the exception of the Act of 1785, the most important piece of legislation on behalf of education ever passed." Thus were created new institutions, such as the Ohio Agricultural and Mechanical College (now known as The Ohio State University), Michigan State University, and Purdue University.

In the twentieth century, with the end of World War II in sight, Congress passed Public Law 346, the Servicemen's Readjustment Act of 1944, which quickly became known as the GI Bill of Rights. The law was intended to serve a variety of needs for returning veterans, such as inexpensive home loans, but no part of it proved more consequential than the college education it offered. Over the next decade, millions of young men from all social classes, many of whom had never thought a college education possible, flooded the nation's campuses.

Including Wooster's. Just as the V-5 cadets had skewed Wooster's enrollment during the war years, the vets turned the campus into a different place than it had ever been. The influx began slowly in 1945 as the war ended, with twenty-one veterans, eight of them women, in the fall. The first surge came in January 1946, when 150 new male students, 140 of them veterans, registered for the school year's second semester, which brought the enrollment to 290 men and 585 women. That fall, came a flood. Of the 1,236 students enrolled for the 1946–47 academic year, 436 were veterans, including 9 women. Of the vets, 75 had spent enough prewar time in college to graduate that year; 132 were freshmen.

Lowry considered 1,000 an ideal size, but the College agreed to an emergency enrollment of 1,100, then found itself so inundated by desperate former GIs that it went over 1,200. At that, Wooster declined an astonishing 2,700 applications from men, and the admissions office gave up counting before spring the number of female potential students it refused; registration had been closed early for girls largely because of a shortage of dormitory space. The increasing number of male students also ended anxiety among administrators that Wooster was in danger of becoming something of a "girls' school." "Looking down from the balcony at the assembled crowd at the Freshman Mixer," read a fall 1946 alumni magazine article, "it was good to see boys' heads cropping up among a clump of girls' heads. In former years . . . somewhere along the outer edge, if you looked very hard, you might spy one solitary line of five or six of the masculine representation huddled together for protection."

Although some of the veterans were the usual college age and most of the rest not much older, these could hardly be considered boys; these were men. They had been shot at and had watched friends die. Moreover, many had come home to wives and sweethearts, eager for long-delayed romance and starting families. In fact, one in every five veterans in the big postwar classes was married. Since the College was not going to put husbands and wives, and sometimes their babies, in Holden or Kenarden, it had to find someplace for them. Married students were first housed in Miller Manor and Livingston Lodge, which were obviously not big enough; responding to desperate administrators, citizens of Wooster took in the first wave of students, single as well as families. (When couples vacated Miller, twenty-four girls who had been dormed in Hygeia Hall moved in.) But the longer term answer became "the units," World War II–vintage Quonset huts (named for their first construction site, Quonset Point in Rhode Island), half-moon–like prefabricated structures of corrugated steel that the federal government was selling off at $1,000 apiece. These measured 48 feet by 20 feet, with about 720 square feet of usable floor space in wide-open, eminently flexible interiors. The units were dropped into three spaces, between Douglas Hall and Kenarden Lodge (now the site of residence halls); between Holden Annex and the Stadium (now a parking lot); and on most of the grassy block behind Scovel Hall, bordered by Bever, Pine, and University (now the site of Freedlander Theatre and Wishart Hall).

Each family, husband and wife and often a baby or two, had a modest living room, a kitchen-dining room combination, and a single bedroom. A gas heater, hot-water heater, electric stove, and refrigerator were furnished through "government surplus," along with most of the beds and mattresses and kitchen tables; public utilities were included in the $34 monthly rent (taken from the $120 a month the vets received from the government). Then the College put out an emergency call to Wooster residents for "luxuries"—dressers, desks, easy chairs, lamps, and baby furniture—and sent trucks to pick up the contributions gathered from local attics and spare rooms. Given the all-for-one, one-for-all postwar sensibility, wives of the married veterans became part of the College culture. Some took courses along with their husbands; some worked in various campus jobs. They saved a few pennies on milk, meat, and eggs by setting up a cooperative store in the basement of Livingstone Lodge. For entertainment, the families played cards or went to the movies, sharing babysitting with each other or hiring college girls. A fleet of baby buggies lined the quadrangle during the 1946 opening convocation.

Single veterans, too, were part of the dormitory overflow. Those who had bunked in the hitherto unused "loft" of Douglas—"loft" was a generous name; it was essentially an attic—moved into the three Douglas Units, each of which had been converted into eight double rooms with a study for every four men. Altogether, by the end of 1946, when every unit had been made ready, the College held title to thirty-six family units and ninety-six dorm units.[1] They were not spacious, and not gracious, but certainly a lot better for the vets than facing the Wehrmacht in Belgium or being entrenched Japanese on Tarawa.

One of these ex-GIs was Al Van Wie. Fresh out of service, the first person

---

1. Because not enough full-scale dormitories had been yet built to deal with a larger enrollment, some of these units housed students into the late 1950s.

in his family to attend college, this upstate New Yorker thought he'd like to see the Midwest. He wrote to Ohio Wesleyan, Denison, and Wooster, none of which he knew anything about, and Wooster was the first to return his letter; so he applied. "I got on the train, I came out here sight unseen. I didn't know a person on campus." On one of his early nervous calls home, he told his stepfather, "These are either the nicest people I've ever met, or they're phonies. [His stepfather] said, 'Let's take the first one. I think that will be borne out.' He was right." And it turned out all right for Van Wie, who graduated from the College, married a Wooster girl, Judy Tilford (whose father was a longtime mayor), then returned to serve as head basketball coach for fifteen years and as director of athletics for twenty-one years.

Van Wie was appreciative of what the GI Bill meant for him and his fellow veterans. "It allowed all kinds of people, Al Van Wie included, to come to college. Let's face it. Wooster was white, Presbyterian. Now all of a sudden, with the GI Bill, you had all kinds of nationalities that came. . . . Some of them were married. And I'll tell you, that shook some faculty up. These guys wanted to get on with it. They didn't care about a community sing. It's Friday night, if they wanted to sit around drinking beer and playing poker, they were going to sit around and play poker." And the rule that no Wooster student was allowed to drink alcohol? "You talk about some guy's been in the service, been in battle, and you're going to tell him that?"

For the eighteen-year-old girls entering this postwar atmosphere, though, customs seemed not to have changed all that much. During summers, a group of Senior Counselors sent off cheery letters to incoming freshman, like this one from August 1946:

> Wooster girls try to combine comfort and style, and in the rainy season, which occurs all year 'round on the Hill, they usually stick to comfort. All kinds of raincoats and hats are worn, with boots or old shoes to complete the picture. Umbrellas are a rarity. . . . Hat, gloves and purse dress you up on Sundays and formal tea occasions, with white gloves being an all-year favorite. Small dances, informal teas, and lectures usually call for afternoon dresses. . . . We always dress for dinner on Sunday and often on Thursday, which is faculty guest night in the dormitories. . . . For the first time in four years, we have the good fortune to say that formal clothes will be in pre-war demand. Lucky freshmen! You'll go formal to the Big Four reception and to other evening receptions.

. . . [F]or only fifty cents a year you can have a different picture each month from the Lending Library of Art—for that touch of culture in your room. . . . What with the war won, the Navy gone and vets back, Wooster plans to have its first normal college year in four years. That means dates, dances and more dates. But that means rules, too.

That autumn of 1946 brought a new tradition of cheer to the College— students voted 757 to 128 in favor of electing a Homecoming queen for the first time, after nearly three decades of official Homecoming celebrations. She was Olivia dePastina, a psychology major from Trenton, New Jersey, head cheerleader and leader in a flock of student activities. Her selection was reported under a six-column banner headline on page one of the student *Voice,* and she was pictured in three different issues. It is illustrative of changing mores that the election of a Homecoming queen was a very big deal in the 1940s, '50s, and early '60s, the nominees pictured, the election numbers reported above those for Student Government Association president. By the late '60s, the choice was barely mentioned in the *Voice,* and by the '70s the honor had given way to "Outstanding Senior Woman" and "Outstanding Senior Man."

The late 1940s introduced another order of school spirit—an accelerated new life for Wooster's marching band. Although the College had a band throughout the twentieth century, and it marched at football games for much of that time, the story of the modern band began in the late 1930s. When it was decided at that time that girls could join, Dean William Westhafer questioned allowing them to appear in trousers. Band director Stanley Davis offhandedly responded that if girls couldn't wear trousers, the boys would have to wear skirts—or perhaps real Scottish kilts. This led to a Homecoming Tag Day effort that raised about $250, enough to buy fewer than three uniforms. Soon a College trustee and the donor of the newest dormitory, Babcock Hall—the sauerkraut king Birt Babcock—offered to buy as many of the $90 uniforms as needed. A firm in Glasgow filled the order—heavy Scottish wool, cockerel feathers, and sporrans—and shipped them off. That was just in time for the start of World War II, and the ship carrying Wooster's new band uniforms was sunk by a German U-boat; undeterred, Babcock paid for a second order. The band first wore the new uniforms for a concert in the spring of 1940, and it was evident at once that the boys had a difficult time—think Tom

Sawyer and Huck Finn—learning to sit gracefully in their skirts. As for the MacLeod tartan that has come to represent the band—and the College: it was not historic. Since Wooster's colors were black and gold, and its teams had recently been named the Scots, and its heritage was Presbyterian, the College sought an appropriate tartan. The MacLeod clan—noted among other things for having lost the seventeenth-century battle of Worcester, but having survived to this day—fit the black-and-gold bill. Since then, the band members, women and men alike, have always been outfitted in the authentic kilt uniforms.

But it is a different band. In the 1940s, directed first by Davis then by Wally Franks, also the longtime director of music at Wooster High School, it usually numbered from fifty to sixty students. The first of the late 1940s changes could be traced to the nineteenth century, about the time John Philip Sousa made marches fashionable, when a man named Frederick Ellsworth Bigelow wrote a march called "Our Director." For unexplained reasons, hundreds of schools and colleges—most famously Harvard—adopted it as their sports fight song. Wooster was one of these, and for many years the band played it after every Scot touchdown. But in the winter and spring of 1948, a husband-and-wife team, students John and Dixie Weitzel—who had already won campus fame with their score for a *Gum Shoe Hop*—spent hour after hour in a small music practice room tinkering with what they hoped would become a fight song exclusively for Wooster, to the point of dropping in a "Loch Lomond" musical phrase near the end. They succeeded. John and Dixie (her given name was Annelu, but no one called her that) titled their march "Hail to the Black and Gold," and they scored it for the band. Well into the twenty-first century it can still be heard after Scot touchdowns:

> Hail to the black and gold, cheer, cheer for the clan,
>   Keep your eye upon the goal line,
>   Watch 'em drive, watch 'em win, sure they can,
>   Drive on to victory, hold the banner high upon the hill,
>   So we'll hit the high road and they'll take the low,
>   To the glory of Wooster Scots.

The second event was the arrival in 1949 of Stu Ling, who went on to direct the band for thirty-five years. One of his early master strokes was to write Wooster-centric lyrics for a popular tune associated with the singer-band leader Phil Harris. The song, called, "Are You from Dixie," began, "Are you from Dixie, are you from Dixie, where fields of cotton beckon to me." Ling's version began, "Are you from Wooster, are you from Wooster, from the school we love on top of the hill." The catchy tune and special lyrics were a hit with students, many of whom could sing it decades after they had become alumni. Ling quickly raised the roster to over a hundred, before it settled at about eighty players. As high school bands became more imaginative, players came to college better prepared, and in 1967 a summer band camp helped ready them for increasingly complex routines. Bagpipers were introduced after World War II, first a team imported from Cleveland for a Homecoming game, eventually an entire unit of accomplished students. Wooster's majorettes were the "MacLeod Lassies," the alumni magazine reported, in uniforms "whose brevity (or lack thereof) . . . was strictly monitored by the Dean of Women [Marjorie Golder] up through the early fifties." The best of the musicians were incorporated into a symphonic band, which gave concerts in Wooster and at alumni gatherings on tour. Ling also created a jazz ensemble.

Upon Ling's retirement in 1984, Nancy Ditmer arrived to take the band to even bigger and more adventurous efforts. The symphonic band made a weeklong tour each year and has performed in more than half the states as well as Canada. In 2005 the marching band reached an astonishing 188 members—more than 10 percent of the student body—having since settled at about 125. Besides Scot football games and high school festivals, the band played at a 1988 Buffalo Bills professional game, which included appearing—albeit briefly—in a scene from the movie *When Harry Met Sally.* As for the authentic uniforms—only a handful of colleges nationwide have anything similar—in 2012 they cost about $1400 apiece. Even with what is now a band endowment, replacements are only ordered as needed. For example, Ditmer said, "if we need additional kilts with a certain waist size or doublets [jackets] in particular sizes, we focus on [those] purchases." As for the sight of the kilt-clad band leading the football team down the hill into John P. Papp Stadium, money can't buy that.

School spirit was well and good in the heady post–World War II days, but as the vets began to arrive in force and the College was both growing and changing materially, Lowry found it not an easy time. He certainly had not bargained for a group of war veterans who wanted to "get on with it"—collect their college degrees in the fastest time possible and begin earning a living, having lost years of youth fighting for their country. He made certain to let the veterans know they would be welcome—and he let them know as well that he was prepared to compromise. Under the subtitle "Post-War Plan of the College," the 1945–46 catalog, published in the summer of 1945 said:

> The College of Wooster is now engaged in studies of its educational policies and practices in order that they meet the special needs of its students in the post-war world. Plans are underway for a new program of work at the junior and senior level embodying certain features of independent study. But the program will be flexible enough to allow a veteran to complete his college course under the usual college program if he so decides. [In other words, vets need not take on I.S. if they don't want to.] It is expected that proper housing will be available for those who are married.

As Lowry set about invigorating the institution, the fall of 1946 brought to the College four people of lasting note. Two were among its greatest scholars of the century: Bill Kieffer, a Wooster graduate and former instructor at the College whom Lowry lured back from Western Reserve University and who became one of the most distinguished in Wooster's long line of distinguished chemists; and historian Bob Walcott, an elegant easterner with three Harvard degrees, a gentleman-scholar and intellectual of the old school whom former colleagues remembered with reverence into the twenty-first century. A third was the new dean of women, Marjorie S. Golder—known to one and all (except to her face) as "Ma" Golder—a rules-keeper who during her two-decade career at the College, it is fair to say, terrified not only the girls in her official charge but also the boys. A fourth was a new teacher of speech, recruited from Capital University by Bill Craig, a colleague there. This was Garber Drushal, who just over a decade later would succeed Lowry as president.

Most important to the new president was Independent Study. Having committed intellectually to his Independent Study dream, Lowry understood that it could be difficult to sell such an imaginative program to the institution—faculty, students, and alumni alike. The faculty, as faculties do, offered mixed views. They spent endless hours, as faculties do, in discussions about how to institute, then actually execute, this plan. Win Logan, then a young instructor in speech who over the years became one of the College's most respected professors, described it in a later faculty evaluation as a threshold problem: "There was a pleasant and secure feeling about the design of Wooster, a place where confidence in the past and present sometimes made innovation a bit difficult." But the real difficulties were obvious, starting with the fact that many on the faculty considered themselves overworked already, and some seemed—amusingly enough—troubled by the possibility that students would know more about specific parts of their subject than they did. A few called it placing the cart before the horse, scholarship without seasoning. As a pragmatic issue, others wondered how they would fit this time-consuming effort into the curriculum, since in some departments required courses already consumed nearly two-thirds of the four-year degree requirement. And, quite troubling, would the library and the science facilities prove adequate to the increased research need? The possibility even existed that the challenges of I.S. might drive away both professors and prospective students.

As Lowry lobbied hard for I.S., his strength of personality counted heavily—he was confident and popular—and everyone was aware that the new leader had almost assuredly staked his nascent presidency on the concept. He promised the faculty that I.S. would make them better teachers as they pursued, along with their students, the newest developments in their disciplines. The day of decision was April 16, 1945 (the day after the campus memorial service for Franklin D. Roosevelt, who had died April 12) at a two-and-one-half-hour meeting whose minutes were "respectfully submitted" by William I. Schreiber, professor of German and secretary to the faculty:

> Mr. [Frank H.] Cowles, for the Planning Committee, moved, and Mr. [Roy] Grady seconded, the adoption by the Faculty of the recommendation of the Sub-Committee on Upperclass Years:
>
> I. The sub-committee recommends that the program of "Independent Work" (if adopted by The College of Wooster) be required for all four-year students. . . .
>
> II. If the system of "Independent Work" be adopted . . . such "Independent Work" shall be understood to be the equivalent of approximately one-fifth of a student's work. . . .

(Note. No action was taken but it was generally agreed that the average "Senior Thesis" might be about 12,000 to 15,000 words—except for problems in the sciences—and that unpadded quality rather than length was to be desired.)

After it was explained to the Faculty that this plan . . . was not to be an extra burden on the faculty, . . . the new plan was adopted.

The silver bullet Lowry used with the faculty was the research leave. It was an extraordinary pledge for a liberal arts college where teaching had always been paramount. It promised faculty an academic year's leave every five years, assuming an accepted research project. Unlike at a university, where teaching loads were balanced to allow the expected research—and where at the best places and with the best scholars research tended to overwhelm instructional commitment—at Wooster teaching and I.S. advising would still dominate a professor's academic year schedule, but an unbridled year for appropriate research was a tantalizing prospect. Further, because a number of instructors would be away from campus in any given year, the faculty roster would necessarily be increased, suggesting an influx of new blood. (See chapter 19 for discussion of progress in I.S. projects and achievements of the faculty leave program.) In the spring of 1948, one of the earliest recipients of a research leave, Clayton Ellsworth, who would succeed Aileen Dunham as head of the history department, set out to explain, in the *Alumni Bulletin,* its value: "Why should a professor in a small college be encouraged to do research work? The first job of any teacher is to teach his subject with authority, clarity, and, if possible, with artistry. . . . Ordinarily the curricular and extra-curricular duties of the teacher in the small college do not permit him much uninterrupted time for research during the school year. . . . Research work [over a sustained period], written as it is for a professional audience, forces an individual to read widely, to sharpen his powers of observation, selection, criticism, and expression. It increases an appreciation of what has been done, and what remains undone. If the research is well done, it brings prestige to the professor and to his college, and ultimately may be of value to society."

From its beginnings, I.S. had to find its footing. During its incubation period, I.S. was encouraged but not required for any students, and most given the option declined. In the class of 1948 (those who had entered in the fall of 1944 and some returning veterans), only nineteen students completed

I.S., a majority not willing to try the experiment and others abandoning projects for various reasons, including lack of material available in the library, confusion about the requirements, or just plain discouragement. Three programs were completed in English, history, and Spanish; two in biology, religion, and sociology; and one each in speech, philosophy, political science, and psychology. In the class of 1949, only eleven finished I.S.: six in English, three in history, one in Spanish, and one in philosophy. It was not before the class of 1950 (excluding veterans), whose members entered in the autumn of 1946 and began I.S. as juniors in the autumn of 1948, that all students were required to complete an Independent Study project.

Helping introduce the alumni body to I.S., the June 1948 *Wooster Alumni Bulletin* carried an engaging essay from Patricia Henderson, class of 1948 and one of the daring I.S. pioneers. She explained: "I think most of us [tried I.S.] for the somewhat negative reason that we were afraid we'd miss something if we didn't. . . . The culmination came, of course, in the writing of my senior thesis, a painful process in its feeling of incompetency and entailing the preliminary joy of playing solitaire with some 2,000 note cards!" And she wisely summarized:

> I do feel sure that several things are vitally necessary if it is to succeed: . . . an enthusiastic and sympathetic faculty, conferences with the adviser at *regular intervals* in order to counteract the natural tendency to put off what is not immediately pressing; increased library facilities. These are things the student has a right to expect of the college. On his part, he had the responsibility of realizing that this is not a pre-digested program; it requires active choosing of the food, cutting it to manageable proportions, and vigorous chewing. . . . If such a program can be made to work on this campus, it will be a stride of inestimable value in educational progress. Give it a chance.

Since Lowry's vision of Wooster's future depended so much on I.S., he needed not only to persuade the campus-based faculty and student body, but also an alumni body that had done very well, thank you, without it. Like all new presidents, Lowry spent considerable time on the road during his first year or two, speaking to alumni groups. He had the advantage of not having to introduce himself—he had, after all, taught many of those alumni—but he did have to sell I.S., or explain, in non-lofty terms, what it was, and perhaps more important, what it was not. It was not, as he said repeatedly, "an intellectual hothouse for cultivating Phi Beta Kappas." He told a *Cleveland Plain Dealer* reporter in the spring of 1948, "This word 'independent' causes the plan to be misunderstood in some quarters. The word is not a synonym for loneliness." In the February 1945 issue of the *Alumni Bulletin,* the new president wrote: "I hope Wooster may attract its fair share of normal guys and girls who could not possibly be Phi Beta Kappas, but who with reasonably good minds and unmistakably good hearts, want to come to their best in terms of what talents heaven gave them." With this optimistic take on an academic program unlike that of almost any other college in the nation, Wooster was ready to move into the postwar '50s.

CHAPTER 3

Not as Quiet as It Seemed

As the College along with most of the nation settled comfortably into the 1950s, the veterans were graduated mostly, and Independent Study was ensconced, and America liked Ike. Gone was not only the fighting of World War II but also the rationing and other home-front sacrifices. The economy was booming as Detroit manufactured cars instead of tanks and planes, and new homes sprouted across sprawling suburban developments. Since the average cost of a home in 1950 was $8,450 and the average cost of a car was $1,510, on their average annual salaries of $3,210 most workers could keep up, even if only fathers worked outside the home, and mothers stayed home to cook and clean and raise what would come to be called the Baby Boom generation—especially with a gallon of gasoline costing 18 cents, a loaf of bread 12 cents, a quart of milk 20 cents, and a pound of hamburger 30 cents. Wooster's tuition seemed a reasonable $247.50 a semester, and including room and board, an entire academic year might cost a little over $1,000, plus laundry and social expenses—which the College estimated at between $120 and $200. But there were unsettling developments. As Winston Churchill had warned as far back as March 1946—"From Stettin in the Baltic to Trieste in the Adriatic, an iron curtain has descended across the continent"—America's wartime ally, the Soviet Union, was now the enemy in a Cold War that would last into the 1980s. Some events seemed too far away to notice, as when in 1954 a French garrison surrendered in the hills near Dien Bien Phu; and the French gave up their Indo-China colony, which divided into three countries, Cambodia, Laos, and Vietnam, the last itself dividing into North and South.

It might have appeared a distant threat in 1950 when the United States
sent troops to defend South Korea against an invasion from North Korea,
but every college campus, including Wooster's, could feel the impact. The
Selective Service system instituted a test to be taken by male students,
guaranteeing a deferment from the military draft—as short as one year or
all the way through graduate school—depending on how well a student
did; even an I.S. oral might not have seemed so important. The nation's
anxiety about the threat of communism was exacerbated in the early
1950s as a freshman senator from Wisconsin named Joe McCarthy, re-
peating his lies about Communists in the State Department and the army,
ruined countless lives from his meteoric rise in 1950 to his humiliating
flameout in 1954. The postwar Red Scare even intruded on Wooster: in
the late spring of 1949 the chairman of the infamous House Committee
on Un-American Activities decided on a "textbook checkup" in the nation's colleges. Some institutions acquiesced, some refused, and Lowry
responded with butter-wouldn't-melt-in-my-mouth charm. He offered
this public statement about the request:

> We would find that difficult to honor. We have as a special feature of
> our college a program of independent study in the junior and senior
> years, the freshman and sophomore years leading directly to it. This
> program encourages students to their own investigation and wide use
> of the library. Hence collateral reading at the College of Wooster is,
> in the nature of things, potentially every book in a library of 110,320
> volumes. We believe that the committee would not want us to go to
> the expense and labor of listing these volumes. We hope that everyone
> understands that the 70 colleges asked to submit lists of books were
> picked at random—drawn out of a hat as it were—and that there is
> neither honor nor stigma in the invitation. As far as Communism is
> concerned, a Christian college can have no truck with it because Marx-
> ism and Christianity simply do not mix.

At campuses across the nation, the most daring student challenge to
authority was a panty raid. Students were listening to Sinatra and Ella, Patti
Page and Doris Day, Eddie Fisher and Johnny Ray. One of Wooster's musical highlights of 1954 came in December when the Buddy Morrow band,
which had scored an enormous hit with "Night Train," packed Memorial

Chapel, the crowd so wild that students were literally flipping hymnals in the air. After the performance, it was discovered that one of the band members and the girl singer had been making melody on the chapel stage and had left a near-empty whiskey bottle open on the piano. Hopeful that this would not end big-time performances on campus, Student Senate president Don Hartsough timidly entered Lowry's office to alert him to the violation of campus decorum. "Oh, that," the president responded dismissively, sensing the student enthusiasm. That year, 1954–55, turned out to be full of musical treats. In October had come the Trapp Family Singers—not as famous then as they became after the movie "The Sound of Music" was released a decade later; the following February the great composer Aaron Copland; and in March the Sauter-Finnegan big band. The academic year's cultural highlight came November 18: a chapel lecture by the acclaimed British historian Arnold Toynbee. Visiting the United States to mark the publication of the final four volumes of his ten-volume masterwork, *A Study of History,* he lectured in New York, Washington, and Boston but at no relatively small site except Wooster, a tribute to Lowry. (It was a sign of the times that when a picture appeared in the alumni magazine of the two of them with Aileen Dunham, head of the history department, the caption read, *Dr.* Toynbee, *Dr.* Lowry, and *Miss* Dunham.)

Through the decade, the College maintained strict control of its students. According to the 1952–53 handbook, a student could take eighteen chapel cuts per semester, averaging one a week, with a $5 fine imposed on the nineteenth and 50 cents for every other. Twice-a-month attendance at church of one's choice was required. Class cut penalties—faculty members were supposed to take attendance, of course—were tied to the number of credit hours offered in a class; a total of thirty cuts in a semester or forty in a year would cost a credit hour. The handbook sweetened the rules by describing the traditions for couples who decide to "go steady": "When that fateful day arrives when a lassie is pinned, she and her beau may attend church together. The girl passes out lollipops and the boy cigars to all their friends making her 'pinning' official. Then comes the 'sweetheart serenade' from the fellow and his section at which time the lassie's 'one and only' must render her a solo." Students seemed amenable to the rules. An opinion poll conducted by a political science class found a bare majority in favor of loosening hours for girls, the most popular choice being a 1 A.M. weekend curfew. Asked what to do with any extra money at the College, more than one-third suggested a new gym or field house, with a student union the second choice. A new dormitory for boys was barely mentioned, even though some boys were still assigned to the deteriorating postwar units.

The rules did not loosen over the decade. From the 1959–60 student handbook: "The drinking of alcoholic beverages by students in residence is prohibited." Students could not have cars unless they were married, lived with their parents, commuted each day, needed a car for I.S. or a job, or were seniors after Thanksgiving break. However stringent these rules seemed when taken together, they "only served to enhance the income of off-campus drinking establishments," remembered Gene Bay, who became a Presbyterian minister and Wooster trustee. "It is a wonder that no one was killed in a drunk driving accident." Girls' hours varied from 8 P.M. weekdays for freshmen (until Thanksgiving when it went to 9 P.M.) to 11 P.M. for seniors; their curfew was midnight on Friday and Saturday. "Each dance or party is to be chaperoned by at least two couples. . . . At all dances, at all open houses in the men's dormitories, and on all hay rides, etc., there must be a member of the faculty or administration among the chaperones." Intriguing rules applied to women's dress:

> Blue jeans, slacks, or Bermuda shorts . . . may not be worn to classes except for lab work and field study. They are not to be worn on Sunday at any time on campus. . . . They are not to be worn to any meals in the dining halls with the exception of daily breakfast, Saturday lunch, Sunday breakfast and supper with long coat and daily lunches during examinations. Bermuda shorts are to be no shorter than two inches above the knees. . . . Shorts other than Bermuda are not allowed on campus, except for the tennis courts and then a long coat must be worn to and from the courts.

And finally, "Sun-bathing Rules—

a. Sun-bathing is permitted in the following places: 1. The balcony at Babcock—2. The yard behind the French House—3. The court at Holden—4. The balcony at Wagner.
b. Sun-bathing attire is limited to shorts and halter or bathing suit— nothing less.

c. The roofs at Scot Cottage and Westminster are not to be used for sun-bathing.

d. Only women are allowed in these places designated for sun-bathing.

e. Two demerits are given for sun-bathing in places not on the approved list.

f. Sun-bathing in Holden Court before 2:00 P.M. Sunday is prohibited."

As student handbooks indicate, men's sections and women's clubs drove the 1950s social scene. National fraternities and sororities had been expelled from campus during the teens, in considerable part because of fierce opposition from the College's great benefactor of those years, Louis Severance. Since social groupings are almost inevitable, sections and clubs took their place, calling themselves "local" fraternities and sororities, even taking Greek names. Association was easier for men, since nearly all of them lived in the neatly divided seven sections of Kenarden Lodge, with Livingstone Lodge housing Eighth Section. The clubs, not tied to living arrangements, drew less than half the membership. For instance, in the 1953 *Index* 418 men are pictured by section and 189 women by clubs. In the 1959 *Index,* section pictures show 477 men, club photos 229 women. In the photos from both years, the men were neatly dressed in jackets and ties, the women in blouses and skirts. It is remarkable how these pictures contrast with section and club pictures from the more rebellious 1960s and early '70s, when hair was long for both men and women, the neat dress code had given way to sloppy sweat shirts and jeans or shorts for both sexes, and careful poses had been replaced by exaggerated showpieces. For the 1970 *Index,* one section posed in underwear, another offered only snapshots of various members, and for another the editors ran two blank pages with the explanation that the section did not furnish any pictures.

Here is a listing by each club and section for those two sample years, with Greek name and number of members pictured: Clubs—Ekos (Epsilon Kappa Omicron): 25 members in 1953, 35 in 1959; Imps (Zeta Phi Gamma): 26 in 1953, 28 in 1959; Kez (Kappa Epsilon Zeta): 18 in 1953, 34 in 1959; Peanuts (Pi Kappa): 27 in 1953, 36 in 1959; Pyramids (Delta Delta Rho): 28 in 1953, 34 in 1959; Signets (Sigma Gamma Nu): 23 in 1953 (not included 1959); Sphinx (Lambda Alpha Sigma): 26 in 1953, 31 in 1959; Trumps (Chi Alpha Chi): 16 in 1953, 31 in 1959. Sections—First (Beta Kappa Phi): 28 members in 1953, 39 in 1959; Second (Kappa Phi Sigma): 63 in 1953, 69 in 1959; Third (no Greek name): 59 in 1953, 71 in 1959; Fourth (Phi Omega Sigma): 46 in 1953, 43 in 1959; Fifth (Phi Delta Sigma): 47 in 1953, 70 in 1959; Sixth (Phi Sigma Alpha): 52 in 1953, 48 in 1959; Seventh (Kappa Kappa Kappa): 52 in 1953, 67 in 1959; Eighth (Alpha Gamma Epsilon): 71 in 1953, 70 in 1959.

Section and club formals were highlights on the social calendar, which meant that, except for basketball, Severance Gymnasium was in a near-constant state of decoration. Sections rehearsed long hours to prepare for competitive serenade contests. But their competition was strongest during intramural sports events, especially what was euphemistically called "touch" football. Members of Second Section recalled winning the championship for three straight years in the mid-50s, led by the passing of Bob Tignor (who became a College trustee), the receiving of Bob Voelkel (a varsity basketball star), and the defense of Blake Moore (a third-generation Wooster student, whose grandfather had played on its first football team in the nineteenth century). The highlight was an overtime victory against favored Fifth Section, whose star receiver and passer, Bud Barta and By Morris (later director of admissions) were both varsity basketball regulars.

The official handbook encouraged a certain level of hazing: freshmen were required to have candy, chewing gum, and lollipops available for their "slave masters," the sophomores. But that was mild compared to Hell Week initiations, during which paddling was de rigueur for both sexes. Many years later, women remembered such Hell Week experiences as club members hiding in closets then jumping out to frighten pledges, pledges forbidden to see their boyfriends, instant singing performances around campus, wearing "balloons on our behinds." For men it could get rougher: all-night scavenger hunts that included waking up leading Wooster citizens or roller skating down ramps in freezing weather at Cleveland's Terminal Tower.

All of these anecdotes might be considered examples of old-fashioned fun and games for college students. Illustrative of the changing ethos on campus, though, was the near quarter-century tenure, beginning in 1956, of Viola Startzman Robertson as the College medical director. When Vi Startzman arrived at Wooster as a freshman in 1931, she told Roy Grady, the head of the chemistry department, that she aspired to be a doctor, whereupon Grady told her bluntly that girls didn't become doctors. Still, Startzman majored in chemistry, avoiding Grady's courses and supported in her ambition by Professor John Chittum. It took her six years after graduation, though—working as a lab technician bacteriologist and earning a master's degree in chemistry—to accumulate the money and nerve to apply to medical school at Western Reserve University in Cleveland. As one of four women in a class of a hundred—nearly all the others were in the Naval Reserve and had their tuition paid—she graduated on the accelerated wartime schedule, completing four years' training in three. After interning at Babies and Children's Hospital and teaching pediatrics to Western Reserve medical students for five years, she returned to Wooster to practice.

It wasn't easy. The city had one female doctor, Eva Cartwright, an anesthesiologist, and a couple of the city's best-known physicians declined to work with Startzman. But Bill Schultz, with whom she had taken college classes, offered to help, and Robert Wright allowed her to use his offices rent-free during mornings while he was performing surgery at the hospital. Startzman won patients by word of mouth (she remembered Lois Freedlander, wife of a future College trustee, bringing her two daughters), but just as her practice was growing—and soon after she married Dr. James Robertson, a widower with four young sons—she accepted the tempting invitation to help build the pediatric practice at the Cleveland Clinic. Then Dean Taeusch persuaded her to return to Wooster, explaining that the College had lost its part-time doctor and now needed someone else, perhaps three mornings a week, because a group of nurses, living on the top floor of Hygeia Hall, "did most of the doctoring."

Clearly it wasn't that simple. Startzman reorganized the health system, moving the five full-time nurses elsewhere, so Hygeia had twenty-two beds for patients. The first major test was a flu epidemic in 1958, when Hygeia quickly filled, and Startzman made the rounds through quarantine areas that she set up in the dorms. She also discovered that students might, for example, arrive reporting a bad cold, but the problem was actually trouble with parents or, worse, clinical depression. She and Betty Shull, the invaluable clinical psychologist, counseled many students and occasionally called a student's family (after telling the student) to recommend further treatment. Startzman also remembered with a smile that many I.S. papers were written from a Hygeia room by students who came in complaining that their dorms were too noisy.

Startzman took on another task in the late 1950s and early '60s that was not in the job description: "Very little was known by the students about human sexuality. It was amazing how little they knew, really, and yet when you think of the society from which they came, no one else knew very much either. So I did a lot of counseling in the office and also had a few classes in which I would discuss human sexuality and human relationships, and pregnancy, of course, and venereal diseases, and that whole kind of thing that we sort of take for granted." Was there any concern from Galpin Hall? "The thing that amazed me was how wonderful the administration was in never questioning what I was doing. Howard [Lowry] stayed away from students really. He liked students, but he didn't know students, didn't really know the adolescent or the young adult. So whatever I said or did was without question. Bill Taeusch [probably knew] and he went along with it."

How did the classes come about? "One or two students would come and say, 'Dr. Startzman, we don't know how one gets pregnant. What happens? Would you come and talk to a group of us?' So we'd have meetings in the dorms, late, like 9 o'clock. I'd sit with them in their rooms, and we'd discuss it very informally. Eventually the boys got to know about it, so we'd have their meeting down at Hygeia. Then later we had [meetings] together. . . . Bev Asbury [minister at Westminster who arrived in 1962] and I gave a once-a-week course, [about] eight weeks, to engaged couples or couples who thought they were going to marry, and we gave them both the medical point of view and also the religious and theological point of view." As the 1960s brought different views of sexuality, and wider knowledge, Startzman did what she thought appropriate, which was to provide birth-control pills and to fit diaphragms, always after determining that the woman and man were serious and contemplating marriage. Pregnancy often caused deep anxieties. In the '50s if a girl became pregnant by a fellow student, both often left school. This only happened a handful of times, but Startzman and Racky Young, the dean of men, would help them transfer quietly to other colleges. In the 1960s, the doctor counseled pregnant students on the choices of marriage, or placing a child for adoption, or even abortion. In this last case, she wanted the student to discuss the options with her parents, but some students refused. If a young woman insisted on ending her pregnancy—this was rare, but it happened—Startzman arranged for a facility where this could be done safely; after a few days the woman could return to class with a "medical situation" explanation. "The administration, to the best of my knowledge, never, ever questioned one of those," Startzman said. Don't ask, don't tell.

The academic year 1952–53 brought to Wooster one of its most erudite—and popular—young professors. His name was Robert Peters. His credentials were impeccable: bachelor and master's degrees from Magdalen College, Oxford; bachelor of Music from the University of Durham (England); additional master's from the University of Adelaide (Australia); doctoral program in progress at the University of California, Berkeley; book forthcoming on the teaching of history. Further, he had been elected a Fellow of the Royal Historical Society and a Fellow of the Royal Asiatic Society. He had taught at two of the most prestigious preparatory schools in England: Eton College, Windsor, and Gresham College, Norfolk. His ambition, he said, was to chair a Department of History at a liberal arts college.

Peters was assigned sections of the introductory western civilization course, where his lectures were so popular that students were known to return to hear them a second time. He was, according to the faculty, a congenial colleague and gracious host, his personal library awe-inspiring. Awed as well were the female students whom the worldly thirty-four-year-old dated; one of them, a senior and the daughter of a prominent lawyer, was rumored his fiancée. Indeed, he charmed the whole town. Although his specialty was medieval church history, he gave spellbinding talks to the Kiwanis Club and the Exchange Club on the coming coronation of Queen Elizabeth II and dazzled groups as varied as the local chapter of the American Association of University Women and the 447th Military Police unit. As if his academic credentials were not sufficient, once it became known that he was an ordained Anglican priest, he was invited to officiate a communion service at St. James Episcopal Church. It was hardly surprising that his stellar performance led the College's Teaching Staff and Tenure Committee to recommend that his contract be renewed. All in all, this young man seemed too good to be true.

Robert Peters was a fraud. When Dean Taeusch discovered this in the spring, he confessed to the Board of Trustees: "In my sixty years I have had to eat humble pie, but never before has my pastry been so full of raspberries and crust." The dean's first inkling, about the time of spring vacation, came from the Episcopal bishop of Pittsburgh, who had heard from a mutual friend that Peters worked at Wooster; he informed Taeusch that Peters had gotten into trouble with the church there, left voluntarily for Canada three years earlier, and was not supposed to return. The dean wrote officials at Oxford and Adelaide, who responded uniformly: his letters of recommendation were forged and degrees false. Hot on the trail, Taeusch used the pretext of a routine check of four faculty members who were not U.S. citizens to ask Peters for his registration card. Peters said he couldn't find the card but offered a registration number, which immigration in Pittsburgh said was false. Two days later, immigration officers arrived to take Peters to jail in Cleveland prior to deporting him to Canada; when Canada refused to accept him, he was deported to his native England. Dean Taeusch completed his soulful report to the board: "We who have been responsible for the conduct of this business have tried to proceed with the Christian charity that is due to every son of God. In that spirit, I omit now nonessential information about his love affairs and his debts [he left upward of $3,000 in unpaid bills] . . . Perhaps in the new reign of her majesty, Mr. Peters can be put on the right track."

Wooster was embarrassed, needless to say, but it turned out to be in very good company. Peters—his actual name was Parkins, and he was at least a decade older than he claimed—lived a life so confidently outrageous that it seems, literally, incredible. He appeared to have been married four times, always to much younger women, and divorced probably twice; he was convicted and jailed for bigamy. Actually trained as an Anglican clergyman, he was once deported from Switzerland as an undesirable alien; he lived and taught in Ceylon and Australia and in Canada until his faked credentials were discovered. Then, *after* his Pittsburgh and Wooster outings, he not only entered Oxford's Magdalen College with false credentials but also married in the college's chapel there, and Magdalen paid for the wedding and a champagne reception, which was attended by heads of colleges and other distinguished guests. It took the eminent historian Hugh Trevor-Roper to unmask him—in England, at least. For in 1960, seven years after leaving Wooster, he was teaching at Hope College in Michigan, an affiliate of Wooster's in the Great Lakes College Association; he had an offer to teach the following year at the University of Texas flagship campus in Austin. Found out at Hope, he was deported again, and that's the last traceable record of Robert Parkins.

In 1910, when Mrs. John S. Kennedy, the donor of Kenarden Lodge, visited the College to view the new boys' dormitory, she insisted on staying in a Wooster hotel. The city's accommodations were so bleak, however, that President Holden picked out the biggest downtown hotel room available and redecorated it from carpeting to wallpaper for her benefit. It was clear that something better ought to be available for College alumni and guests. By 1940 Prexy Wishart had actually collected funds for such space, but nothing much happened. Sometime in the '50s, the board chairman, Robert E. Wilson, discussed with Lowry a lodge that would accommodate College guests. The story may be apocryphal, but when Lowry is said to have protested that the College had other, more pressing needs, Wilson insisted that he wanted his friends to have a decent place to stay. So he donated $450,000 to construct the lodge, requesting that it resemble his Georgian Colonial home in White Plains, New York. At the dedication ceremony on September 9, 1959, Waldo H. Dunn reminisced about the Wilson family's contributions to the College (Bob Wilson's father had been a favored professor of mathematics) and intoned: "Through it will flow a stream of people young and old, the great and the lowly as well as the average 'in between.' There will be singing and laughter and good fellowship. Here will come alumni to renew old memories and friendships. Here will come strangers to make their first acquaintance with Wooster, and to decide whether or not they care to become comrades with us in promoting the welfare of this College. Here there will be life, movement, color, rest, and refreshment, as the stream of human life flows happily through its corridors."

The building was called the Wooster Inn, and over more than half a century it has served the College in many ways. The thirteen guest rooms and two suites have accommodated trustees, alumni, and parents, as well as visitors to the Ohio Light Opera and a host of other Wooster events. The Board of Trustees and its committees have met there, and it was for decades the regular site for Board dinners. Its dining room saw countless interviews with prospective faculty members and was the regular meeting place for any number of groups, including the Women's Advisory Board of the College and retired faculty; it has long been one of the city's upscale restaurants.

All of this came at a price. From 1959 until past 2000, the College lost millions of dollars operating the Wooster Inn. Although the board repeatedly discussed efforts to stem the financial bleeding, and the administration changed management with some regularity, it never dealt with essential savings. For one thing, the Inn kept its prices modest to benefit both regular guests and the College, which was picking up the tab for trustees and potential faculty. For another, it was not serving liquor, which is the high-profit item in any restaurant. Most costly of all, the College was trying to operate the Inn as it did the English or philosophy department. That is, every employee at the Inn was an employee of the College, which included salary when the College was closed, full health benefits, qualification for fifteen paid days off after working twenty-three hours a week for ninety days. Its computer system didn't function; thousands of dollars in untracked gift certificates hung around. It was an untenable model.

In 2003, a year in which the Inn lost about a half-million dollars, Bob Walton, vice president for finance and business, took a personnel action that was to have long-range consequences: He hired Ken Bogucki as executive chef; six months later, in spring 2004, Bogucki became general manager and began trimming costs. Before long, with the economy tanking and a necessity to find savings, the College made a significant financial decision. It established the Wooster Inn Management Company, which would own the building and lease operation of the Inn—and everything inside—to Bogucki, who set up his own firm, KMB Management Service Corporation, to run it. Since July 1, 2009, employees have been off the College payroll, working instead for Bogucki, a few full-time, most part-time (almost none students), using rules fit for a hotel/restaurant rather than a college. An entrepreneur, Bogucki established regular catering relationships and a popular weekly community event called Party on the Patio. In a city with a burgeoning number of quality restaurants, Bogucki's kitchen has more than held its own. To get the Inn a liquor license, he literally walked the neighborhood carrying a petition which led to a referendum that approved the license. This produced his most profitable new venture, the remodeling of a modest meeting room in the basement of the Inn, now called the Pub. It is an intentionally high-end space, not fit for student budgets, and it quadrupled projected earnings in its first two years. The College now has the same Inn for its guests, with more attractive amenities—and without losing money.

It should be obvious that Wooster's is a busy faculty, so perhaps one must ask what these teacher-scholars did in some of their spare time. In the February 1954 edition of the *Alumni Bulletin*, Dorothy Mateer, professor of English, explained why she and her colleagues deserved a club.

Why a Faculty Club anyhow? Why does a relatively small Faculty need one? The clearest answer lies in the fact that we're a pretty hardworking faculty and therefore find ourselves rotating between our separate classrooms or offices and homes with but passing glimpses of our colleagues except in committee meetings. As a result, we lose out on a chance for a kind of professional gossip and informal exchange of ideas that cements individual members of a Faculty into a cohesive group aware of what is "past or passing or to come" for Wooster in particular and for liberal arts colleges in general.

Opportunity arrived when the home of Edmund Secrest, the late director of the Ohio Agricultural Experiment Station (now the Ohio Agricultural Research and Development Center) and College trustee, came on the market; Bob Wilson offered to buy it for a club if the faculty would pledge to cover maintenance and operating expenses, which it did. The following fall, the club opened with a dining room for weekday lunch, a lounge, bedrooms available for male faculty, and a guest-room rental for alumni and friends. It was largely furnished by gifts from trustees and Wooster residents, and College students spontaneously contributed its prized possession, a sterling silver tea service. A few years later, the College decided it needed the space and demolished the former Secrest house, eventually using its lot, on the corner of University and Beall, for the Scheide Music Center. When Lowry Center opened, the faculty moved to a second floor room, named the Taeusch Lounge in honor of the former dean, a place for weekday lunches and an informal meeting spot for conversations and newspaper and magazine reading. In the twenty-first century, however, the administration took over the space, renaming it the Tartan Room, and the faculty club was no more.

It could also be asked, what students did in their spare time; among the many possible answers, one would have to be visiting the Shack. In 1915 Bill Syrios, an immigrant from Greece, founded a little snack bar in a small, unobtrusive building on Pine Street. He named it the Sugar Bowl, but everyone called it "the Shack." From sundaes and salads, the menu grew with the Shack's popularity, which was largely attributable to Bill's popularity. He proudly watched his three children graduate from the College—Anna, who became a physical education teacher, in 1948; Menelaus William (known as "Min," later "Bill"), a lawyer, in 1950; and Gus, a businessman, in 1952—before he died in 1957. In its heyday during the 1940s and 1950s the Shack was jammed during chapel hour, in the late afternoon after class, and from nine o'clock in the evening, when students began to desert the library, until near ten o'clock when the girls had to be in their dorms. The key difference between the Shack and the on-campus

Student Union—besides Bill's personality—was smoking; you could do it
in the Shack and not in the Union. Anna, who lived in the family apartment above the Shack nearly until her death in 2012, believed it was not
a coincidence that the Shack's attraction to students slipped when Bill's
death ended the "family touch." "My dad was like a father to the college
kids," she once said. "He had a fantastic memory. He knew their favorite
drinks [soft drinks and coffee], and who was dating whom. He loaned
them money and usually got repaid." The Shack went through a variety of
operators, and a brief name change to the Pine Street Café, but it gradually
lost touch with students, and local residents became its dwindling group
of customers. Even a beer license, won after a hard-fought struggle with
neighbors, didn't help. Too much competition developed over the years:
students could smoke and drink alcohol pretty much where they wanted
to; a club called the Underground began operation on campus; and Lowry
Center, with a number of attractions including Mom's Truck Stop, opened
in 1968. The building survived into 2012 as a small restaurant, but as a
neighbor of a campus that was expanding, its prospects were dim.

CHAPTER 4

Celebration and Dismay

As the decade of the '60s began, with bubbles of unrest ruffling the mostly placid waters of the earlier decade, the College's leaders looked positively toward the Centennial coming in 1966, and, needless to say, a fund-raising drive keyed to the big event. The goal was set at $20 million, a relatively modest amount, one that the trustees and President Lowry felt confident they could reach. Yet, in contrast to the sophisticated financial machinery that would soon become so much a part of every college's operation, attracting funds for Wooster then seemed almost unseemly, a touch beneath notice. Lowry himself did much of the fund-raising, and his friendships and charm appeared to suffice. Luck did help a little: Mabel Shields Andrews, widow of a Cleveland industrialist, saw the campus for the first time accidentally, when she came to town to visit the Agricultural Experiment Station. She met Lowry, and in a surprisingly short time the College had a new dormitory, Andrews Hall, and a few years later, Andrews Library. But the development—that is, fund-raising—arm of the College was, to put it mildly, lean, and the people running it tended to be retired Presbyterian ministers or missionaries.

Lowry was growing a bit anxious by 1962 when the ten-year Centennial Campaign was six years old and had raised about $5 million—although records were spotty enough that no one was certain of the exact figure. At that stage, only two-thirds of the trustees had contributed, and some had not even been approached. So he turned for help to G. T. "Buck" Smith, class of 1956, who was then working in the provost's office at Cornell University. Smith had grown close to the president as a Wooster student—he helped decorate the Lowry Christmas tree, and when Lowry returned home from a foreign leave, Smith arranged a parade up Beall Avenue and a rally in front of the president's home complete with pep band recruited by band director Stu Ling. (The president was driven from the railroad station by Louie Noletti, a College staffer who chauffeured him everywhere; Lowry never learned to drive.) As Smith returned from Cornell, a fund-raising consultant recommended that Wooster reduce its goal, but Lowry saw that step as an admission of failure; instead he fired the consultant and instituted a reorganization. Cary Wagner, then vice chairman of the board, agreed to replace U.S. Steel president Benjamin Fairless, who was totally inactive as chairman of the campaign; Winslow Drummond, a retired college president who was the vice president of development, was reassigned to seek funds around the country; and Smith, twenty-six years old, became director of the Centennial Campaign.

Who were potential contributors? Alumni not likely, because they were considered tapped out, having provided most of the funds for a renovation of Kauke Hall the previous year. One promising group was citizens of Wooster and Wayne County, and under the leadership of Don Noble, chief executive of Rubbermaid, they contributed about $500,000 toward a speech building named for a man they revered, Prexy Wishart. Then, out of the blue one day, came a call from a man in Toledo, named Ward Canaday, who was unknown to Wooster. Canaday, chairman of Willys-Overland and renowned as the father of the Jeep that helped win World War II, invited Lowry and Smith to lunch in Toledo; there he told them that he wanted to honor Dr. John Mateer, who had saved his wife's life at the Henry Ford Hospital in Detroit. Since Mateer's father, Horace, had taught geology and biology at Wooster for forty years, Lowry said a new biology building would be a good choice. Of the $1.5 million it would cost, Canaday quickly provided $250,000, and another patient of Mateer's, Mrs. Eleanor Ford, Edsel's wife, matched that; most of the remainder to build Mateer Hall came from borrowed funds, repaid over the next half-dozen years.

For all the attention Lowry had paid to the Presbyterian Church and its ministers, the churches of Ohio had not been significant contributors to the College. They became something of a fresh source to tap, with limited success. But there was one gigantic exception: Trustee Chuck Dilley introduced the College to Josephine Lincoln Morris. An involved member of Cleveland's Fairmount Presbyterian Church and an active philanthropist, Jo Morris was primarily concerned then with the emerging civil rights movement. At a reception at Dilley's home in the winter of 1963, seated next to Lowry and informed of his serious hearing problem, she was heard to announce loudly, according to Smith, "I have a helluva long list of things in which I'm interested, and Wooster's nowhere near the top." She was moved, however, to make a major starter gift to honor Frank Ferris, the longtime pastor of Fairmount who had subsequently taught at the College. To complete funding for the Ferris chair, a dinner was arranged at the elegant Wade Park Manor in Cleveland on Monday evening, November 25, 1963. It was the day of John F. Kennedy's funeral, the end of a weekend of national mourning. At first, the dinner was to be cancelled, but then Morris decided that the positive event would raise everyone's spirits; there was 100 percent attendance, and the $250,000 goal for the Ferris chair was reached within a month. The next year, Morris joined the Board of Trustees and contributed to the College in countless ways; when she retired from the board nine years later, she was succeeded by her daughter, Marjorie Morris Carlson, a 1963 graduate of the College, who served nearly forty years, including a term as vice chair.

It actually took a sharp rebuke to Lowry's pride to force increased attention to the College's long-range financial outlook. In the late 1950s, after an influx of Ford Motor Company stock had suddenly made the Ford Foundation the world's largest foundation, it set out to stimulate American higher education through challenge grants to leading colleges and universities. Lowry thought Wooster deserved to be among them—Independent Studies surely distinguished his college—but despite that program and the fact that he was well known in the East, Wooster was passed over in both the first and second waves of grants. The principal reason, it appeared, was the lack of a well-planned ten-year profile, especially when it came to financial prospects. Garber Drushal, who had recently become dean of the College, and Smith, now the chief development officer, went to work on a plan, and to put together the numbers Lowry reached into his economics department for a young professor named Hans Jenny. Invited to apply again, Wooster submitted its ten-year plan in 1963 and received a $2.2 million challenge grant; this was eventually matched with $5.5 million from other sources to become a critical part of the Centennial Campaign.

Getting the campaign to its goal, however, was a close thing. The climax was to come at the finale of a year-long centennial celebration, an all-classes reunion, with three tents arrayed on the playing field between the gym and Douglas Hall, and as many as three thousand expected for lunch. Lowry had just landed a $1 million gift from Foster McGaw that was to help build a new chapel—and he was to announce it publicly for the first time. Administrators also expected to mention a $600,000 bequest from Bob Wilson, the longtime board chairman, who had died the year before. But as the lunch began, Wilson's widow, Pearl, believing that she was not being shown proper respect, bolted from the party; Smith found her grieving at her husband's grave in the Wooster Cemetery and persuaded her to return. Thus, Lowry could announce both the McGaw gift and the Wilson bequest to a thrilled audience—and that the campaign had passed the $20 million mark. He was so pleased that he invited Pearl Wilson and others back to his home, where he broke out a bottle of his best Catawba grape juice to celebrate.

Lessons learned from the Centennial Campaign perhaps encouraged Lowry to tighten his administrative structure. The College had not had a vice president from 1901 to 1948, when Lowry appointed Harold Dalzell; Dalzell was succeeded in 1954 by Joseph P. Harris, and Winslow Drummond followed in 1960. All came from ministerial backgrounds and to the extent their responsibilities were known, it was for fund-raising. The centennial drive had begun under Harris, about whom one prominent trustee later commented: "The what and why of this vice presidency [was] something of a mystery to the board, . . . and [he] was soon to disappear from the scene." The academic leadership of the College historically came from the dean, a role Elias Compton filled from 1899 to 1921. Upon Compton's retirement, Prexy Wishart, who openly expressed his willingness to leave important academic decisions to the dean, chose John Kelso, who served eight years; Kelso was succeeded by William Westhafer, who served (although lacking a PhD) until Wishart's retirement in 1944. As dean, Lowry selected Bill Taeusch, his colleague in English, Harvard-trained, who had been teaching at Western Reserve. When Taeusch retired after seventeen years, Lowry, looking for a guide in science, brought the chemist Clark Bricker from Princeton; the match did not please either Bricker or Wooster particularly well, and he left after two years to teach and continue research at the University of Kansas.

Here, Lowry produced a surprise. He appointed Garber Drushal, who had spent seventeen years in the speech department; Drushal was popular with the faculty, but a professor of speech was not what many colleagues had in mind for their academic dean. Intensely interested in politics, Drushal had been elected president of the Wooster City Council in 1959 and moved his departmental position to political science in 1963. The next year, when Drushal and Lowry created an associate dean position to deal largely with Independent Study and faculty leave issues, the president recommended hiring Fred Cropp. Cropp, who had graduated from Wooster a decade earlier, was a geologist at the University of Illinois and returned to the College in the part-time associate dean position and as a professor of geology. In 1966, Lowry reorganized the administration with three vice presidents, starting with the elevation of Drushal's title to vice president for academic affairs. He named Hans Jenny as vice president for finance and business (previously vice president for budgetary affairs), and Smith as vice president for development, in recognition, Lowry said, of their efforts through difficult financial times, actions that earned applause from the trustees. All of the three continued with essentially the same responsibilities, just loftier titles. Having learned to respect Cropp's skill and energy, Drushal promoted him to dean. This group would remain intact for more than a decade.

Something else was troubling Lowry—as through the years it troubled many alumni: the deadly plague overtaking the campus's glorious arbor. "I would rather lose two good professors than one of those elms," he was supposed to have said. They, the trees, were going, though. In 1951 nearly five hundred elms were counted on campus when the dreaded Dutch elm disease was first known to strike. About eighty-five diseased trees were removed, and another seventy-five fell victim to campus construction. In 1963, for the first time, the disease reached the elms on Quinby Quadrangle, and as dying trees were removed the issue of how to save the rest or replace them was first discussed at Board of Trustee meetings. The campus grounds supervisor, Vernon Craig, reported that the fungus, *Ceratostomella ulmi,* was spread by the European elm-bark beetle, *Scolytus uultistriatus,* and there was no known cure. The instant Dutch elm disease was identified on a tree, in hopes of saving its neighbors, dead or dying branches or even the whole tree was removed in an effort to eliminate breeding places for the beetles, and DDT was sprayed in the early spring. Over the years, the weapons used to save College trees have included new plantings, disease control, pruning, and tree removal, but the struggle never ceases. In about 2002 the ash borer, a beetle native to Asia, appeared in the United States, and by 2009 it had surfaced in Wooster; the College began inoculating its half-a-hundred ashes with a systemic chemical that it must continue to apply periodically to save the trees' lives.

The best thing to happen recently to the College's beloved trees was the 1987 creation of a tree endowment, which allows donors to honor the College or memorialize loved ones, making possible both new plantings and ongoing care. In 2008, about three days before vice presidential candidate Joe Biden was scheduled to arrive, along with about forty-eight hundred visitors and national television cameras, a storm hit Wooster, pulling trees from their roots and flinging limbs in all directions. The entire ten-person grounds crew went on clean-up duty, and by the time of Biden's visit, the campus was spotless. The tree endowment covered the cost, estimated at $16,000. And the grounds crews and endowment appear to be winning. In 2012, more than three thousand trees watched over the campus.

As those magnificent elms were dying on the quadrangle, they suffered another painful demise in the court of public opinion. In October 1960, a *Voice* editorial argued that the "Love Song"—the recognized alma mater—had outlived its usefulness, inappropriate in both words and music; it criticized the "extreme sentimentality of the words, the closing 'Yoo-hoo,' the reference to Wooster University." Ralph Plummer had scribbled the song in one day in 1906, with a lyric testifying that Wooster was then in fact a university; the song had become the acknowledged alma mater, although never officially designated as such. Now the newspaper offered a $25 prize for the composition of a new alma mater. The contest, which drew several entries from alumni, faculty, and students, was won by two seniors, Sue Marshall as lyricist and Pat Carson as composer. Their contribution was titled "The Elms Are in Their Beauty":

> The Elms are in their beauty, the paths unwearied still;
> The lives of men they witness, a promise they fulfill.
> O Wooster thou hast heard us true, and found within us
>   wisdom new;
> As time reveals our debt to thee, we'll sing thy
>   praises true.

Inevitably the effort to unhorse a cherished tune like the "Love Song" sparked backlash, as evidenced by letters, even essays, in the alumni magazine. Before long the musical tribute to the elms—like the elms themselves—largely disappeared from the campus. And alumni events at the College still end, "Ever remembering, never forgetting, our love for you, dear Wooster U."

Although such sideshows occupied more of Lowry's time than he might have liked, his principal pleasure always came from the intellectual world. One high-level achiever was Dick Noble, class of 1964 (and son of a College trustee), who became Wooster's first Rhodes Scholar since 1921—and the only one until 1979, when Jennifer Havercamp became the College's first female Rhodes Scholar.[1] Probably the most famous student of the era, as it turned out, was a graduate of the class of 1961, a native Ohioan who had transferred to Wooster as a junior in 1959. John Dean served as White House counsel under Richard Nixon and testified at the Senate Watergate hearings in 1973 that he had warned the president of a growing cancer within the presidency. Dean later returned to his alma mater as a guest lecturer. At some point in the mid-1970s, his I.S. paper, which ordinarily would have been archived at the College, disappeared and has never been traced.

In the mid-1960s, Lowry found a fascinating intellectual challenge through an idiosyncratic professor of religion, Bob Smith, who had come to Wooster in 1960. (He was not related to Harold Smith, professor of religion since 1948.) Although Smith was an ordained Presbyterian minister like the other religion faculty, having earned both divinity and PhD degrees from Yale, "I am not at all a theologian at heart," he said years later, reflecting on his career. As a faculty member, he received an automatic place in the local presbytery, the organizational body of the Presbyterian Church for the Wooster area, but he found its meetings, focused on the needs and governance of churches, meant nothing to him, so he stopped attending. After he received a polite letter from the presbytery reminding him that he was missing required sessions, Smith responded with an equally polite message that he would demit, that is, give up his ordination, which in no way affected his status at the College. As a Yale grad student, he had spent a year working on archaeological projects in Jerusalem and Jordan, and at Wooster, he and classicist Vivian Holliday developed a course in ancient civilizations that they team-taught.

When the College received an unexpected $25,000 bequest in 1966,

1. Wooster's class of 1921 produced two Rhodes Scholars, Earl Meadow Dunbar and Marshall Knappen. Two men (only men were eligible then) were known to come close, John Compton, class of 1949; and Larry Caldwell, class of 1962, both finalists.

Lowry, who in those financially stressful times could have dropped the funds directly into the operating budget, instead offered it to Smith for an archaeological project. Wooster thus became the only private college in the country to mount a dig in the Middle East, or, possibly, in the world. After a preliminary trip to Jordan, Smith settled on a dig at the site of Pella, a village on the eastern slope of the Jordan Valley seventeen miles south of the Sea of Galilee, whose existence could be traced back for nearly four thousand years. Over the next months, a weather station was established and a farmhouse renovated there to provide a photography studio, kitchen, and pottery storage rooms. A Ford tractor and two dump trucks were shipped from the United States. By early 1967, a team of professionals and students, plus about a hundred local workers to do the heavy labor, had been assembled. In the spring of the academic year 1966–67, six Wooster students spent six weeks studying archaeology in Jerusalem, Israel, then moved to Pella to join the dig. (The students slept in tents in the farmhouse's courtyard.) "It really went very well," Smith recalled. "Most of the students turned out to be excellent. . . . So they made good records in the field for us, they followed instructions. . . . [We] got a lot of things accomplished, excavated a reasonable but not absurd amount. . . . The whole expedition, somehow we managed to do it on $25,000."

It was already getting uncomfortably hot in the Jordan Valley as the spring session ended May 20, but Smith planned a summer term that was to include students and some eager Wooster faculty. That day, in a letter to Wooster, he wrote: "No doubt at home there is considerable consternation over the Arab-Israeli tensions, but here in Jordan life goes on quite normally and there is widespread belief that the present crisis . . . will pass." Two days later in a visit to Israel, he found a note from the American consulate: "To all American citizens in the Jerusalem area; the local situation appears serious. American tourists are therefore advised by the Consulate General to make plans to depart at an early date for a more secure area."

Wooster's Pella dig was about to become a victim of the Six Days War. The students scattered, most of them finding refuge with a Wooster faculty couple, Arn Lewis, the art historian who was on leave in Beirut, Lebanon, and Beth Lewis, a European historian. In a hasty return to Pella, Smith found Jordanian troops digging artillery emplacements, but he was assured they were "only practicing." On May 28, he cancelled the second session. After the war, which began June 5, Smith visited the campsite, finding that "the war had passed Pella by." A quantity of material was shipped to Wooster for processing and study, and Smith returned to Pella in November 1967, planning for a 1968 dig. But given a drying up of funds and general anxiety, Wooster's expedition entered a hiatus. It was not until "twelve long years" later, Smith said, that the College mounted a second trip, this time in cooperation with the University of Sydney, with funding from the National Geographic Society and the National Endowment for the Humanities. Wooster dispatched teams for three years, skipped 1982, returned to Pella in 1983 and then in 1985, to tie up loose ends. Sydney, with Australian university research support, continued the work. Considering the sizes of his undergraduate student teams and modest finances, Smith was proud of what Wooster accomplished: "What we did was not only uncover more of a city that . . . would otherwise be subject to gradual, continual looting, but we also published several reports that give scholars the benefits of what we learned in terms of the ancient artifacts and pottery . . . what we found in tombs, in debris from ancient occupations. . . . I feel pleased with the reports we were able to publish."

In a twenty-first century when people work actively into their seventies and eighties, it is easy to forget that Howard Lowry was a few days short of his sixty-sixth birthday at the beginning of summer 1967. In one way he remained the original Howard—he had not lost his taste for the company of attractive young women; pretty undergraduate women could still get swift access to his office or dinner invitations, and one in particular, only five years out of college herself, was his hostess at the end. Nonetheless, to many of those closest to him, he had for some time seemed an old man, easily tired, a bit forgetful, hard of hearing. Close friends even suspected—after the fact—that he had actually suffered mini–heart attacks or mini-strokes that had never been acknowledged, let alone treated.

Lowry's poor health could have been exacerbated for any number of reasons, but one, certainly, was the 1960s' outburst of student protest, a general unrest on campuses nationwide that spread to Wooster. The original protest movement can be traced to a group of young men from North Carolina A & T University (what is now called a "historically black university") in Greensboro, who in January 1960 sat down at a segregated lunch counter in a Woolworth five-and-dime and would not be moved. Before long, white students in considerable numbers joined blacks in civil rights protests; the Mississippi summer of 1964 brought many whites—including students and faculty from Wooster—to help in voter registration campaigns in that segregated state (three students, two of them white from the North, were murdered). Different but related campaigns for student rights, what became known as the free speech movement—for changes in how campuses should be governed—began in the fall of 1964 at the University of California, Berkeley, and in following years it reached across the country. After the 1965 U.S. military escalation in Vietnam, student—and faculty—protest against the war grew increasingly angry and occasionally violent. Wooster's campus was by no means as unsettled as many others, but its tenor changed noticeably. In perhaps the worst affront of all to Lowry, students were even challenging the College's stand on religion. All of a sudden, it seemed, this was not the personal, academic, believing campus he had known and loved since 1919.

Lowry was a scholar who had become a college president, only one of the eminent presidents whose training and experience had ill-equipped them to cope with the new era. Student protest drove away many distinguished men—among them George Beadle at Chicago, Nathan Marsh Pusey at Harvard, Jim Perkins at Cornell, Doug Knight at Duke, and Grayson Kirk at Columbia. The most successful of their successors were trained as lawyers, in effect, crisis managers: Kingman Brewster at Yale, Ed Levi at Chicago, Terry Sanford at Duke, Derek Bok at Harvard, Bill Friday at the University of North Carolina, Morris Abrams at Brandeis. (They were not all lawyers: Steven Muller, a political scientist by training, guided Cornell through crisis and later successfully led the Johns Hopkins University; Drushal, a professor of speech and later political science, took command at Wooster.)

Gordon Tait, then a relatively new but increasingly influential professor of religion, remembered Lowry's administrative style: "He was a master at having public meetings. Students would say, 'Blaaaahh, blaaahh.' He'd say, 'Okay, let's have a public meeting, Tuesday at eight in the chapel.' He would show up, and he was at his best in terms of deflecting any criticism. 'Oh, yes, you make a good point, and I'll take that up with faculty, and we'll have a talk about that.' And of course, nothing ever happened, because he didn't want anything changed." Faculty agitation grew, and at some point Tait, as chairman of the Faculty Committee on Conference with Trustees, was designated to bell the cat—that is, inquire about when the president might consider retiring. Decades later, he squirmed as he related the meeting: "I went to Howard Lowry and asked him what his retirement plans were. He just sat there shocked. Finally, he said, 'Gordon, Gordon, where are the amenities?' Only a Matthew Arnold scholar could come up with that. Not, 'what the hell's wrong, Gordon,' but, in a whisper, where are the amenities. In other words, 'Where is the respect for the institution, and for me, and for what we stand for.' And I tried to explain, weakly, where I was coming from. And he just kind of shook his head. And I got out of there as soon as I could, decently." Tait's faculty colleagues agreed that the best that could be hoped for from the exchange was that it has caused the president to think about retirement. He did. He told the trustees in the spring of 1967 that he planned to retire after one more academic year.

In roughly the same period, one of Lowry's closest confidants, Buck Smith, was coming to a similar conclusion. Smith remembered one of their final dinners at the Greenleaf, a Wooster restaurant popular with faculty, at which Lowry inevitably ordered the "chippy-cheese" (melted ham and cheese) sandwich. He had asked Smith to peruse copies of two talks, a commencement address at Ohio Wesleyan University and his annual baccalaureate address at Wooster. The Wooster talk was called "On the Relevant" and the Wesleyan one, "The Apprentice's Secret." Smith said he contended that the baccalaureate was "not appropriate for The College of Wooster. These are your kids. You're scolding them . . . [about] living a life that is only being loyal to that which is relevant to you. The other talk is inspiring, embracing of the listener." In the event, Lowry made the switch, which worked both in Delaware, where the audience seemed untroubled by any scolding, and in Wooster, where the audience appreciated the Lowry they knew. In his final peroration Howard Lowry at The College of Wooster, he offered:

> In short, the apprentice's secret was life. It was by no means secret, and the aim of education is to put it in a man's heart so it lasts him all his days. We have never assumed here that a senior with a diploma is an educated man. Who, indeed, ever is? He is a potentially educated man, who knows how to continue his education to the very end of his life. . . .
>
> For whether we like it or not, we are all apprentices. This is our permanent assignment in a world that will always outrun even our keenest minds and the highest levels of our competence. . . . Our inevitable and permanent role as apprentices should keep us humble, but it should

exalt and not depress us. The endless knowledge that weighs upon us should engender in us no despair. . . .

There are the still-beckoning frontiers of medicine and science, of social justice, of population control, the production and distribution of goods, the enigmas of automation, our whole political tone and structure, the clearing of the air we breathe, the vexing problems of education, the nation's biggest business. . . . We are apprentices at service to our fellow men, for all our community endeavors and the devotion of many hands. . . .

Ladies and Gentlemen of the Class of 1967:

. . . It is bad form now to love a college. You are supposed to love the abstract things—like truth, and freedom and justice. But not a little piece of earth, or the homely memories of the changing seasons, or the times you had or the people you knew. No one is supposed to put roots down or have the sentiment of belonging. . . .

For belonging has its apprenticeship too. Unashamedly, this morning I express the hope that you will belong here. It will be good for Wooster, and it just may be good for you. At least the house will be always open.

The next Sunday, June 11, Buck Smith and his wife, Joni, drove Lowry to Delaware, where he gave the "Relevant" commencement address at Ohio Wesleyan. On the trip back, he suggested dinner at the historic Granville Inn, Smith remembered, "to celebrate the closing of my mouth." A few days later, he began a trip to California to visit his friend Gretchen Harmon. Although he almost never traveled by airplane, on these recent journeys he did, so eager was he to see Harmon. There was a brief stopover in Oklahoma City to visit Florence Wilson (donor of the Lowry Center book store), and at the airport she took his picture, raincoat folded over his arm—the last photograph ever taken of Howard Lowry. Then on to San Francisco. On the Fourth of July, 1967, Howard Lowry was gone.

PART 2

Changing with the Times

CHAPTER 5

Scientia et Religio ex Uno Fonte

In the *Voice* of December 9, 1960, appeared a statement that can be observed as a turning point in the history of religion at the College. It covered some seventeen hundred words, signed by nearly all of the forty-four Presbyterian Scholars. To be a Presbyterian Scholar—and more of them chose Wooster than any other Presbyterian-related college—was a big deal for young people who had been grounded in their local churches and had survived a national competition to receive the award. These were not the antiwar protestors or hippies who became so visible later in the '60s; rather, these students were so scrupulous that while the statement declared full support from thirty-nine of the forty-four, the students noted one of their number who disagreed with the statement, another who didn't think it went far enough, two who questioned a single element, and a fifth who simply announced neutrality. So their carefully crafted, more-in-sorrow-than-in-anger letter attracted the attention of everyone at the College, including Lowry, who, according to his biographer, considered this "his worst ordeal as president."

The Scholars began by decrying "the mutual inability of the administration and students to express their purposes and desires in terms understandable to each other. This lack of communication is basic." They contended that unlike in earlier generations, even students of strong religious convictions chose Wooster for its academic strength, not its church connection, and, "at present much of the exposure to Christianity at Wooster is superficial because it makes no more than a passing attempt to relate Christianity to the problems, questions, and issues in the student's mind." They complained that Westminster Presbyterian Church, trying to be both a church and a college chapel, did not satisfy either need. They sought not ending a religion requirement in the curriculum but rather "expanding the choice of courses." And they contended that faculty quality could be improved by withdrawing the rule that "it shall be the declared policy of the College to employ as regular members of the Faculty only men and women who are active members in good standing of some evangelical Christian church."

Then they offered some remedies for what they called the College's "intellectual provincialism": Establish "departments in Eastern and African [studies] to broaden the student's understanding of the world in which he lives." Increase "the number of foreign students. " Decrease "the percentage of Wooster graduates on the faculty and in the administration." They also suggested "a college chaplain who could devote his full time and energy to his campus ministry."

The Scholars' statement led to a committee formed by the Student Senate and the Student Christian Association, which took its cautious conclusions to the Board of Trustees the following March. In a subsequent report, delivered in chapel on May 15, 1961, five months after the statement, committee members told their fellow students: "We tried to indicate [to the trustees] that much of the dissatisfaction which has been expressed on the campus this year has arisen out of the belief that Wooster can do a better job of living up to its ideals, and not out of the belief that Wooster should change its basic ideas or goals. By doing this we hoped to make it clear that the specific recommendations for changes in college rules . . . represent more than just normal student griping."

In the chapel report, the committee declared, "First, we recognize that the church which supports this college does so because it believes that God became man in Jesus Christ. . . . Whether or not an individual student at Wooster accepts or rejects this belief can never affect the fact that this belief is the reason for the church-related college." This statement itself was perhaps a leap of faith that many students and faculty might not accept; in any case, the report contended that the College's true religious sense could not be maintained by forced rules. For example, the requirement that students attend the church of their choice at least eight times a semester should be changed to "the college encourages" such attendance, which "we feel would eliminate the present hypocritical attitude." Dealing with the religious restrictions on faculty, which might keep some professors from accepting positions at Wooster, the committee was extremely cautious; it suggested that the rule might be eliminated but might even be retained if "concern over the academic standards of the school could be largely alleviated without making an actual rule change." Finally, the committee dealt with "that overworked word, communication ... that the most important change for the health of the Wooster campus is the creation of a climate of opinion in which general campus discussion about college problems and intelligent student efforts to effect changes, is considered by all to be normal and natural."

The March 1961 meeting of the board had already portended a significant new element. President Lowry announced that James Blackwood, the pastor at Westminster for nine years who had been a stalwart within the church and a respected citizen of the city, would leave Wooster as soon as he could find another post. Blackwood later wrote that after the Presbyterian Scholars suggested he could not handle both the church and student chaplaincy, "nobody had to tell the pastor he was done for. He had known that a long time." Later that year, he left for a pastorate in Florida, where, among other things, he turned his writing skills to preparing a definitive biography of Howard Lowry. Blackwood's two successors over the next decade, Bev Asbury and Ray Swartzback, turned out to be extraordinarily successful at both the pastorate and the chaplaincy.

As anyone with a passing interest in the College's history knows, nearly all of the changes the Scholars sought have been realized: the religion question was removed from the faculty application in 1978; the first Jewish faculty member, historian David Gedalecia, joined the College in 1981, and others have since; an official chaplain, Linda Morgan-Clement—a Presbyterian—came aboard in 1996; scores of foreign students enrolled; a curriculum encompassing all world religions was developed. The Scholars' letter didn't bring about these changes—some came decades later—still, it was an opening. Change resulted because new minds came to the administration, faculty, and Board of Trustees, and certainly because the world outside left Wooster no choice but to look at itself, and the world, differently—to become and remain, in a word, relevant.

Needless to say, religion and the College have been intertwined since even before its beginnings. On the very first page of the first volume of Wooster's history, Lucy Lillian Notestein conjures up this image of a Presbyterian minister, J. A. Reed, in the autumn of 1865, as he looked, beyond the valleys of the Applecreek and Killbuck, to the hills. . . . With heart full, he dismounted, and at the edge of the woodland fell on his knees to give thanks for such beauty. Rising, he was startled with a new thought. What a site this would be for a college! What a place this for youth to come to for study, where in this view across the hills they might constantly be reminded of the glory of God! Again he sank to his knees. Might this be God's leading touching his heart? . . . that He might open the way for this college. . . . linked with that of the Church and its ministers.

The next year, the University of Wooster was officially organized. After being turned down by a Cleveland minister in their search for the first president, the trustees settled on Willis Lord, professor of didactic theology at a Presbyterian seminary in Chicago (it became McCormick Seminary). Lord's letter of acceptance spoke of "a new seat of liberal yet Christian learning" and closed, "I deeply feel the need of the hearty confidence and cooperation of the board and especially of the light and power that come only from God." On September 7, 1870, after prayers and hymns, Lord delivered an inauguration address startling in concept for its time: he took the controversial stand that women should be allowed to attend along with men, and he equated the study of modern languages with Greek and Latin. More, he insisted upon scientific study—Darwin's published theory was barely a decade old—which in no way conflicted with belief in God: "The hand which laid the foundations of the earth and balanced and lighted the stars in the heavens is the same hand that traced the lines and pages of the Bible; and that therefore, by no possibility, can the testimony of these great records conflict. There may be human misrepresentations of both; but there can be no jar in their real contents." President Lord's call seemed fitting for the new school's motto: *Scientia et Religio ex Uno Fonte*—Science and religion from one source.

A great number of things about The College of Wooster changed in its first three-quarters of a century, but one didn't: Lord's five successors—Archibald A. E. Taylor, Sylvester F. Scovel, Louis E. Holden, John C. White, and Charles F. Wishart—were all Presbyterian ministers. The first president not to be a minister was Howard F. Lowry, yet he was a devout Presbyterian layman, active in church leadership both on campus and nationally—he was a trustee of both the Pittsburgh and McCormick theological seminaries and a member of the church's Board of Foreign Missions.

In his first "Adventure in Education," published in 1945, Lowry left no doubt about his views in a passage titled, "Religion and Education": "At the heart of Wooster's adventure is the Christian religion. . . . In many ways, therefore, led by a faculty of Christian men and women, Wooster is a training in practical Christianity. . . . The glory of God would be badly served by second-rate courses in the arts and sciences. Wooster denies that there is any real incompatibility between a Christian education and a liberal education." Lest it be misunderstood, Wooster's national reputation under Lowry was what he intended: it was seen as a church-related college of liberal thinkers with high academic standards. Beth Irwin Lewis, the daughter of missionary parents who spent many years on Wooster's faculty and in the administration, said she was almost forbidden to apply to the College in 1952 because her extended family considered it too liberal.

Lowry's successor, Garber Drushal, who was raised in the Brethren Church, appeared to think it necessary to become a Presbyterian as he became president of the College. Henry Copeland, who followed Drushal, was a devoted Presbyterian who, in his inaugural address, "A Place Apart," stated, "Wooster was founded by Presbyterians who had the conviction that the Prophets, the Evangelists, the Apostles, and the Incarnate Word had provided glimpses of the timeless and the infinite and that divine principles of truth and righteousness ought to be incorporated into human affairs." Copeland made religion a central element of many speeches and so often ended talks with prayer that friends complained he left his audience reluctant to applaud. The next president, Stan Hales, was an Episcopalian, thus the first leader of the College who was not a Presbyterian; in search committee discussions as he was approved in 1996, it seemed apparent that he was Christian, but no one even raised the question of his religious choice. Hales's successor in 2007, Grant Cornwell, said he was raised an Episcopalian, then added, "Now I'm a philosopher. I have my own religious practices and beliefs."

In the early years of Lowry's presidency, Westminster Presbyterian Church was led by C. John L. Bates, a stately Canadian and the son of missionary parents, who became a civic leader in Wooster and whose wife, Jean, founded a popular nursery school.[1] In 1952, the year Blackwood succeeded Bates, an informal census of Wooster students by religious preference counted 604 Presbyterians, about half the student body. The next highest denomination was Methodist, 112, followed by Congregational, 63; there were, among others self-identified, 18 Catholics, 2 Jews, 1 Buddhist, and 1 Universalist.

The 1960s, as everyone knows, led to many changes in the United States, in organized religion not least, and the Presbyterian Church nationally was in the progressive forefront. A considerable number of its clergy took active roles in the civil rights movement and gave early support to campaigns against the Vietnam War and in favor of the women's liberation movement. With such new priorities, certainly including how it would spend its money, and a rising skepticism about religion among students, in 1963 the church released a study called "The Church and Higher Education." This recommended, among other things, that Presbyterian colleges no longer demand that faculty be "active members of some evangelical Christian Church" and that the curriculum be broadened to include "a mature classroom encounter with the Judaic-Christian heritage." The latter had already become a part of the Wooster curriculum; the former took longer.

It was hardly surprising then that by the late '60s the Presbyterian Church decided to cut loose its colleges. In 1968 the General Assembly of the Presbyterian Church USA (not yet united with the southern church) voted that synods should relinquish control, accepting "the wisdom of the synods divesting themselves of the particular responsibilities for direct election or confirmation of trustees or the exercise of other responsibilities that represent latent powers over the governance of the college. The capacities for responsible action by both synod and college seem to be enhanced when the autonomy of each is recognized and when a mutual working agreement becomes characteristic of the relation." On June 20, 1969, the Synod of Ohio passed this motion: "The Synod of Ohio, through proper action of the judicatory, will release any owners of the College of Wooster and its assets to the Board of Trustees . . . and will give to the

---

1. The nursery school was founded in 1946 as the Junior Women's Club Nursery School. Since 1974, when the College took ownership, it has been called The College of Wooster Nursery School. After the Bates family left Wooster, the school was headed by Esther Young, Clare Adel Schreiber, Lynn Akam, Carol Stewart, then Joyce Murphy.

Board of Trustees . . . the full freedom of electing its Board of Trustees." The College's lawyer, Dan Funk, drew up the first change of incorporation detail in more than a century, which the board approved and was filed with the state. Whether any students noticed is problematic.

To its 1968 declaration, the Assembly had added that if any colleges wanted to remain church-related, they could adopt new covenants of affiliation with the synods. On Wooster's behalf, Drushal negotiated such a covenant, which had two benefits: It pleased a large portion of the faculty by making clear that the College was freed from church ownership, and it also pleased important trustees and donors, as well as many alumni, because the covenant officially maintained Wooster's ties to the church, the importance of which Drushal well understood. Citing "a great deal of misunderstanding" about the new order, in the fall of 1969 the relatively new president and relatively new Presbyterian said, "It should now be clear that The College of Wooster still remains a church-related institution of the United Presbyterian Church, USA, and that this relationship is expected to grow and develop through the years." Every five years since, the covenant has been renewed (now with the Synod of the Covenant, which consists of the Presbyterian churches of Ohio and Michigan) without much ado and without a great deal of responsibility on either side; the synod makes a token $10,000 annual gift to the College, which in turn gives it to Westminster.

It cannot be ignored that these changes were occurring in a time of national turmoil on many fronts—notably civil rights advancements in a stubborn South and furious protests against the Vietnam War—and inevitably the Wooster campus would be swept up in this unrest. Still, to an element on the Wooster board the College need not yield completely either to broad national change or to unwinding ties with the church. The Board had tasked the Committee on Religious Dimension, chaired by trustee Juliet Stroh Blanchard, to undertake a long-range study of the relationship between the College and the church, and on May 31, 1968—less than two months after the assassination of Martin Luther King Jr. and on the eve of the Robert Kennedy assassination—it began its report:

> Basic Assumptions—Wooster is a Christian college. "Our educational experience has been, is now, and shall be rooted in the deep conviction of Protestant Christianity." This commitment has been stated unequivocally in various ways in the Charter, Catalogue, and many College

publications and documents. . . . The Committee accepts these statements as the philosophical framework within which to examine the religious life of the College . . . Without resolving all of the ideological differences, the term "religious dimension" is interpreted not as something peripheral, or optional, or adjunct to the pursuit of knowledge, but as an integral part of the intellectual, personal, and social life of the college community . . . To put it very directly, if Wooster is, in fact, a Christian college, it ought to be different from other independent liberal arts colleges which make no such claim or which consider church-relatedness a handicap.

The twenty-six page report ranged across relations with the national Presbyterian Church and with Westminster, church-sponsored events on campus, the quality of the religion department, and student activities and standards of conduct. It accepted the idea that a certain number of church attendances should no longer be required but came down in favor of a required "chapel," even though "its form, content, and title be revised to be more consistent with prevailing conditions." It recommended an official Committee on Religious Dimension—which the board established and which remained part of the board's governance structure for more than four decades. The report concluded: "The College of Wooster, conceived, nurtured, sustained by Christians for a century, in this new day seeks to be Christian in a pertinent, vital fashion."

The committee evaluated the Department of Religion at the College as "outstanding." All of its eleven faculty members—all male and four of them part-time—owned divinity degrees; eight had earned PhDs (Aurelia Takacs, who held degrees from Oxford University, Union Theological Seminary, and Columbia University, was the first woman to serve in the department, as a leave replacement in 1960–61.) It offered twenty-one different courses and averaged thirty to forty majors every year. The committee reserved special praise for the department as a "counseling resource." "A discussion of religious and personal questions of individual students is a large part of the work [of the faculty]." Its model was Art Baird, the leading, and at times single, proponent of teaching "religion" as the department's most important task and assuming a pastoral role. He inspired many students in the classroom, and a certain element of them turned to him for counseling outside the classroom.

Yet, by then, the faculty, chaired by Gene Tanner, who had come to the College in 1953, was assuredly reinventing itself. Baird's position led to some tension within the department, since his colleagues preferred a more academic approach and considered counseling better left to pastors. One of them, Harold Smith, a scholar of world religions, declined to teach sections of the New Testament. Bob Smith, a scholar of ancient civilizations, became so uninterested in the routines required of a Presbyterian minister that he gave up his ordination. Gordon Tait, a scholar of religious history, authored both a fiery essay on Prexy Wishart's ideological victory over fundamentalist William Jennings Bryan for leadership of the Presbyterian Church in 1923 and an important work on John Witherspoon, the Presbyterian minister who led New Jersey's delegation to the Continental Congress and signed the Declaration of Independence.

Not accidentally, in 1969 the Department of Religion became the Department of Religious Studies. As would be expected, change was coming to the curriculum. Historically, some courses on the Bible had been taught by ordained Presbyterian ministers without PhDs, and until the '60s students could fulfill their religion requirements with a semester course in the Old Testament and a semester course in the New Testament. It did not please scholars in the department that Virgilius Ferm, who had come to Wooster in 1927 and headed the philosophy department until his retirement in 1964, had taken upon himself the responsibility for teaching some of the more thoughtful courses in religion, dealing with the history of Christian thought and the philosophy of religion. By the late '60s, though, the religious studies scholars had taken over, and the yearlong religion requirement could be fulfilled with such courses as Christian Theology or American Religious Groups, which included Catholicism, Judaism, and various denominations of Protestantism.

Over the years, both course offerings and requirements continued dramatic change, and the 2011–12 catalog is illustrative. Courses in the religious studies department were presented in two areas. The first, called "Religious Traditions and Histories," offered such courses as "American Religious Communities, Chinese Religions, African Religions, Hinduism, Buddhism, Islam, The Life and Teachings of Jesus, The Life and Thought of Mahatma Gandhi, Global Christianity, Native American Religions and Culture, Third World Feminist Theology." The second area, "Issues and Theories in the Study of Religion," offered "Ethics in a Social Perspective,

Women and Religion, New Religious Movements, Religion and Spiritual Biography, Christian Ethics, Religion and Film." Biblical Hebrew could fulfill the foreign language requirement. And the only theology requirement for graduates of the College was called "Religious Perspectives," in which "students . . . complete a course from any department or program that examines the religious dimension of humankind in relation to issues of cultural, social, historical, or ethical significance."

In one of those coincidental but quite wonderful turns of fate, the '60s upheaval in religious consciousness at the College—and elsewhere— brought to Westminster Church two ministers who could not have better fit the tenor of the times. The first was Bev Asbury, Blackwood's immediate successor in 1962; the second was Ray Swartzback, who followed Asbury in 1967 and served until 1972.

Asbury's journey to Wooster was unusual. A Georgia native and graduate of the Yale Divinity School, he landed at a liberal Southern Baptist church in Zebulon, North Carolina, at the age of twenty-four; inconveniently for the liberal young pastor, North Carolina was turning sharply conservative. Asbury's efforts on behalf of civil rights and labor unions led to establishment pressures that his church could not withstand, and, he recalled later, "I was asked to leave the state of North Carolina." He moved to Westminster College in Fulton, Missouri, where he became a Presbyterian, and soon took a Presbyterian pulpit in Webster Groves, a St. Louis suburb. The Yale chaplain, William Sloane Coffin, recommended him to Wooster's Westminster search committee. He was scouted by Bill Craig, chairman of the College's speech department; they hit it off, and he was offered the Westminster pulpit.

Soon Memorial Chapel was packed every Sunday, and popular demand led to the reprinting of his sermons. In Wooster, he led a civil rights march from campus downtown, and he took a dangerous journey to Hattiesburg, Mississippi, along with religious studies professors Tait and Harold Smith, to support voting rights for blacks. But perhaps more important he became a trusted counselor to students: a Danforth Foundation study indicated that he was advising more students than ministers at any other campus in the nation. He also shared with Vi Startzman, director of the medical center in Hygeia Hall, programs in pre-marriage counseling.

When Asbury left at the start of 1967 to become the first campus chaplain at Vanderbilt University, his surprising successor was Swartzback.

"Ray made me seem like a conservative," joked Asbury, whom Swartzback invited back several times to preach at Wooster. A World War II veteran wounded in the Battle of the Bulge, Swartzback began his career at twenty-six in a working-class, white, industrial area of Cincinnati, with a pulpit that had gone unfilled for several years. A 1954 cover story in *Presbyterian Life,* titled "The Church Nobody Wanted," chronicled his success at building the congregation from zero (his wife was the only person in the pews the first Sunday) to the hundreds. Then this young white man took over a black church in inner-city Detroit, which, during the riots of 1967, was the only structure in its neighborhood left undisturbed.

Swartzback, who told the Westminster search committee that he would serve no longer than five years, was attracted by the fresh opportunity but almost shell-shocked by his new surroundings, as he later described: "From a congregation steeped in the black experience, a congregation that knew how to syncopate, I found myself toe-tapping to the strains of Bach. From a support community composed of domestic workers, assembly-line hands, and political activists, I found myself confronting thirty-five retired missionaries, a host of PhDs, a smattering of students, and a goodly number of town persons—all deeply committed to the world of books."

Fortunately for both Swartzback and Wooster, he arrived just as a growing number of white students were angered by the Vietnam War and the relatively small black student population was angered by what seemed a lack of administrative effort to increase diversity. Perhaps unique at the College, both groups grew to trust him. So when the campus seemed on the verge of eruption after the killings at Kent State, and when black students threatened to disrupt Homecoming, Swartzback was a steadying influence. In 1972, true to his word, he left the College to serve in Glenville, a largely black area of Cleveland, from where he went to a similar church in the New York City borough of Queens, before retiring to a small farm in southern Ohio, where he spent much of his later years devoted to his lifelong hobby of carving wooden songbirds.

Like those of other principal elements of the College, the religious perspective of the Board of Trustees changed dramatically over the years. The University of Wooster was incorporated in the state of Ohio on December 18, 1866, by the Synod of Ohio of the Presbyterian Church, and its first board declared: "Resolved that we enter upon the work of establishing the University of Wooster with the single purpose of glorifying God in promoting sanctified education and thus furthering the interests of the church and its extension over the whole earth." Since the Synod of Ohio continued as the College's owner of record until the 1960s, it officially appointed all Board members, although approval of the board's own choices had long been a formality. At that point, according to the bylaws, at least 75 percent of the board's members were to be "communicant members" of the Presbyterian Church, and as many as five of its thirty-six members were Presbyterian ministers. (Almost never did a year go by in those days that at least one Presbyterian minister in Ohio was found worthy enough to receive an honorary degree from the College, and one year there were four.) The bylaws have been amended several times to reduce the Presbyterian requirement, first to 50 percent, then to 33 percent, then to 25 percent. No other religious qualification appears in the bylaws, and it is impossible to tell when a Roman Catholic was first elected to the board, but it is probable that, in 1974, Harold Freedlander, one of the city of Wooster's most prominent businessmen and philanthropists, became the first Jewish member.

It didn't seem to matter that not until 1969 did the board officially control the College; the differences were internal and moved with the times. Every board meeting and every board dinner into the twenty-first century began with a standard Christian prayer; now the prayer can be Hindu and offered in the language of Nepal, or the gathering can be welcomed with a Unitarian Universalist reading. The longstanding Committee on Synod Relations fell out of date as the College became independent. When in June 1969 the board replaced it with a Committee on Religious Dimension, the committee was led for its first eight years by Juliet Blanchard and bulwarked by fellow trustee Chuck Dilley—staunch defenders of the religious history and customs of the College. Blanchard told the board in June 1970 that the committee needed to offset the rumor—presumably from the 1968–69 negotiations—that "the churches have kicked out the colleges."

The committee met regularly with the chairman of the Department of Religious Studies, the pastor of Westminster, and, eventually, the College chaplain, along with other interested faculty and students. In later years, led by John Compton, a renowned professor of philosophy at Vanderbilt University (and son of Arthur Compton), and Gene Bay, senior pastor of the Bryn Mawr Presbyterian Church, it performed a significant role for the board, monitoring and reporting on both the changes in campus procedures—the end of required church attendance, reduction in the number of days for chapel attendance, the change in name from "chapel" to "convocation," the elimination of regular convocation—and also efforts to bring religion and spirituality to the College in new ways. In short, it served as a connecting link between the College as it had been—dear to large numbers of alumni—and the College as it was becoming. Ultimately that ended, too. The committee survived until 2011 when a reorganization of the board allowed it only ad hoc status, subsuming its responsibilities into two other committees, those of academic and student affairs.

That newer religious dimension of the College took another consequential turn in 1995. When dedicated trustee Henry R. Luce III (whose grandparents were Presbyterian missionaries in China) wanted to honor Henry Copeland upon his retirement as president, Copeland suggested endowing a College chaplaincy. Luce did, insisting upon naming the position the Henry Jefferson Copeland Campus Chaplain and Director of Interfaith Campus Ministry and adding the concession to history that the holder be a Presbyterian minister. Until this endowment, the role had been filled in eclectic ways. Some years, the minister of Westminster accepted the dual functions of pastor and chaplain; as responsibilities grew, an associate pastor at the church, Cynthia Jarvis and Barbara Battin among them, served as de facto chaplain. It was one of Copeland's insights that the College would benefit from separating the chaplain's role from the church, and the Luce endowment made that possible.

As it happened, the connection to Wooster's history and the concession to modernity were nearly perfect: The first, and only (to 2012), campus chaplain was a Presbyterian minister, Linda Morgan-Clement, born in Hong Kong and raised in the United States, a classic tie to the missionaries who had gone to China in the nineteenth and twentieth centuries, gone from Wooster to carry Christianity to the Far East, then frequently sent their children to the College and not infrequently returned to Wooster in retirement. That said, she was every bit a modern American woman. Morgan-Clement came to Wooster with no specific marching orders—it was not clear whether she was to be pastor only to students or to the entire campus—and she spent years creating her position. For example, she and the dean of students, Ken Plusquellec, himself an ordained Presbyterian minister, fairly quickly agreed that the College of Wooster Volunteer Network, students who work in the community, seemed appropriate to campus ministry, so she took charge of that. She also focused on building a multi-faith campus ministry, rather than an interfaith one, which she believed locked students into "silos," Muslims in one place, Jews in another, Christians in another.

Assigned to windowless space in the basement of Lowry Center, she went to work on diversity—what she called the "critical non-mass"—meaning that none of the faith groups, even Presbyterians by this time, was big enough to go off on its own. Although by no means do all students, whatever their faiths, belong, the College has, for instance, an active Newman Club for Catholic students and an active Hillel for Jewish students. A nun serves as the campus Catholic minister, and the national Inter-Varsity Christian Fellowship supports a full-time staff member. Rabbi Joan Friedman, a scholar of religious history and a tenured faculty member, holds trifurcated status: one-third time a member of the Department of Religious Studies, one-third in the Department of History, and one-third an advisor to Jewish students. The year 2007 brought for the first time a Muslim to the annual Theologian-in-Residence program. Morgan-Clement also teaches—Feminist Theology and the Theology of Peace over the years as well as a course titled "Inter-Faith Dialogue."

One of Morgan-Clement's proudest contributions to the College was to develop a multi-faith baccalaureate service. Over the years, baccalaureate had come to seem vanilla—a Christian framework, usually with a Presbyterian minister preaching, but, as sensitivity grew for all faiths, without mention of the sacred. Then, with student input, the service became welcoming to parents of all religious faiths, with, for instance, names for the sacred in many faiths spoken and used. In 2011, the baccalaureate speaker was Rabbi Patricia Karlin, one of Stanford University's chaplains. Morgan-Clement's baccalaureate prayer that day began: "May our praise rise like incense and our gratitude soar like music, Gracious Creator. We have come to this place from across the globe; drawn together for the lives of our seniors, a shared love of learning, and dreams of a better world. We thank you for binding us together across oceans of difference—Obvious and invisible, Explored and denied, Respected and repressed—All of which have become a part of this place that we call Wooster. We are grateful for so much."

CHAPTER 6

"Quite Astounding Women"

Yvonne Williams, professor emeritus of political science and black studies and former dean of the faculty, recalled a vivid introduction to the College in 1959:

> I was very much in awe of many of the women who were on the faculty. They were quite astounding women when you think about it. People like Dorothy Mateer, Fran Guile, Ibby Coyle, Maria Sexton, Miss Dunham. They were amazing women. I was sensitive to that, having come from my experience at Harvard. [Yvonne spent a year at the overwhelmingly male Harvard Law School before deciding to earn her PhD.] So they made a real impression on me. And chairs of departments. Aileen Dunham in history. Dorothy Mateer in English, Fran Guile and Pauline Ihrig in French. When you think about these women in the context of the whole of academia, Wooster was the kind of school that did not, I think it was their Presbyterianism, they did not want to attract too much attention. So, a person like Maria Sexton was never given the credit she was due, in terms of her accomplishments with the Olympic team, the Olympic Committee.

Yvonne Williams and her husband, Ted Williams, a skilled chemist and extraordinary teacher and mentor, played significant roles at the College for four decades. Ted we will talk about elsewhere. But it is useful here to skip through time and talk about Wooster's women of an earlier era and more recent eras.

The career path of female scholars at Wooster has been something of a roller coaster. As Yvonne Williams discovered in awe, many of the most important members of the faculty were women at a time when almost no leading university or liberal arts college could make that claim—or, it appeared, even wanted to. Here is a sampling of the roster Howard Lowry found upon the beginning of his presidency in 1944: four full professors, Rebecca Mary Thayer in English, who had joined the faculty in 1918; Aileen Dunham, in history, 1924; Mary Z. Johnson, in political science, 1926; Eve Roine Richmond, in music, 1926. At assistant professor rank, there were Pauline Ihrig, in French, 1923; Elizabeth E. (Ibby) Coyle, in biology, 1926; Eva Mae Noonan, in classics, 1927; Frances V. Guille, in French 1937.[1] The full faculty included twenty-three women, about one-third of the total, although of twenty-three departments, only three were headed by women. Among the remarkable elements about this roster was that it went almost unremarked-upon either at the College or anywhere else. In a lecture summarizing his half-century career, the University of Texas historian Dick Graham (Wooster class of 1956) recalled of his undergraduate days, "Aileen Dunham . . . was a formidable person both in class and out of it. I was too naïve and unobservant to notice that as a woman with authority she stood out in America at that time."

As at other colleges, men always predominated on the faculty, but how had Wooster assembled such a roster of women professors? Absent any contemporary record of the mind-set among top administrators, the question today produces only speculative answers. The central figure here is Prexy Wishart, at once a staid minister and a humane moderate—witness his successful clash with William Jennings Bryan early in his Wooster presidency. Except for Professor Thayer, appointed the year before he arrived, all of these women joined the faculty under Wishart's leadership. Many were known quantities, honored graduates of the College—Ihrig; Coyle; Guille; Richmond; and Dorothy Mateer, a member of a prominent Wooster family, whom her friend Howard Lowry brought back in 1949. As a group, they held doctorates from distinguished universities: Johnson and Noonan from the University of Chicago; Ihrig, Columbia; Thayer, Cornell; Dunham, a native Canadian, from the University of London. But

1. Pauline Ihrig graduated from the College in 1923, first in her class. Howard Lowry graduated second.

those same universities rarely accepted women to their faculties in the 1920s or '30s, which meant that finding a job above secondary school was a challenge. Mateer did well, rising to become director of the high school at The Dalton School, one of New York's most elite private schools, but taught at no college until her appointment at Wooster. Their difficulty in reaching higher education positions was one reason they would work for lower salaries, which Wishart, reasonably, from the Wooster budget standpoint, took advantage of.

Another important thing they had in common: nearly all were single— in contrast to male faculty members, who were assumed to be raising families. Guille and Helen Kaslo, who came to Wooster in 1951, married for the first time later in life, but most of the group remained single. Some lived alone—Dunham, for example, in a modest, well-tended house on Palmer Street that she willed to the College. Coyle spent years resident in Holden Hall. Clare Adel Schreiber, who lived more than seven decades in Wooster as a faculty wife, head of the nursery school, prolific writer, and community leader, speculated, "They were not terribly happy about their lives. I think they did a lot of private quibbling about it. But nothing much happened." It cannot be said definitively that they chose to devote their lives only to scholarship, but there is evidence that they saw themselves as making such a decision. When Beth Irwin Lewis, a prized student of Dunham's, returned with a PhD from the University of Wisconsin, her mentor said, "You've failed me." How did I fail you, Lewis wondered. The answer: "You got married." A member of the same class as Lewis, Priscilla Courtelyou Little recalled small gatherings of history honors students at Dunham's home, where she spoke of "how difficult it had been to make her way as a woman in the academic world." Once, Little remembered, the longtime head of Wooster's history department poignantly observed, "You couldn't be married and be a professor, too."

Whatever their choices, these women built distinguished careers, and students at Wooster were the beneficiaries, even if the rest of the world didn't know much about them. Fran Guille, however, alone of all the redoubtable women on the faculty during this era, turned research into fame. Frances Vernor Guille, a twin who lived much of her life with her sister in Wooster, graduated from the College in 1930, earned her master's degree from Western Reserve University in 1936, and over the next decade bounced around the College's administration and faculty, as an assistant in the alumni office and as an assistant dean of women while teaching French part-time. She left in 1947 to complete a doctorate at the Sorbonne in Paris, which focused on the life of Francois-Victor Hugo, author Victor Hugo's son. While she was examining family documents at the home of Jean Hugo, Victor's great-grandson, he referred several times to a diary that he thought had been kept by his great-aunt, Adele, and although he offered several leads to its existence, Guille could never run it down.

In 1955, by which time she was a professor of French at Wooster, Guille read in a French literary journal that a diary of Adele Hugo existed in the Pierpont Morgan Library in New York City. Apparently the twenty-five hundred pages—scraps, really—had been treated as junk after Victor's death in 1885; a London dealer sold them to the Pierpont Morgan. Before she had even seen the diary, Guille wisely obtained permission from the library to work on it and permission from the Hugo family to publish it. Later, she remembered "being more frightened than elated" when she saw the pages, most undated, rarely in chronological order, hard to read—sometimes written in what seemed to be a code. After getting the package microfilmed, she spent a year's research leave, 1956–57, in front of a reader at a friend's guesthouse in Florida, aided for part of the time by her Wooster mentor, Professor John Olthouse. She also spent weeks on the Channel Island of Guernsey, where the Hugo family had lived, and traveled to Nova Scotia, where the besotted Adele had chased after the English army officer with whom she was in unrequited love. And the shape of a volume of the diary began to form in Guille's mind.

Not until 1968, thirteen years after she had first determined that there actually was a diary, was the first volume of *Le Journal de Adele Hugo* published. Guille was in Paris on May 7, 1968, when the publisher called and asked if she wanted the first copies delivered to her Paris lodging. "Oh, no," she recalled. "I ran (in spirit, for I went by bus) to the Rue de Cardinal Lemoine and carried away ten precious copies. As I started home with my loot, I noticed many police cars on the streets near the Sorbonne." It was the start of the 1968 Paris student uprising. The book, however, was noted nowhere except in the academic community, until one day a young French film director idly picked it up in a Left Bank shop. After reading Guille's mini-biography of Adele, which was the introduction to the diary, Francois Truffaut, the most acclaimed auteur of the French New Wave, was intrigued by its cinematic prospect; he spent six years off and on creating a script, and in 1975 he directed *The Story of Adele H*—with a prominent onscreen credit to Frances V. Guille. Given the coveted New York Film Festival closing slot that October, the movie enchanted a sold-out audience in Lincoln Center. Vincent Canby, the chief critic of the *New York Times*, called "Truffaut's profoundly beautiful new film" the "highlight" of the festival. Explaining Adele's inability "to cope with the truth," Canby continued: "she kept a coded journal, only recently deciphered. It is this journal that is the basis for Mr. Truffaut's most severe, most romantic meditation upon love." The difficult-to-please Pauline Kael exulted in the *New Yorker:* "[It] is a musical, lilting film with a tidal pull to it . . . a feat of sustained acuteness . . . and it's Truffaut's most passionate work."

On the evening of the showing in New York, President Garber Drushal gave a small dinner party in Guille's honor at the Plaza Hotel. With her was her husband of two years, Walter Secor, a longtime professional acquaintance who had retired as professor of French at Denison University. (Secor, a widower, and Guille had first established a personal friendship when they ran into each other in a Parisian café.) After the movie ended, Truffaut, a small man with unruly hair, in black tie, emerged on the stage to cheers. In his curtain speech, he credited Guille as the editor of the source and beckoned her to stand in her box to be saluted by the audience. Later that evening, Carol Dix, a Wooster trustee, and her husband, Ray Dix, publisher of the *Daily Record,* hosted a reception in her honor at a hotel across Columbus Avenue from Lincoln Center. Francois Truffaut—who no doubt could have attended any number of other parties—arrived with his gorgeous twenty-year-old star, Isabel Adjani—and they stayed. What better capstone could a professor of French from a small liberal arts college in the Midwest have for a career—or for a life. A few days later, Guille began to feel uncomfortable in her Kauke Hall office. "What does a heart attack feel like?" she asked her husband, and requested he take her to the hospital. Eight days after the most momentous evening of her life, Fran Guille died.

By that time, nearly all the astounding women who awed Yvonne Williams had retired, in almost every case without being replaced by other women. Just as certain national economic and social conditions had brought so many women to the faculty in the 1920s and '30s, other conditions helped reduce their number in the '60s and '70s. Soon after World War II ended, men flooded into graduate schools; at the same time, given the mores of the era, many young women who might have pursued graduate degrees chose instead to marry and raise children at home; thus, men filled the pipeline leading to faculty positions. In Lowry's final year as president, Wooster's expanded faculty consisted of twenty-seven women, almost the same as in his first year, but now ninety-six men, more than twice as many as that first year, and still only three of twenty-four departments were chaired by women.

Among the few women who joined the faculty in those years was Vivian Holliday, who grew up in a South Carolina village and enrolled in a tiny women's college at which the students wore uniforms, intending to major in elementary education. But she "kept exploring," went on to earn a doctorate at the University of North Carolina, and arrived at Wooster in 1961, to succeed Eva Mae Noonan in what was then called the Department of Greek and Latin. (Six other women came at the same time, but only one stayed more than a year or two.) Although Holliday brought a doctorate, she received only the "instructor" rank, which was given to men who were still working on their dissertations. But the young classicist demonstrated her academic ability and charm quickly and was soon invited to join select social company. Lowry knew that many of the visiting dignitaries who lectured at the College wanted to unwind with a nightcap, but he did not want to serve alcohol at the president's house. So he would call on his friend Dorothy Mateer to entertain a group at her apartment in a remodeled barn at the corner of Beall and Bowman. "I sat there mesmerized," Holliday remembered. "I couldn't ask questions, but whatever was mentioned at Dorothy Mateer's, when the bookstore opened the next morning, I would be there to buy the book."

While a few women joined the faculty every year during the 1960s—Deb Pacini (Hilty), as instructor in English and later secretary of the College, in 1964, and Thalia Gouma-Peterson, the eminent art historian, in 1968, among the more notable—the decade brought significant retirements: Richmond in 1964, Dunham in 1966, Mateer in 1967, and Ihrig in 1970. Although Betty Friedan's *The Feminine Mystique* appeared in 1963, it took years to filter into the national consciousness; "women's liberation" was only becoming a national byword as women paraded on Fifth Avenue in 1970 and *Ms. Magazine* was founded in 1971. At Wooster, many women felt marginalized. For support, a number of them, led by Beth Lewis, who served variously as a faculty member and administrator (and was married to a faculty member), began in 1972 to meet weekly for lunch in a small dining room at Lowry Center—what they called the "Women's Table"—occasionally teased by male faculty passersby. The next year, Lewis organized a women's lecture series (for instance, historian Helen Kaslo Osgood spoke on the correspondence between Abigail and John Adams) that brought guests from nearby universities to discuss common interests.

Inevitably, fresh attention to women's issues found its way into the academic program. As early as 1971–72 the catalog listed an interdepartmental course in history and religious studies that examined the traditional definitions of masculinity and femininity through physiological and psychological dimensions. The next year Hilty and the historian Jim Turner—widely credited as the man most responsible for promoting women's programs at the College—taught an interdepartmental course, "Women in History and Literature," and classicist Holliday taught "Sex Antagonism in Western Literature," tracing its history to the Greeks and Romans. By 1978, the faculty had approved a minor in women's studies, its introductory course "Women in Contemporary Society," taught by Turner (who died in 1986). The minor offered courses on fiction by women, women's history, women in sports, and a junior-senior–level seminar.

The faculty tide also began to rise again in the late '70s. A turning point could be found in 1976, when two leaders of the new era of powerhouse women joined the faculty: Carolyn Durham, a University of Chicago PhD (and a Wellesley classmate of Hillary Rodham) in French, and Joanne Frye in English—someone really different, a single mother of two small children, hired so late that her name was added out of alphabetical order at the end of the faculty roster in the catalog. In the 1970s, too, husbands and wives came to the faculty together: Barbara and Jim Burnell in economics, Beth Lewis in history and Arn Lewis in art history, and Susan and Dick Figge in German (although they had to share one position for a while).

Faculty women agreed that the Henry Copeland presidency, which began in 1977, brought a wave of women who made an indelible mark on the College over the next several decades—among them, in 1978, Yvonne Williams returning with her PhD to political science and black studies; in 1981, Josephine Wright in music and black studies and chemist Virginia Pett; in 1987, physicist Shila Garg, who later became dean of the faculty and interim provost, Nancy Grace and Debra Shostak in English, and Elena Sokol in Russian studies; in 1989, Madonna Hettinger, a medieval historian; in 1992, Jenna Hayward in English and Lori Bettison-Varga, a geologist who became president of Scripps College. During this time, too, family-friendly administrative modifications were implemented. Faculty meetings were moved from 7:00 P.M. to 4:00 P.M. so parents did not have to leave home in the evening and arrange for child care. In earlier years, faculty members who were parents did not bring their children to campus; it just wasn't done. But bit by bit, strollers became nearly as commonplace on campus as they had been during the postwar veterans' era, and the sounds of children were known to ring in Kauke halls. "All of a sudden there were children all over campus," Hayward noted, adding, "and the students loved it."

As women reached a critical mass on the faculty, the 1988–89 catalog listed no fewer than twenty-four women's studies courses taught by twenty faculty members. So in early 1989—more than five hundred women's studies programs existed by then at American colleges—the Women's Studies Curriculum Committee at Wooster sought to elevate its program to a major. From its start in the 1970s, when courses focused simply on information about women's lives, the committee's proposal said: "Women's Studies—and the feminist scholarship on which it is based—began a second process as well. . . . Feminist scholars question, for example, the notion of history as a study of power—structures dominated by men . . . and they question traditional periodizations based on predominant male experience." Noting that the minor cross-listed women's studies courses with fifteen different departments, the proposal said, "Women's Studies is thus an interdisciplinary area of study that is unified by a feminist perspective." On the evening before their presentation to a faculty meeting, the committee's leaders went to dinner at the Wooster Inn. "Everyone was nervous," Nancy Grace remembered. "There was a fair amount of 'why wouldn't it pass,' but there was the potential for surprise attacks." The next day, with Joanne Frye confidently presenting the plan, and a number of men speaking in favor of it, the faculty approved. Having won a major, the committee elected for women's studies to remain a program rather than a freestanding department. It was so interdisciplinary, its leaders believed, that to give the program as much flexibility as possible, it needed to reach out to many departments for its faculty.

And women's studies continued to be a discipline in motion. In 2008, the program returned to the faculty, seeking a new name: "The title

'Women's Studies' no longer accurately reflects what we do; instead, we propose the title 'Women's, Gender, and Sexuality Studies [pronounced Wigs].'" It explained:

> Women's Studies developed as the academic wing of the Second Wave of the U.S. Women's Movement in the 1970s. Initially feminist scholars concentrated on consciousness-raising, feminist pedagogy, recovering women's history and their artistic and literary contributions and fostering political activism, on behalf of women. These still remain important goals. . . . We have [now] come to realize, for instance, that masculinity and femininity are so intricately related that it is impossible to understand one without the other. . . . Feminists of color have profoundly changed the assumptions. . . . In addition the transitional nature of women's issues has become more apparent in an era of globalization . . . [and] a binary division of sexes into male and female have been called into question by Lesbian/Gay/Transgender Studies and Queer Theory . . .

The name change was approved—as was a new course known as "Queer Lives." This change had been debated intensely within the program. On the one hand, it allowed new attention to the role of men in a culturally changing world, as well as an increased focus on gays, lesbians, bisexuals, and transgender people, their history and how their experiences are shaped and understood. On the other hand, it reduced the concentration on women's experiences and history, their creativity and contributions, and how discrimination has operated. Some women on the faculty believed, after all the change, that discrimination, even traces of sexual harassment, continued to exist at Wooster; yet it cannot be doubted that the place of women at the College has changed for the better. And it is difficult to find a more vivid example of how Wooster's culture, and its academic program, has evolved over the decades.

CHAPTER 7

The Journey to Diversity

On the occasion of the fortieth reunion of the class of 1963, June 7, 2003, alumni and friends from many classes gathered in the Gault Recital Hall of the Scheide Music Center for a panel discussion. The panel brought together three men of the class who entered the College in the autumn of 1959, had been outstanding undergraduates, and had built outstanding careers afterward. The fourth was a man who arrived, coincidentally, as a young teacher that same fall of 1959 and became one of the most influential professors in the history of the institution. The classmates were Clarence Reginald "Reggie" Williams, James "Jet" Turner, and Reginald "Reggie" Minton. The professor was Theodore Roosevelt "Ted" Williams. The audience was largely white; the panelists were black. Before the discussion had ended, some in the audience had shed tears, others had gasped in shock. Members of the mostly white audience heard things most of them had never known; they were innocently unaware of what the young men had gone through on campus, in the community.

The original conception of the panel—the idea came from Doug Hole, a white classmate, former roommate of the three students, and basketball coach Mose Hole's nephew—was for some sort of chronology, which made how it played out more stunning. In his introduction, Reggie Williams said, "We want to give you some idea of what we saw, felt, and experienced personally, with the civil rights era as a backdrop. You will each have your perspectives. . . . To get the full understanding of how it was to be black at Wooster, you might want to imagine that all of your classmates at Wooster were black except for nine of you." Reggie Minton talked about his experiences as one of the few black students. He recalled walking across campus one day with a friend, a white woman, whose parents saw them; they with-drew her from school. (He had begun to understand life's difficulties much earlier; living in the projects in his hometown of Bridgeport, Connecticut, he had witnessed his first murder at the age of eight.) Turner was assigned to tell what it was like to be a College student in the city of Wooster, where a black man could not get his hair cut during business hours, even in the three barber shops operated by black men. Reggie Williams described what the College meant to his career, twenty-seven years as an air force officer, executive vice president of the insurance giant USAA (United Services Automobile Association), president of the San Antonio Area Founda-tion—and trustee of the College. Soon after his graduation, he and a group of white friends from Officers Candidate School were refused service in a Dallas restaurant; he had a plate of roast beef hurled at him, and his friends wanted to break up the place but decided that would get them kicked out of the air force.

Those were among the stories the audience heard that day, but there is a lot more to the story of Wooster and African Americans, much of it troubling, a great deal positive as well. In his 1870 inauguration speech, Willis Lord insisted that neither race nor gender would restrict the Col-lege. The first Negro student, Clarence Allen, graduated in 1892 (a century later, the College created the Clarence Allen Scholarships for minority students), but enrollment of black students over the years was spotty. In 1951, the College undertook what would become a brief exchange program with predominantly black Fisk College in Nashville, Tennessee, but it was not until the mid-'60s that Wooster decided it could use its faculty and student strength and interest to aid Negro higher education in the South. A lot had changed since 1951. The U.S. Supreme Court declared segregation unconstitutional three years later in *Brown v. Board of Edu-cation of Topeka,* and extensions of the doctrine were passing through the Court annually. National Guard troops were required to desegregate Little Rock Central High School in 1957. Four girls attending Sunday School were killed when a bomb ripped the 16th Street Baptist Church in Birmingham in 1963, and in that hot summer hundreds of thousands of people, white and black, marched on Washington, where they heard Martin Luther King Jr. proclaim, "I have a dream." In the aftermath of President Kennedy's assassination that same year and under President Johnson's firm hand, Congress approved the Civil Rights Act of 1964; and the 1965 march from Selma to Montgomery, Alabama, led to the Voting Rights Act later that year. Through all those years only a handful of black students attended the College; in the early '60s Wooster actually enrolled more African students than African American, and from 1961 to 1966, the total number of African American students was twenty-eight.

A turning point in this racial history—both for the College and for the city—arrived during the years 1959 and 1960. Here was a town of fourteen thousand, with a disproportionate number of PhDs—the College faculty and scientists at the Ohio Agricultural Experiment Station on the other hill at the south end—and a limited number of black families, a few dozen, probably not as many as the number of churches in which the citizens took much pride. It was welcoming to the Amish families who shopped there—Wooster was central to the largest Amish population in the world—their horse-drawn buggies lashed to parking meters, filling the angled parking spaces on East Liberty Street on Saturday nights. Yet Wooster and Wayne County were not hospitable to all. When the Seventh Day Adventists held a conference at a downtown movie theater a few years earlier, protesters bombarded them with eggs until police finally stepped in. The atmosphere at the College was unquestionably far more enlightened, but the fact was, it had never hired a black faculty member.

John Chittum and his wife Alma were teetotal Methodists and dedicated pacifists; one of their sons was a conscientious objector during World War II. They also stood firmly for human rights. As chairman of the chemistry department in the 1950s, Chittum believed it was time for Wooster to appoint an African American (or Negro, as the operative language had it) to the faculty. Setting out to find a chemist worthy of that fine department, he tapped logical sources, and at Howard University, the famous institution in Washington, D.C., he was directed to one of its stellar graduates who was completing his PhD at the University of Connecticut.

Ted Williams had considered a career in industry, but opportunities then for African Americans were, to say the least, limited. He had several offers in higher education, including one from Villanova, which his wife, Yvonne, had hoped for because she had grown up in Philadelphia. When he visited Wooster, he liked it, liked John Chittum, and bonded with Bill Kieffer; Yvonne resisted, but she agreed to give Wooster a two-year trial. There remained, however, a problem: the application form included the question, "Do you use alcohol?" Ted decided he had to be scrupulously truthful and answer "yes," because, as he told his wife, "all chemists use alcohol." Chittum grilled him about the "alcohol problem," but they worked it out.

The Williams family, the Chittum family, and others at the College were surprised, however, when Ted and Yvonne and their two young daughters found it difficult to find a home; one woman had agreed to rent to them, but when she discovered they were black, she withdrew the offer. Then Chittum learned that Pauline Ihrig, professor of French, was to go on leave to France, and she readily agreed that the Williams family could rent her home.

When Ihrig returned, and the Williamses needed to look again, Dave and Marty Moldstad, both in the English department and planning to be away for the summer, offered their house on Sherwood Drive in the northern part of Wooster. On Mother's Day 1960, as the Moldstads returned from church, they were greeted by neighbors gathered next door to protest the renting of their home for two months to a professor at the College. The discussion was heated, the language harsh at times; Dave Moldstad suffered an anxiety attack and was hospitalized. Despite this outburst, the Moldstads were undeterred, and at first the Williamses thought they would accept. "But then I thought of myself with these two small children," Yvonne remembered. "And I wasn't going to have them holed up in a house all summer afraid to play in the yard." It happened that the retired College physician Wilder P. Ellis and his wife, who had been foreign missionaries, were planning to spend the summer taking their three grandchildren to visit lands where they had served. The Ellises lived in Shreve, a Wayne County village with fewer than a thousand residents, where no African American family had ever lived. They talked to their neighbors and local business owners, who said they would welcome the Williams family. When the Wilders returned, they wrote in the *Daily Record*, "One business man who has lived here all his life said, 'Their living here was the best thing that ever happened to this town.' Everyone practically was singing their praises, telling how they had attended the different churches and contributed their talents, and how warmly they had been welcomed, and liked. They endeared themselves to our neighbors."

The Mother's Day protest inspired a host of letters to the editor, all of them condemning the outburst, some citing similar incidents, some accusing the community of hypocrisy for its cultural self-regard. Without rancor, President Lowry wrote in the newspaper: "We believe it would help if before such persons are judged . . . they could become known to those judging them for what they are—cultivated, attractive and highly gifted human beings. We believe that, once they are known, they would be received in Wooster as first-class citizens and people it is a privilege to know." Then came an editorial in the *Daily Record,* titled "The Time Has Come": "The people who precipitated the Ted Williams demonstration Mother's Day Sunday have forced the community to ask itself what its position is going to be on race matters. The fire burned slowly at first. Now people are talking and are frankly asking themselves how they stand. . . . It isn't right that a few people should be forever 'explaining' this community. The people should be compelled to look into a mirror."

After the summer in Shreve, the Williamses' peripatetic Wooster housing adventure was not over. For the next academic year they rented from Mose and Bee Hole while Mose took his first leave. That led to another summer, which the Williamses spent in what had been post–World War II veterans housing behind the stadium. The following autumn, Mary Compton Rice rented them the legendary house on College Avenue in which Elias and Otelia Compton had raised their notable family. That stay lasted four years. Then one day, Mose Hole came to Ted and Yvonne and said, "Bee says the house is getting too big for her. We're going to move, and we want you to buy our house." Yvonne chuckled as she recalled the most reasonable offer. "At the time we just kind of laughed because we didn't have any money. But we scraped together, and my Mother helped a bit, and we made it." In that house in the 700 block of College Avenue, Ted and Yvonne raised four daughters and entertained colleagues for nearly forty years. After Ted's death in 2005, Yvonne lived there alone until 2011, when she moved into a spanking new condo not far from Sherwood Drive.

In his nearly half-century career at the College, Ted Williams became among a handful of the most influential figures in its modern history. Any number of people considered him their best friend. He was recognized and honored nationally for his abilities as both chemist and mentor. He was always in demand as an I.S. advisor. And he was a recruiter par excellence. One day he ran into a girl from Massillon named Debra Schwinn, a high school senior with super grades who was a classically trained violinist as well as a bluegrass fiddler. She aspired to become a doctor and planned to enroll at Case Western Reserve. A little time with Ted, and Deb Schwinn was soon a chemistry major at Wooster. She earned her MD at Stanford and became dean of medicine at the University of Iowa.

Perhaps no better description of Williams's place in College history can be found than the tribute by President Emeritus Henry Copeland before a capacity audience in the McGaw Chapel at Ted's memorial service Dec. 3, 2005. It is worth quoting at length:

> When he came to Wooster, the College was a small and more inti-mate place. . . . Ted was drawn into this intimacy, and in later years he fought to recreate it, for example through his afternoon jogs with students, his Friday afternoon "seminars," and the perpetual open house he and Yvonne held on College Avenue for students and alumni. Ted also shared Howard Lowry's vision of Independent Study as a program designed to challenge students to come to their best, according to each of their capabilities. . . .
>
> Ted's care and concern for the College were evident in his daily inspections of the campus as if to reassure himself that all of its moving parts were still functioning. He often began by having coffee with Howard Raber, Phil Williams, and Bill Snoddy, then meeting his eight o'clock class, and afterwards seeing a steady stream of students in his office.[1] Thereafter, he would stroll through the Galpin offices one by one, then on to Mom's Truck Stop and the Faculty Lounge. . . . Ted and Yvonne's back door was always open between 11:00 P.M. and midnight for anyone who wanted to talk over the day's events. . . .
>
> My second observation is that Ted was an unrelenting critic of the institution. Presidents, deans, department heads who did not hold the institution to its highest standards; colleagues who refused to take a 7:45 or eight o'clock class . . . ; and, of course, the institution as a whole when it did not live up to the commitment that . . . Wooster do its part in full measure in the pursuit of racial equality. Ted held the institution accountable for this goal, and as a result, he was often frustrated and disappointed. But as Deborah Hilty once remarked, "He was the con-science of the campus." . . . Wooster is in his debt.

1. Howard Raber was director of food services, Phil Williams was director of grounds, and Bill Snoddy became vice president of finance and business.

Although Wooster had taken cautious steps during a time of racial upheaval, the recognition that its effort should be greater is described in a 1967 "progress report" from the ad hoc Faculty Committee on Negro Education: "Wooster, as institution and as a collection of diverse individuals, shared with many other institutions and people a strong awareness of, and at times an involvement with, the civil rights struggles in this country in 1964–65. . . . Out of this concern, in the spring of 1965, a group of faculty members began informal discussions in this area [they gathered for the first time in history professor Bob Walcott's living room], which were followed in June by a charge from the Dean to inaugurate a summer study." From this came the faculty committee, which investigated both off- and on-campus diversity opportunities for the College.

After examining cooperative possibilities with several predominantly black schools in the South, including a regional tour, Wooster settled on an exchange program with Miles College just outside Birmingham—largely because it needed help so badly. Because of a lack of PhDs among its faculty and a woefully inadequate library, Miles did not have academic accreditation; it had no dormitories; nearly everyone in its all-black student body held jobs, many full time, and students dropped in and out regularly. Yet it produced 60 percent of the black teachers for Birmingham's segregated school system. In 1966, two Miles students spent the summer at the College, and two Wooster students worked with Upward Bound in Birmingham. That summer, three Wooster faculty—historian Hayden Schilling, art historian Arn Lewis, and Tom Raitt of religious studies—visited Miles for a week, lecturing and observing classes. During the academic year 1966–67, Ruth Smyth of Wooster's mathematics department spent her sabbatical leave at Miles. "Wooster and Miles turned out to be a good fit," Schilling said. "Neither of us was pretentious; we both had a church background [Methodist at Miles], and we both believed that the world could be better." Lewis remembered, "We were innocent. In the mid-'60s we were suddenly confronted with a problem we felt we had to take seriously. We took it seriously, but we were not prepared to deal with its complexities."

One illustration came when Louisa Stroop, a junior, became the first Wooster student to attend Miles during an academic year, the second semester of 1966–67. The College gave her no preliminary counseling. "I think Wooster was a little naïve just shipping me down there without much preparation," she recalled years later. "I was told when I got there that I needed to be careful, that it was dangerous." Stroop lived in the president's home, never left campus by herself even to shop, became the only white face in the college choir—and never had an untoward experience. That same academic year, a Miles student named Solomon Oliver Jr. transferred to Wooster after some heavy recruiting. In his freshman year, he took French from a young Wooster graduate, Mary Lou McCorkle, who quickly spotted his ability. So did John Munro, who had resigned as a Harvard dean to work at Miles, and he arranged for Oliver to attend summer school at Harvard. McCorkle encouraged him to transfer to Wooster, but Oliver was reluctant, knowing little about the Midwest. Into the summer she pushed, telling him to call Dean Drushal collect, which he was nervous about. Having used up most of his excuses during the call, he told the dean he couldn't pay much toward his education. "Let us worry about that," Drushal said. Oliver did transfer, excelled as a double major in political science and philosophy, went on to law school at New York University, came back to Wooster to teach for three years, and became a federal judge, ultimately chief judge of the Northern District of Ohio, as well as a trustee of the College. He also married Louisa Stroop.

The Wooster-Miles exchange program—both faculty and students moving from one to the other—prospered for about three years, then tapered off. The College was hard-pressed to provide all the scholarship money needed for Miles students, and faculty members found the continuing administrative chores diverted them from teaching and research. For its part, Miles set up exchange programs with four other colleges. But the relationship remained warm. Both Miles's president Lucien Pitts and its chief academic officer Richard Armington received honorary degrees from Wooster. (Armington became the first black man elected mayor of Birmingham.) In the meantime, Wooster stepped up its recruiting of black students, and the faculty established a black studies curriculum.

At Wooster, as at many other colleges in the 1960s, an understanding was rapidly growing about the largely unexamined place of black people in American culture, and in 1967 the faculty had created its committee on "Negro Education." The chairman was Arn Lewis, its other members Paul Christianson, Tom Raitt, Jack Carruth, Bob Walcott, Hayden Schilling, Ruth Smyth, Fred Cropp, and Frank Miller. They understood that the road would occasionally be bumpy. Christianson, a professor of English, remembered that when they realized that no special preparation had been made to introduce the few black students to campus life, a group of faculty members decided to invite them to an informal party at the home of Carruth, a professor of music. The students arrived, "and the doorbell rang and we thought, 'What do we say?' . . . [T]hey didn't know where they were and we didn't know how to talk to them. It was a very self-conscious time." Still, the faculty tried what it knew best: academic work. Christianson offered English 399, "Readings in American Negro Literature," in the fall of 1968. Jim Hodges, a Georgian with a PhD from Vanderbilt University, taught the first black history course, History 281, "Afro-American History," the following fall. The class met in the basement of Andrews Library with about twenty black students, most of those on campus, enrolled and about seventy white students. "There was some tension," Hodges remembered. "The white students were venturing into uncharted territory where the black students were far more confident, and they challenged the white students occasionally to defend naïve positions." In the spring of 1969, the faculty voted to establish an Afro-American studies major.

It was a consequential year for race relations at Wooster. Black enrollment increased significantly, to sixty-eight students. In chapel on November 6, the cochairman of the Black Students Association, Ken McHargh, presented the Black Students' Manifesto. McHargh remembered years later what members of the association wanted their fellow students to understand: "Whereas students generally were talking about beer in the union, and coed dorms, things like that, we were talking about integrating black cultural history into the College fabric, whether or not it was through the eyes of black historians and black educators, getting more black faculty members and black administrators on campus who had a voice and who we thought were underrepresented during that time, and dealing with institutional and social issues of race." McHargh, who had grown up in Akron in a black neighborhood, paying little attention to the civil rights movement, came to Wooster in the fall of 1966 as a basketball player and was quickly hit with culture shock—a dozen or so black classmates, no support systems for an urban black kid, no one to take problems to except Ted Williams.

Less than three weeks after presentation of the manifesto, the faculty voted to support "an all-out effort by the campus community to recruit Black and third-world students without delay. The faculty recognizes that this will require additional scholarship funds and it supports every effort to raise the necessary funds." The Board of Trustees devoted an informal session at its final meeting of the academic year 1969–70 to a "discussion on racial understanding." Introducing the session, President Drushal noted that in 1963 (the year the reunion panelists graduated) Wooster enrolled three black students. The number had risen to 34 the year Drushal succeeded Lowry and by 1971 had reached 120. Then he presented somewhat related steps the College had taken that produced both positive and negative results: "[We have] also brought to the campus in significant numbers the sons and daughters of blue-collar workers. This fact, together with the rising tuition at Wooster, has introduced a kind of economic polarization to the campus; and in the eyes of some this factor is responsible for as much tension on campus as the racial factor." He concluded, "In creating a student body which reflects much more closely than before the racial, ethnic, and social composition of American society, I do not believe we have surrendered the ideas that sustained Wooster for 100 years but are living up to these ideals in new ways. We have, at the same time, created a situation that is going to challenge us all." After its discussion, in official action the Board of Trustees "reaffirm[ed] its continuing commitment to the education of Black and other minority students as a manifestation of our Christian concern."

Although commitment was sincere, implementation was sporadic. In the fall of 1970, two black professors were recruited: Lewis Jones in history and Russell Jones in political science. The next year, black students took their case directly to the Board of Trustees, listing three main grievances: an inadequate curriculum for black students, too few blacks brought to the faculty, and no full-time black admissions officer. In 1973 the faculty authorized, and the trustees approved, a black studies program, making Wooster one of the earliest liberal arts colleges to have one. In 1982 Copeland formed a Committee on the Quality of Life for Black Students, which was to concentrate on admission and retention of black students, seek an increase in black faculty, support broader black programming, and in general attempt to eliminate racist attitudes and behavior both on campus and in the Wooster community. According to a follow-up report fourteen years later, some progress had been made in quantifiable areas: the number of black faculty, for example, had grown from 5.5 positions among a total of 136 in 1982–83 to 9 positions out of 143 by 1996–97.

Yet, neither goodwill efforts nor academic changes created the equality that new groups of African American students had come to expect. Protests occurred sporadically, including 1986 demonstrations by both white and black students against apartheid in South Africa. The theme of this campaign at colleges around the country was divestment—that is, institutions should divest their stock interests in corporations that did business in South Africa as long as its government maintained racial apartheid. Wooster faced a particular problem: Canton's Timken Corporation—whose foundation was one of the College's major supporters—continued to operate in South Africa, insisting that its efforts helped alleviate harsh conditions for black people. Delicate negotiations undertaken between the administration and student protest leaders—some private financial information was even shared with students—diffused the campus crisis.

But in the thirtieth anniversary year of those 1959 freshmen, racial tensions boiled over closer to home. A clash during an intramural basketball game in mid-February—which resulted in the resignation of a campus security officer over an alleged racist threat—led to campus rallies and marches during the next month, protests against claimed racism both in the city and on campus. The culmination came on April 20, 1989, when a group of black students entered Galpin Hall through its unlocked doors about 7:00 A.M., before any administrators had arrived. They offered a list of relatively moderate demands: primarily to increase the number of black faculty and psychological professionals, and to add financial services for black students. Over the course of the day, President Copeland and Dean of Students Ken Plusquellec met quietly with the students three times, including an afternoon conversation just outside the doors at Galpin as students were toting in pillows and blankets, presumably prepared for an overnight stay. Copeland, who had worked to increase the number of black faculty without this urging, reiterated his pledge and told the students, "Take whatever time you need. I stand ready to talk."

The black students emerged after thirteen and a half hours, and their leader, Mark Goodman, offered a calm statement. "We, the Black student leaders, have consistently struggled for recognition, respect, and substantive change ... [and] we have received support from every sector of the campus community. ... [W]e have conducted ourselves in a manner which has encouraged communication and maintained our integrity." He went on to cite no fewer than sixteen areas of positive change on campus—from "suspension of classes to discuss racial issues" to "increased office space for the Office of Black Student Affairs"—and praised the College administration: "During the past three weeks, we have witnessed more changes in attitude toward black students and concerns than have taken place within the [preceding] twenty years; of this we are proud."

Alert to how the circumstances might be perceived off campus, Copeland immediately dispatched a memo to the Board of Trustees: "I declined to endorse a Black Studies requirement for graduation. . . . [I]t is the faculty's prerogative to decide this matter. . . . I agreed to go forward with the process which should lead to the appointment of a Black psychologist or counselor. . . . On the condition that there had been no damage to Galpin Hall, I agreed not to penalize, prosecute or otherwise punish any student involved in the protest." And had there been any damage? Two people who worked in Galpin had special memories of the siege, which they recounted with smiles. Bill Snoddy, vice president for finance and business, reported that the students, who had apparently ordered pizza during their stay, carefully cleaned up his office and left a note saying they hoped they had not disturbed anything. Sally Whitman, then working in the Office of Admissions (now executive assistant to the president), said the only damage she knew about was to the copying machines. The students had jammed all the new-fangled machines; not knowing how to clear them, they moved from one copier to another as each clogged. It didn't take long for experienced staff to clear the jams, and Galpin functioned normally the next day.

Enrollment of African American students continued to bounce up and down. The total fell to 74 in 1984 but reached 108 in 1991. Seven years later, the number fell to 66, then got as high as 90 by 2003, and was down to 68 in 2007. In 2005 President Stan Hales convened a Diversity Task Force, supplemented by an ad hoc Committee on Campus Diversity; their goals were to come up with short- and long-term plans to increase domestic minority and international student enrollment. One major product of their work: Wooster joined more than three dozen of the nation's most prominent colleges and universities (among them Oberlin, Bryn Mawr, Carleton, Northwestern, Cornell, UCLA) in cooperation with the Posse Foundation, which recruits bright minority students across the country and arranges their admission as a group to attend one institution; involved students are part of their own posse and do not feel alone in a challenging environment.

Wooster's first posse cohort—twelve African American students from Atlanta—enrolled in the fall of 2008, and soon after their 2012 graduation, many of them were already participating in alumni activities. By 2009, the African American enrollment total was 114, and by the 2011–12 academic year it had reached 166. The number of Hispanic/Latino students—the category was not measured separately until 2008—totaled more than 30, and the number of Asian and Asian American students about 40. (Some 133 students did not identify by race, so those individual categories could be higher.) Reflective also of President Grant Cornwell's global outreach, the international total passed 80. By the 2011–12 academic year, the overall minority and international enrollment could be counted in the several hundreds within a student body of about two thousand.

Although over four decades black studies became a vital element of the academic program, it shouldn't be a surprise that the road was uneven. First came the Faculty Committee on Negro Education in 1967, then the first courses in 1968, then faculty approval of an Afro-American studies major in 1969. That fall, as listed in the 1969–70 catalog, the major included joint courses with the departments of art, economics, English, French, history, philosophy, political science, religion, sociology, and speech. The major was administered by an Afro-American Studies Committee, consisting of five professors: Dave Moldstad as chairman, Ron Hustwit, Jim Hodges, Hayden Schilling, and Ted Williams. Then came a shocking turnaround: near the end of the 1972–73 academic year, the faculty's Educational Policy Committee recommended the establishment of a Black studies department, which the faculty voted down, 57–38. Tempers were raw. At the same meeting, the faculty voted by secret ballot, 52–23, to eliminate even the Afro-American studies major.

This led to a special faculty meeting three days later. It was, according to the minutes,

> interrupted by the appearance and speeches of Black students who were protesting the discontinuance of an Afro-American Studies major and the failure of the faculty to establish a Department of Black Studies . . . [and] demanding to know why individual members voted the way they did and why the votes were by secret ballot. . . . Mr. [John] Gates [professor of history] moved that a committee be appointed to meet with the Black Students Association over the weekend to try to

interpret the vote of the faculty on the two issues, to attempt to create a Black Studies program, and in general to keep communication open between the faculty and the students.

One week later, voting 84–7, the faculty adopted the report, which authorized a Committee on Black Studies (including administrators and faculty chairs) and "establishes that the following courses would be continued: Black America (history), African History (history), Afro-American (history), Political and Social Philosophies of Black America, Racial and Ethnic Minorities, Black Politics, Civil Liberties, Afro-American Literature, French Literature of Africa and the Caribbean, Black Religions, Black Theatre, Black Church Music, Jazz." Shortly afterward, the Board of Trustees authorized an official program in black studies.

The first step in building this new program was to choose someone with both the ability and clout to organize it. Ted Williams was on leave at UConn that summer, so Fred Cropp, vice president for academic affairs, flew to Hartford to ask his wife, Yvonne, to take on that task for a year, while the College sought a director. Yvonne had gotten her undergraduate degree at Penn State University, then became one of the first two black women admitted to the Harvard Law School, which she left after one year to marry Ted and attend graduate school. She had earned a master's degree in political science but not yet a PhD when Cropp persuaded her to fill the interim position. "I was trying to get as broad a representation of departments as seemed reasonable," Williams recalled. "The institutional attitude to me is the amazing thing because I think it was a very positive and supportive attitude. There were certainly skeptical individuals, of course, and there were one or two who were really unwilling to cooperate, but in general we had wonderful support from the administration and pretty good support from the faculty."

In 1978, when the first person chosen as director, Ben Berry, left after four years, Yvonne returned to reorganize the program and redesign the curriculum, while completing her PhD in political science at Case Western Reserve University. "That was the most exciting time," Williams remembered. "I learned so much . . . to be able to sell what I wanted to do I had to understand the various disciplines. . . . I think we managed to develop a very strong core curriculum, and then our program really became a kind of model for the small liberal arts school." In the first two decades, a number of appointments important to both black studies and other departments were made: Annetta Jefferson in English and theater in 1974 as the program was being organized; Josephine Wright, who became the longtime department chair, a joint appointment with music in 1981; and Alphine Jefferson, who had directed the black studies program at Southern Methodist University, jointly with history in 1989. The number of African Americans on the faculty did not top the nine in the late 1990s—Wright never let the administration or her faculty colleagues overlook that—but if one included biracial faculty members as well as those of African, Indian, Chinese, and Latino backgrounds, the minority roster was nearly double that in the first decade of the twenty-first century.

A further milestone was reached when black studies became a full-fledged department in 2000—thus guaranteeing the relatively new discipline an increased level of academic legitimacy, as well as a certain permanence. From "black studies," the department became known as African American studies, then Africana studies, which fit the College's increased attention to globalism. Under this name, the department now could offer such courses as "Black Nationalism," "Marxism and Africana Radical Thought," and "Martin, Malcolm, and Mandela." It cross-lists courses with, among others, the departments of art and art history, music ("Gospel Choir"), philosophy, and political science ("The Constitutional Law of Civil Rights") and with the program in women's, gender, and sexuality studies ("Africana Women in North America: Earliest Times through the Civil Rights Movement"). If some African Americans still sensed the sting of discrimination at Wooster, their status had clearly touched the dreams of Willis Lord and the aspirations of Clarence Allen and had traveled a long road from the tribulations the three freshmen and the young professor faced in 1959.

CHAPTER 8

New and Renew

No college could remain the same structurally over decades, but it is noteworthy that every single academic building on Wooster's campus has been either constructed or largely remodeled since 1960—some of them put to entirely new, almost ironic uses. A few buildings of older vintage have disappeared, notably Hoover Cottage, built in 1884. Some older structures have survived with relatively modest change, remarkably Holden Annex, thrown up as a temporary residence for women in 1927, which continued to house women nearly a century later.

The oldest building still standing exemplifies Wooster's willingness to adapt its resources to the times. Built in 1900, the Frick Library survived the 1902 fire that destroyed the College's principal building, Old Main, and served as the College's library until 1962. To clear space for the new Andrews Library, at the northwest corner of Beall and University, two buildings had to go. One was Hoover, home to generations of freshman girls; it was torn down, its place on campus adjoining the libraries taken by grass, trees, and a parking lot. The other was the student union, which the College obviously needed (Lowry Center did not open until 1968). First, the observatory that had topped the union building since the nineteenth century was removed—its telescope is now in the city's Freedlander Park—then the structure was jacked up over steel beams and towed around the corner to University, where it became known as the Temporary Union Building, which of course students called the TUB. After Lowry opened, this facility was repurposed again as the Rubbermaid Student Development Center. With the opening of Andrews, the original Frick library was converted into an art museum and the home of the studio art department. Then, when a new art center/museum opened in 1997, the building was reconverted into a library, now the Timken Science Library in Frick Hall, and the home of Wooster's significant collection of science-related intellectual material. The College's newest library, the Flo K. Gault Library for Independent Study, opened in 1995, seamlessly connected to Andrews. (Details on the College's libraries and how they have modernized technologically appear in chapter 10.)

The building that since 1997 has housed the art department is another illustration of imaginative remodeling. Generations of students remember the original structure as Severance Gymnasium, built in 1912 to look outside as much like an academic building as any other. Its basketball court—bleachers closely surrounding the floor, fans in the front rows with their feet practically in bounds (players occasionally landed in their laps chasing loose balls), fans in a shallow balcony staring down—was enough to give visiting teams claustrophobia. And the court was decorated for many a festive dance. To visiting swim teams, the pool in the basement was akin to a kiddie pool, less than one-third the official Olympic length and, when it was finally abandoned in 1973, the smallest in the nation used for competition. The building also squeezed in a running track on the balcony; a basement auxiliary basketball court known as the "cage," used mainly for intramural games; locker rooms; coaches' offices; a Turkish bath for faculty; and some dorm space in the rafters for athletes. When the new Armington Physical Education Center opened in 1973, a modest reshuffling, carried out largely by art professor Donald MacKenzie and seven students over a summer, turned the old gym into a home for the studio art department. In the 1990s, a lengthier effort consumed more than a year and united students of art history and studio art after more than twenty years in separate locations. The most striking aspect of the old building is how the basketball arena is used, its main floor divided into studios for painting, printmaking, drawing, and design, with studios for I.S. projects on the balcony. The swimming pool has become a ceramics studio.

Now the remodeled Severance Gym has a new sibling—connected through a striking arch retained in the old building—the Ebert Art Center, made possible principally by a gift from Robert Ebert, whose father was one of the founders of the Wooster Rubber Company (which became Rubbermaid, Inc.). Dedicated in October 1997, it features a curving modern facade of much the same material used in Severance and covers seventeen thousand square feet, more than half the size of the original gym building. It gives the College a spacious, welcoming museum—as one student said, "you get the sense immediately that this is a place where you can spend some time"—with two galleries, storage for the College's permanent collection, and lecture and seminar rooms. A park south of Severance and Ebert, containing an outdoor sculpture, was created by the trustees in 1995 to honor Lolly Copeland, wife of the retiring president, for her contributions to both the grounds and the history of the College.

The old gym is one of three structures named for the Cleveland philanthropist Louis Severance, whose funds—and influence, for he campaigned successfully to banish national fraternities and sororities—changed the face of the campus during the second decade of the twentieth century.[1]

Long before the Severance Gym was repurposed for the art department and museum, however, the College clearly needed more modern physical education facilities. One option for decades was a field house—considered as early as the end of World War II—which many former players wanted to name in honor of "Coach" Boles, the longtime athletic director. Wooster's athletes, however, had to settle for new facilities in a series of steps. First came a basketball arena, called Timken Gymnasium, followed by the Armington Physical Education Center. Not until 2012 was a true field house completed, by then including a state-of-the-art recreational facility. (See chapter 11 for details on the intercollegiate and recreational facilities.) The second of Severance's contributions to the sports program is what alumni know as the football field, originally called Severance Stadium. It is now the setting for not only football and track and field, as it was for many years, but also both men's and women's lacrosse, any number of intramural athletic events, even a club cricket match on occasion. The grandstand was essentially rebuilt in 1995 and the facility renamed John P. Papp Stadium after the principal donor. The now extensive use of the playing site was made possible by the installation of an all-weather artificial turf field and floodlights, thanks to a primary contribution from trustee Ed Andrew and his family.

1. Severance was a devout Presbyterian and donor to many church causes as well as to the city of Cleveland. His son John made the principal gift for Severance Hall, home of the city's internationally famed orchestra.

The third Severance, home to Wooster's esteemed chemistry department, has undergone two major renovations to deal with the ever-changing
demands of modern science. Gas that swept from the chemistry laboratory is thought to have caused the fire that took down Old Main, but the
Cleveland financial angel quickly contributed funds, and Severance Hall,
now safely separated from Kauke Hall, was dedicated in the fall of 1902.
Inevitably, it was tired and outdated when remodeled for the first time in
1960. The initial thought then was to renovate one basement laboratory,
but that required removal of the main heating system, and as a variety of
difficulties arose—coupled with the fact that the structure of the building
was sound—the decision was made to modernize the interior completely.
(Wooster's chemists thought it helped that the chairman and vice chairman of the Board of Trustees, Bob Wilson and Cary Wagner, were chemists.) The process was relaxed. Lectures continued during demolition and
construction, and students performed experiments in any lab available.
A steel strike slowed the work, no stairs were fully ready until late in the
first semester, and the building was unheated until November 15. Workers and professors cooperated fully; when a blueprint conflicted with the
structure, a foreman and John Reinheimer, the faculty liaison, would solve
the problem on the spot.

The second remodeling became the centerpiece of the Campaign for
the 1990s, costing $11.3 million, at that time the College's largest ever single
expenditure. (More than half the donors had been chemistry majors.) The
exterior brick load-bearing walls and terracotta trim around windows and
doors were preserved—"The underlying dignity of the building was a bit
hidden," said Robert Schaeffner, the principal architect—but everything
else was new. An addition on the east side helped increase usable space by
one-quarter, to forty-two thousand square feet. The building ultimately
contained nearly a mile and a half of ductwork; nearly two miles of waste
pipes; nearly three thousand different valves; more than four miles of telephone, fiber-optic, and control-system cables; more than sixty-four miles
of electrical wire; and three hundred laboratory drawers. At one point,
the renovation stood about $2 million over its then $10 million budget.
Bill Snoddy, the vice president for finance and business, and Ted Bogner,
who headed the company performing the remodeling, were respectful, a
bit awed, as they sat down with the accomplished chemists—"the easiest
group I ever worked with, so great to work with," Bogner said—to trim the

budget. Monte Borders, Ted Williams, Dick Bromund, Dave Powell, and Roy Haines, whose tenures at Wooster were measured in decades, readily agreed to modifications. They adjusted duct work, reduced the number of expensive sound attenuators, and eliminated the dry wall planned for the facade, saving about $500,000.

Still, the project was short well over $1 million, and it appeared program cuts would be required of this signature department. Stan Gault was informed, and he called Ed Andrew; they filled much of the gap. Shortly afterward, trustees were discussing whether to proceed with construction on borrowed money, which would taint their rule of building only with funds in hand or pledged. During a coffee break at a board meeting, Gault found Sally Patton, the vice president for development. As Patton remembered, "Stan said, 'you take [him] and [him] and [her], and I'll take [him] and [him] and [her]. Let's get this done.'" Before the coffee break ended, the two of them had collected about $500,000 in pledges, and construction was soon approved. Still, the chemistry faculty refused to budge on one point. It demanded retention of the original blackboards— not merely for nostalgia's sake, they claimed, but because writing with chalk gave a "better feel," and the boards were easier to erase.

The only academic building that has not been adequately upgraded is the 1920s biology center Mateer Hall. It was remodeled somewhat in 1968 with new offices, new labs, a 280-seat lecture hall, and a passageway to Severance Chemistry next door. But "biology" is too simple a term for what these neuroscientists teach and learn in the modern world. A twenty-first-century facility worthy of Wooster's commitment to the sciences ranked at the top of any new construction effort.

No rehabilitating the College had ever done, however, could compare to the monumental task of reshaping its classic academic building, Kauke Hall—twice. Constructed in 1902 on the foundation of Old Main and first used for class in February 1903, Kauke was a magnificent Collegiate Gothic edifice. For its exterior, the architect L. C. Holden (brother of President Louis Holden) used yellow-grey Ohio clay, trimmed with Bedford limestone and grey terra-cotta. Its floors are four inches thick, formed by laying two-by-fours on edge, a strengthening custom common in warehouses of the early twentieth century. But early-twentieth-century standards were not what students and faculty expected by mid-century, not the drafty windows or worn floors, offices shared by several professors making student conferences difficult, wooden stairways so cramped that students often used the outside fire escapes to get upstairs faster. So for the Centennial Campaign, alumni raised more than $1 million to reno-' vate Kauke on the theme "We wore it out, we should fix it." After faculty moved to offices in houses around campus, even the recreation rooms of Andrews and Babcock halls, work began in June 1961 and continued through the 1961–62 academic year.

By the fall of 1962, classrooms were grouped together in the central part of the building, with faculty offices in the wings, inspiring casual and interdisciplinary conversations. The interior walls were finished in pale green and beige and acoustical-tile dropped ceilings improved the lighting. Vinyl floors could be mopped clean, carpeting was added to other floors, inside staircases were made of steel, a freight elevator was available to the handicapped as well as for equipment, classroom chairs were movable. Most faculty members now had their own offices and telephones and no longer had to go to a small room in Memorial Chapel to pick up their mail. "To alumni who remember Kauke over the past few decades, the change will seem miraculous," exulted the *Alumni Bulletin*.

On the outside, Kauke looked much the same, except for one architectural change that no one unfamiliar with the College before 1962 would grasp. The planners had proposed an arch, an open corridor in the center of the building, but funds ran short. As work neared completion, a $30,000 contribution from Charles Delmar in honor of his son who had attended Wooster made possible the final touch—the Delmar Archway. Since autumn 1962, the arch has become part of College culture—a shortcut between classes and dorms, the opening through which freshmen march to their first convocation and seniors to commencement, a drive-through by at least one Volkswagen Beetle, and the countless winter evenings when spirited—and occasionally spirits-fueled—students packed it with snow.

Kauke lasted sixty years before its first renovation but, in a faster world and with more students, just over forty years before the second. What had seemed "miraculous" in 1962 was dated and worn by 2005. This would be the centerpiece of the Independent Minds campaign of the early twenty-first century, an $18 million effort—it began with an $8 million grant from the Walton Family Foundation—now the largest financial undertaking in Wooster's history. Yet before the huge Kauke project could begin, and some around campus wondered why it was being held off, a considerable amount of groundwork—perhaps it should be said "underground" work—was required. It was now considered essential that Kauke be air conditioned, but the necessary operating system, located under the Rubbermaid Center adjoining Holden Hall, was already near capacity cooling other buildings and clearly could not add Kauke. The solution was to create a South Campus Air Conditioning Loop, to service the Freedlander Theatre, Wishart Hall, Scovel Hall, Severance Hall, Mateer Hall, and Burton D. Morgan Hall, where the basement would house the new apparatus. That would allow the system under the Rubbermaid building to shed enough load so that it could air condition Kauke.

But just a moment. As this plan was being conceived, there was no Burton D. Morgan Hall. Morgan was a northern Ohio industrialist with no longtime connection to Wooster, but he had established a foundation, and as it happened two of its trustees—Stan Gault and Dick Seaman— were also trustees of the College. So at this important time the foundation contributed $8 million toward construction of what became Morgan Hall, on the northwest corner of Pine Street and College Avenue. The 2002 completion of the building—which blends with the traditional Collegiate Gothic architecture yet is the most distinctly modern academic structure on campus—opened several avenues. One was that equipment for the new South Loop air conditioning could be installed in its basement. Another was to increase the roominess of Kauke by offloading the departments of economics (including business economics), education, and psychology to Morgan, along with the Office of Information Technology, which occupies its top floor.

At the same time, the city agreed to the closing of University Street at the base of the main quadrangle (similar to the closing of Henrietta Street from Beall Avenue to Bever Street), thus allowing for a campus mall that extended grandly from Kauke to Pine Street. But a further issue existed. Morgan Hall was to occupy the site of Hygeia Hall, which had been the College health center since the 1920s and now was to be torn down. Here another trustee, Bill Longbrake, longtime chairman of the board's Finance Committee, stepped in to make possible the construction of a modern facility on Wayne Avenue, the Longbrake Student Wellness Center. (It is a "wellness center" and not a hospital to avoid certain strict and costly rules.) The Center includes six treatment rooms, eight in-patient beds, a pharmacy lounge, and a conference room and offices. It also has a wing for psychological counseling, but since there is only a single outside entrance to the building, the purpose of any visit is kept private.

Finally, the College was ready to gut and rebuild Kauke. Once again, the faculty moved out, and classes were scattered. The entire academic year 2005–6 was devoted to the remodeling. Since, once again, there would be no major tinkering with the facade, the first task was to optimize the seventy-seven thousand square feet inside. One decision was to avoid wasting academic space on the mechanical devices for heating and lighting, which had not been moved in the 1961–62 renovation, and the now essential air conditioning. Most of that equipment lies in a fifty-by-fifty–foot concrete vault hidden under the grass in front of Kauke; the rest is in attic spaces on either side of the tower classroom. Each room has a ceiling bulkhead that stretches the room's length; these connect from room to room, containing the ductwork and sprinkler piping for fire protection. One lesson the 1902 builders learned from Old Main was that if part of the building caught fire, the entire structure was likely to go. So they divided Kauke into seven distinct parts, fire-protected from each other (a similar idea led to separating Kenarden Lodge into seven sections). The 1961–62 renovation had included slightly less attention to fire security, since by then the College had more confidence in the city fire department and available water than it had in 1902; the latest changes added to the protection.

With a representative from each academic area contributing, the planners decided to divide office and classroom areas, the west side of the building devoted to faculty offices, the east side to classrooms. Another step was to undo a major part of the 1961–62 work: The dropped ceilings were removed and the wood ceiling rediscovered, so rooms looked more like the original Kauke. Obviously, twenty-first-century amenities were added: elevators, ramps for the handicapped, better stairways, better restrooms. The planners introduced a gathering place for students and faculty—the Old Main Café just inside the front of the building, a coffee-and-snacks spot that would have been unheard of a few decades earlier. The wall outside the café is covered with bricks bearing the names of contributors (plaques throughout the building denote donors of offices and classrooms). And the entire building facade was retouched so that while it still looked like the original Kauke, its surface could last another half-century or so.

From the 1960s into the 1990s, the College emphasized renovation of its classic academic buildings over new construction. The oldest, the library, predated the fire. Kauke, Severance, Scovel, and Taylor halls—all of which were dedicated on the same date, December 11, 1902, one year after the great fire—were simply worn down, as well as academically out of date in many respects. Yet they were too fundamentally sturdy to rip down—and attractive and memorable besides. (Upon the opening of Taylor in 1902, the *Voice* rhapsodized, "No better building could be planned than this. The building is a model of convenience and beauty.") To meet modern code requirements, Taylor and Scovel needed upgrades. Additions on the west side of Scovel and the north side of Taylor contained new handicapped-accessible restrooms, new stairs, and an elevator. Scovel's basement was unusable because of regular flooding, and the second floor was so shaky that it could only be partially used; both were fixed. But the main floor, consisting of those two-by-fours standing end to end, remained solid, and layers of old paint were scraped from the brick walls and wood ceiling, restoring the original look. A greenhouse on the south side of the building was torn away. Then laboratories and classrooms were modernized for the unusual departmental bedfellows, geology and philosophy. There was, in retrospect, one regret about Scovel. A cupola at the top of the building—which, had it been salvaged, would have connected the building to its historic origin—was deemed too damaged to save and was discarded.

Taylor served the College conveniently, if not always beautifully. Although it has long been the home of the Department of Mathematics, and more recently was a temporary home for the technology center (now moved to Morgan Hall), much of the building was occupied by speech and theater, which took up fancier new quarters across the street, in Wishart Hall and Freedlander Theatre. Besides its code additions, renovations included fixing a leaky roof, laying a large skylight on the top floor, and moving classrooms and faculty offices to the outside walls to take advantage of natural light. Surely the most memorable place in Taylor was the Scott Auditorium (named for a donor family), home of theater productions ranging from the student-written and -performed *Gum Shoe Hop* to faculty plays to Broadway-style productions. But the auditorium was useful for, and memorable for, other reasons. When the student body grew too large to fit into Memorial Chapel, and chapel attendance was still required, the overflow was funneled into Scott. The self-identified second-class citizens in Scott could only hear and not see the Chapel programs until a camera was placed in the balcony of the Chapel to transmit video. Since the auditorium needed to be kept dark so events on the screen could be seen, after roll call crawling shapes were seen escaping out the side doors; it was also noticed that many couples who were going steady favored the darkened auditorium.

Across the street from Taylor Hall, the corner of campus bounded by University and Bever Streets had been an open playing field, then the site of veterans' housing units after World War II, and in the 1970s became the center of the College's communications and entertainment complex. It now holds two buildings. First, in 1966, came Wishart Hall, home of the Department of Communications and of the Department of Theater and Dance, which were collectively the Department of Speech until 1981. Wishart Hall, named for Prexy, was built with funds primarily from that former president's admirers in Wooster and Wayne County. It is home to a speech and hearing clinic; a dance studio; faculty offices; and the College student radio station, WCWS. In it too is the Delbert H. Lean Lecture Room, named in honor of the longtime head of the speech department, which can seat 300 for faculty meetings and lectures, and the Craig Theatre Library, which houses the collection of Bill Craig, Lean's successor and speech chairman for nearly thirty years. A decade later came the Herman Freedlander Theatre, honoring the most prominent retail businessman in the city of Wooster's history, a staunch booster of both the College and the city.[2] The spacious auditorium, with 400 seats and comfortable leg room, plus a hydraulic-lift orchestra pit and a roomy back stage, offers sharp contrasts to Scott Auditorium; within the building also is the Effie Shoolroy Arena Theatre, seating 135 and used for experimental productions. The Freedlander Theatre offers more than a site for College performances and other large gatherings; as the venue for the Ohio Light Opera, a professional company which every summer for more than a quarter century has attracted visitors nationwide to its presentations of the Gilbert and Sullivan oeuvre as well as Broadway musical highlights, it has become a music-lovers' destination.

2. Shortly after World War II, Herman Freedlander made an anonymous contribution, later disclosed, to build the city's first public swimming pool, with one condition: that it not be racially segregated, as the major private pool in the city had been.

At the turn of the twentieth century, Henry Clay Frick built a home for his mother at the corner of Beall Avenue and Pine; this eventually became the home of the John Overholt family. Left to the College, it was converted in 1941 to a home for the music department and named Merz Hall, in honor of Karl Merz, the nineteenth-century director of the Wooster Conservatory of Music. In a building showing its age, with sagging floors and rooms that did not shield sound, the department persevered for nearly a half-century, until the Scheide Music Center's opening, in 1987. After serving as a student residence hall for five years, the old music building was completely remodeled in 1992–93, thanks to gifts from several reunion classes and yet another from the Gault family; it took on the stately look of the early-twentieth-century home it had once been and a new name, the Gault Alumni Center.

The road to the Scheide Center was rocky. It had been clear for years that one of the College's most significant needs was an appropriate home for its musicians—"theory classes in a tiny, freezing, creaky" annex, and "pianos vying with trumpets and sopranos in happy cacophony" as alumna and concert pianist Anne Mayer described the Merz facility. But it was not for lack of trying that they didn't have a new home. In the early 1980s, Stan Gault and Sally Patton presented to a major midwestern foundation what they believed a compelling case that Wooster needed a music building, but the foundation seemed to prefer science. After they explained that Scovel Hall had been renovated recently, and Mateer Hall was reasonably up to date, foundation executives seemed understanding and even visited the campus. The College was optimistic. Then Patton received a call from a foundation leader, who said he really liked Wooster but he liked science more and the money was going to another college in Ohio for a science building. Gault called it one of his greatest disappointments as chairman. Richard Gore, professor of organ, became central to the renewed efforts. Gore shared a love of Bach and organ music with a New York friend, William Scheide, who along with his grandfather and father had assembled what was called "possibly the finest private collection of rare books and manuscripts in the Western Hemisphere." (Besides being a significant philanthropist for educational institutions, Scheide was a major contributor to civil rights organizations, including the NAACP Legal Defense and Educational Fund, run by his good friend Thurgood Marshall.) Upon Gore's urging, and with Scheide's principal contribution, the music center opened in the fall of 1987—faculty offices,

sound-moderated practice rooms, a courtyard for public receptions, the
Noble Atrium entrance, and the four-hundred-seat Gault Recital Hall for
performances and lectures.

Even the College's "Main Street"—Beall Avenue—received a facelift in
the first decade of the new century. This was shepherded by Bob Walton,
who left a business career in 1999 to become the College's vice president
for finance and business and set about to fix everything on campus from
faculty health benefits to student street-crossing patterns. Soon becoming an
influential member of the Wooster City Council, Walton helped develop the
so-called Beall Avenue Corridor from downtown, where Beall dead-ends at
East Liberty Street, to the extended northern edge of the campus at Bloom-
ington Avenue. Utilities were placed underground, new water and sewer
lines installed, and the street repaved, at a cost of more than $8 million, paid
by a $2 million federal grant and contributions from both residential and
commercial property owners as well as the College. Defining the campus
setting, north from Pine Street, Beall becomes stylish—tree-lined median,
fresh signage, fashionable lighting, and brick crosswalks (which students
are supposed to use [but don't always], and where drivers are supposed to
stop when someone is crossing on them [but don't always]).

It is also worth considering some of the least-renovated structures on
campus. The president's home on University Street looks on the outside
much like it did when it was built, in 1928. Inside it has undergone various
levels of rehabilitation and modification for every new family that moved
in. Lowry, a bachelor whose mother lived with him, did not consume
much personal space. The Drushal family, Garber and Dorothy and three
growing children, redecorated the bedrooms. The Copeland family did
not move into the house for months, waiting while the Drushals built a
retirement home in Holmes County. Over the years, a porch was enclosed,
an addition constructed, a patio enhanced for outdoor parties. In 2008,
Joe Biden, running for vice president, spoke at a campus political rally
and was interviewed by a network news reporter in the living room.

Galpin Hall, the administrative headquarters, where the president, the
vice presidents, and most of the deans and their staffs work, was built in
1931. It looks both on the outside and inside much as it originally did. Yes,
there have been improvements, air conditioning, better lighting and restrooms; an expanded president's suite. Galpin—where the top administrators
work—remains probably the most unremodeled building on campus. So
Wooster.

CHAPTER 9

Homes Away from Home

For Wooster women who remember living in Hoover Cottage as freshmen, in Holden Hall or its Annex as sophomores and juniors, and in Babcock Hall as seniors, or men who lived in Douglass Hall as freshmen and in Kenarden Lodge (or Livingston Lodge) the next three years, twenty-first-century accommodations are dizzying. For one important thing, the housing is coed—a thought so foreign as to be laughable in the 1940s, '50s, even '70s, when an 11:59 P.M. goodnight kiss on the steps of Holden was as close to coed living as most students got. As the College grew, from Lowry's idealized one thousand students to the doubled number in 2012, new dorms—now known as residence halls—obviously were needed. Over a half century, from the late 1950s into the first decade of the twenty-first century, Wooster built nine new residence halls and remodeled three of its most historic. It also added two dining facilities and razed the oldest dorm on campus. Hoover Cottage, built in 1884, was finally considered unsafe as it stood for freshmen women and too expensive to rehabilitate; it was used awhile as a bookstore, then knocked to the ground in 1960. Something else happened as the twentieth century turned into the twenty-first. Student housing and accompanying recreation facilities and other amenities—simply stated, attractive and graceful living conditions unimaginable for earlier generations—became an essential element on Wooster's campus, as similar amenities were becoming de rigueur at colleges and universities across the nation.

After the completion of Babcock Hall in 1935, the College did not see a new dorm until 1954, when Andrews Hall, a men's dorm adjoining Kenarden Lodge, was dedicated, a gift largely from Mrs. Matthew Andrews of Cleveland. The next year brought another, Otelia Compton Hall, named in honor of the wife of the longtime dean and matriarch of Wooster's first family. Paid for largely by contributions from Wooster and Wayne County residents, it was built as a women's dorm at the southeast corner of Beall and Wayne, housing more than a hundred students and including lounges and multipurpose rooms. The next residence hall, Wagner Hall, completed in 1957, came farther east on Wayne Avenue, with a primary gift from Cary Wagner, the board chairman. The most notable architectural fact about Wagner Hall is that it looked unlike its neighbors because it was topped with a flat roof. That might not seem terrible, except that President Lowry despised the shape—so much, said Buck Smith, that if the president was driving or walking past the dorm he refused to look at it. Lowry did not live to see the change, but trustees knew of his distaste, and in 1991 one of them, Ruth Frost Parker, funded the addition of a gabled roof with new windows and lights. Who lives behind those attractive windows? No one. The addition is a facade with no rooms, an unsung tribute to Lowry. In 1966, Compton and Wagner became part of a complex with the completion of Kittredge Hall, connected to Compton, a dining facility that can seat more than three hundred and also is frequently used also as a site for major College gatherings. The opening of Kittredge, combined with the College's principal dining hall in Lowry Center, ended an era of dormitory food service.

The next set of dormitories could be called historic because they marked a turning point in College construction, for reasons good and bad. Built as a trio in the mid-1960s, Armington, Bissman, and Stevenson halls spread along Wayne Avenue east from Andrews, ending with Bissman at the southwest corner of Wayne and Beall. Each of the trio received its name from families with ties to the College, all of whom made contributions to their construction. But the primary funding came through low-interest federal loans, and thus the building process had to follow strict bureaucratic guidelines, from bidding to design. That helps explain why they were, and remain, the least successful residential projects in Wooster's modern history. Still, it is pertinent to realize that the College was willing to accept those strict terms—and build on the cheap—because its finances were so straitened.

A Canton company submitted a surprisingly low bid for all three, which, under the guidelines, had to be accepted. Then it abandoned the project midway, when it went bankrupt, and the Bogner company stepped in to finish the residences as well as possible. Builders sometimes disparage these types as "prison dorms": small rooms, long straight corridors with no definition and little opportunity for interchange in the halls. It didn't take long for word to filter through the student body that these halls were to be avoided if possible. In recent years, they have been remodeled significantly to add amenities, encourage interchange, and reduce occupancy (by turning doubles into singles and triples into doubles). But perhaps their most important legacy is that they helped frighten the Board of Trustees about debt and about building without sufficient funds in sight. Before long, the board declared that it would not construct anything unless funds were in hand or pledged. The new rule obviously reduced the prospect of indebtedness but certainly slowed building plans; clearly, it also left the College in a far more confident and secure financial position.

It can be recorded here that the Armington-Bissman-Stevenson trio helped change Wooster's building plans in another way, too: it established that a hometown firm could be counted upon to meet the College's needs reliably when those out-of-towners failed. Some conflicts are typical of any town-gown relationship: drivers harassing students as they zoom down a principal campus street, the College closing streets to facilitate campus expansion, or off-campus-dwelling students hosting noisy parties. However, the relationship between the College and two Wooster construction companies, Bogner and Freeman Construction, illustrates town-gown cooperation. The Bogner company (now the Bogner Construction Management Company) first served the College as masonry subcontractor on the four academic buildings completed after the 1901 fire. It was general contractor for the first time on Holden Hall, then on the president's home and the second phase of the original Frick library. After World War II, Bogner and Freeman shared most of the work. Freeman remodeled Kauke the first time, Bogner the second; Freeman remodeled Severance chemistry the first time, Bogner the second; Bogner built Wishart Hall, Freeman built the Freedlander Theatre next door. In something of a gentleman's agreement probably brokered by Howard Lowry, Bogner largely worked west of Beall Avenue, Freeman east of it, including major projects like Lowry Center and the first phase of the Armington Physical Education Center. In recent years, Bogner has directed nearly all the

College's projects, primarily as the construction manager, bidding much of the work to subcontractors and supervising it.

An early exception to the new money-on-hand policy, however, even in a difficult financial time, was one building considered essential—a multipurpose student union, which had been an acknowledged goal since Prexy Wishart's time. The long-standing, smallish union, moved to clear space for Andrews Library, was designated "temporary." In 1963, a College committee was already planning services that might be included in a new building; there was even a College Union Emphasis Week—but no union. Finally, in December 1965, board chairman Wagner announced to a full chapel that there would soon be a modern student union and that it would be named after the president. Seated on the stage, Lowry was taken by surprise, pleased but flummoxed. Certain that he would be chiefly responsible for raising the money, he felt guilty about asking friends to contribute to a building named for him; he told the trustees that if they found a transcendent donor he would certainly relinquish the tribute.

In 1966, the College completed its $20 million Centennial Campaign, which had focused on academic structures, but it lacked the funds to pay for a chapel, a physical education center, or a student union, so it launched immediately into what was called the "Essential Extras Campaign." (The chapel is discussed in detail in chapter 12 and the physical education center in chapter 11.) The price of a union was estimated at $2.2 million in 1964, but in October 1966, the bids totaled $3.5 million. Despite its anxiety about debt, the board thought the need was too great not to move ahead. The building was completed in 1968 (Lowry had died the year before), but it carried a debt load of approximately $2.5 million, straining the operating budget. Then in December 1971, Foster McGaw, who had already made the lead gift for the new chapel, after telling Buck Smith that he had spent a "wonderful weekend" with Wooster students during the recent dedication of the chapel, and telling him that he didn't make such decisions but "God makes them," offered $1.6 million as a challenge grant to pay for the student union. Thanks to trustees, and students who did a wintry walk to stir interest and raise funds, the McGaw Challenge was met within sixty days, and Lowry Center was paid for.

And Lowry Center has indeed been a center of campus life for nearly a half century. It houses the campus post office and bookstore. It offers a bowling alley and offices for student organizations. It is the principal dining hall, and it features snack bars and Mom's Truck Stop for meals all day. Its expansive lobby, remodeled more than once, is almost constantly crowded with students seated or sprawled on comfortable chairs, around a fire pit, chatting or now more commonly working on laptops or toying with cell phones. It has become a central gathering place for campus meetings, some of them of historic importance, such as that following the 1970 Kent State killings. It can provide a ballroom or a lounge where faculty can gather. Rare is the day when almost every Wooster student does not come into contact with Lowry.

Not for a quarter-century after the mid-1960s did the College build another dormitory, and it would provide just about as sharp a contrast to the Armington-Bissman-Stevenson combination as could be imagined. This was Luce Hall, opened in 1990 on Beall near Pine, primarily a contribution of longtime trustee Hank Luce (whose father, Henry, the founder of *Time* magazine, had also been a trustee). Like other colleges nationwide, Wooster now realized that students wanted attention paid to their comfort and style in ways once seldom considered. Besides sharing a formal lounge with fireplace, fitness room, and kitchen, the hundred or so residents live in suites that accommodate a half-dozen or more. All suites are designated as living/learning language units—French, German, Spanish, Russian, Chinese, classical studies, and ancient Mediterranean studies. In 2004, the College opened Bornhuetter Hall, a residence hall nearly twice as large at the northwest corner of Beall and Wayne, with a principal gift from trustee Ron Bornhuetter, class of 1953, and his classmates. More modern in appearance than most other dorms, yet more traditional in layout than Luce, Bornhuetter offers study lounges on each floor and a central courtyard. Then in 2008 came Gault Manor, across the street on the northeast corner of Beall and Wayne, its very name suggesting something more elegant than Wooster students had been accustomed to. Another gift from Stan and Flo Gault, Gault Manor quickly became the first choice for upperclassmen. Its thirty-five doubles come with private bathrooms; it offers large common rooms on two floors and four smaller lounges; its recreational space comes with state-of-the-art audiovisual equipment.

One other addition to the formal housing stock was the 1961 addition of a wing at the north side of Holden Hall, which increased its capacity to more than three hundred, making it the largest on campus. That wing was renovated in 2004, and the main building, erected in 1907, underwent

its most significant renovation during the summer of 2005. (Holden Annex, built in 1927 as a temporary building, with no basement and a simple
stucco surface over a wood frame, was still in service in 2012.) A major
remodeling of Kenarden Lodge, which dates to 1911, took place during
the 1991–92 academic year, not only modernizing living quarters but also
adding a workout room and a formal lounge with fireplace. Babcock Hall,
the onetime senior women's dorm and current the center for students
living in the Cross-Cultural Living and Experiences Program, was renovated in 2008–9, with first-floor offices for the Center for Diversity and
Global Engagement and the Office of International Students, as well as
headquarters for Interfaith Campus Ministries.

Over the years, though, as enrollment grew toward two thousand, the
College couldn't build, renovate, or afford residence halls fast enough, so it
made do by buying up houses around its neighborhood to accommodate
a handful of students at a time. The residence application form offered in
spring 2012—information covering forty-five pages—illustrates how the
College has expanded its neighborhood housing options, dividing them
by area: Beall Avenue North, Beall Avenue South, Stibbs Street, Spink
Street, College Avenue, University Street, Independent Senior Housing.
The 2011–12 catalog described no fewer than forty-one different housing
sites, ranging from Holden with more than three hundred beds and its Annex with fifty more to some accommodating six students, or seven, eight,
or nine. Admittedly, this solution sometimes presents problems—parties
can lead to complaints from neighbors, occasional visits from the city
constabulary, and considerable anguish within the dean of students' office.

More significantly, the houses illustrate the remarkable breadth of
imagination and effort among Wooster students. Most of these smaller
units are program houses, in which students with related interests live
together; they are similar to residences like the French House of the 1950s,
which organized only along academic lines. Avery House on Stibbs Street
(off East University) houses seven students, who volunteer with the Wayne
Center for the Arts and provide on-campus events such as poetry readings and a spring concert. The eighteen students who live in the Fairlawn
Apartments on East Wayne Avenue (east of the Inn) manage "the Honey
House program, which aims to educate the College community on hive
collapse disorder, raise honeybees, and sell honey." Crandall House, on

Pearl Street (a block south of the southern border of the campus) accommodates six students who "oversee Bursting the Wooster Bubble, designed to encourage strong and healthy town relations between College students and the larger Wooster community." Hider House on East University accommodates eleven students who belong to "Men Working for Change, where residents seek to grow as men of character and competence as they volunteer their time raising awareness of domestic violence issues . . . and work in the community at local Wooster high schools." The nine residents of Reed House "crochet hats and scarves each month for Every Women's House, Children's Christian Home of Ohio, and patients at the Cleveland Clinic–Wooster." The ten residents of Calcie House belong to the Dream Program, "promoting awareness and facilitating multicultural interactions and understanding of different cultural practices and beliefs among Wooster students." The ten residents of Weber House teach English as a Second Language to individuals in the Wooster community. The ten residents of Colonial House belong to the "Women of Images program and serve as a support network for incoming and current women of color." The ten residents of Corner House "are part of Gallows, which provides substance-free entertainment through regular comedy routines." The fourteen residents of Kate House "plan and implement activities for children and youth at the Attention Center, a Wayne County facility for pre-trial delinquent youth." That's a sample of the College's off-campus houses.

Nearly all of these residence facilities are open to both men and women. The movement to coed housing at Wooster, in parallel with other colleges around the nation, was largely a product of its times, students more aggressively pursuing their wants, those being parietal rules loosened to the point of extinction. The idea had been percolating since the early 1970s, and the trustees approved Babcock and Westminster House as "program-centered living-learning units with men and women in the same building" in 1972. Administrators sold the idea by explaining that it would be discriminatory to offer special programs only to women or men. Doris Coster, then dean of students, remembered leading a group of skeptical trustees into Babcock to demonstrate both the plan's efficacy and its taste. Although women and men could use separate staircases and resided in separate wings, one trustee wanted privacy screens placed at the end of each hall so that women would not be embarrassed if they looked toward the men's wing and saw someone without a bathrobe. Coster chose not to suggest that "bathrobes were of another age." In the event, the College did provide privacy screens; they lasted something less than twenty-four hours.

In the spring of 1978, the Student Government Association and Campus Council both approved a proposal for open visitation. Copeland, in his first year as president, rejected it on the stated grounds that the College lacked the space to increase the diversity of its housing and that students had not adequately considered issues of security and privacy. Less publicly, he still had to consider the views of influential trustees who remained fiercely opposed to coed housing. Administrators also heard from parents who said that their children were sometimes forced to leave dorm rooms—rooms they had paid for—so roommates could entertain friends of the opposite sex. Those considerations failed to persuade a number of outspoken students, and at least one organized march on Galpin Hall occurred. Although student opinion polls seemed split, one student began a letter to the *Voice:* "Once again our college is under the control of narrow-minded politicians whose timing usually manages to outwit the student's desires." Gradual change did occur. A few coed opportunities had become available in program housing, and for the 1980–81 academic year, Stevenson Hall was offered as a "non-program coed residence hall" on an experimental basis.

With program housing in the lead, again gradually, more and more residence halls became coed. Some offered alternate coed floors, some rooms at alternate sides of the same floor; restrooms and shower options varied. What was clear is that students wanted coed residence halls, at Wooster as almost everywhere else. In the early twenty-first century, when students registered their living-space preferences for the following autumn and one dorm—Compton Hall—remained a women's dorm, it was the last accommodation to fill up; Compton soon became coed. "Nobody even asks about it [coed living] any more," said Kurt Holmes, dean of students. By 2012, the College was offering "Gender Neutral Housing." To wit: "Gender Neutral housing is an environment where student housing is not restricted to traditional limitations of the gender binary. Students may choose a roommate of any gender, and will not be asked by the Office of Residence Life to identify their own gender during the selection process. . . . The housing option is open to any students who are committed to the purpose of Gender Neutral Housing and feel it meets their own needs." "Coed housing" somehow seemed old-fashioned in this new world.

As the years went by, just about every new student need—or desire, depending on how this is judged—became fulfilled, save for one. The athletes got their gymnasium, swimming pool, and locker rooms, but they never did get their field house and never stopped hoping for it. As personal physical fitness grew increasingly important for the rest of the student body, a field house or something akin to it seemed increasingly important, as important as Lowry Center had been half a century earlier. Actually student physical fitness was only part of the perceived need. Competition counted. Wooster had watched other colleges build fitness and recreation centers attractive to students—Kenyon, for example, had constructed a $75 million Taj Mahal of sweat. Did similar buildings at other liberal arts colleges make a difference in enrollment? Hard to know, but it might have had a subtle effect. The Board of Trustees regularly talked about the concept; as vice president for finance and business in the early 2000s, Bob Walton actually ordered up a model of what such an edifice might look like. The fantasy plan was for a complex that would connect Lowry Center to the Physical Education Center, a complete student facility, but cost estimates ranged up to $72 million, and that was not going to happen. During the College's turn-of-the-century Independent Minds Campaign, planners did seriously consider seeking a field house or recreation center but finally settled on other priorities. Again, the field house took second place while other needs jumped ahead.

Since the Independent Minds Campaign had ended only in 2005, some thought the potentially big donors might have been tapped out, but new president Grant Cornwell saw a need, and a group of younger trustees agreed enthusiastically. At meetings in New York, five whose careers turned on finance and real estate—Doon Foster, Steve Gault, Blake Moore, Bob Savitt, and Peter Sundman—all but demanded that the College take action. Cornwell remembered being conscious of conservative anxiety about debt and the economy, but "they were telling me, Grant, we have to do this. Let's get moving. . . . Those guys were very comfortable with debt. At that point, they felt that we were not exercising our debt capacity strategically—a more aggressive college would use our balance sheet, and if we did we would be moving along faster." The ball was rolling, but there was further hesitation among some trustees that the coaches would essentially take over the facility. Cornwell calmed them with a slogan coined in the early moments: "Every student, every day." He also made a command decision about the name of the facility. He thought the College seemed too content with acronyms, like PEC (Physical Education Center), which are "inelegant. PEC has no poetry to it." Worried that a building called the Student Recreation Center would be reduced to SRC, he declared that it would be called simply the "Scot Center."

Once the fundamental decision was made, other decisions were required. To comfort those who feared the building would eliminate an autumn tradition—the band marching down the hill as it led the football team to the gridiron—the planners promised that the hill would be reconstructed. It was. A Wooster study team visited recreation facilities at a half-dozen neighboring colleges and garnered some dos and don'ts. A small point: Wooster escaped the climbing-wall fad of the 1990s, which students had tired of by the early twenty-first century. A larger point: Kenyon's huge building was located at the edge of campus, and many students considered it so inconvenient that they began ignoring it and using workout rooms in their dorms. This clinched the positioning of the Scot Center: it would not take space away from the Wayne Avenue playing fields but would be built between Lowry Center and the PEC—in the heart of campus and convenient to residence halls. It could even be connected to Lowry Center someday, if a plan and the money for it became available.

Still, cost—something near $30 million—remained a worry, and presumably it would require that millions be borrowed. Then the bids came in, remarkably a pleasant surprise: the actual construction would cost something over $19 million, about $3 million below what was anticipated. With unexpected funds available, the College added such extra touches as an aerobics studio and a large meeting/dining space as well as a more decorative lobby. Altogether, the Scot Center cost $22.6 million for construction, $4.7 million for furnishings and ancillary items, and nearly $1 million for landscaping—an outside patio, which quickly became a gathering place for students, as well as the band's hill—a total cost of $28.3 million had provided a building more elegant than had been anticipated. Of that, only about $3.8 million in low-interest bonds was needed. Gifts paid for nearly all of the Scot Center: the most consequential came from Trustee Ruth Whitmore Williams and her husband Morris, for what became the Ruth W. Williams Fitness Center; soon Stan Gault's family similarly provided the Gault Recreation Center.

The building is unlike anything seen before on the campus, both in size and appearance. One way to describe it would use numbers: 123,000 square feet, 524 tons of structural steel, 275,000 face bricks, 17,445 square feet of glass, 95.9 miles of electrical and IT wiring, 212,940 person hours of work. The center is topped by a 20,000-square-foot solar array—when built it was the largest at any college facility in the country—that generates 271,000 kilowatt hours of electricity per year, enough to power an entire large residence hall. Almost sheathed in ultra-high-efficiency glass, with a mini-tower designed to play off the iconic Kauke, it features a welcoming lobby with chairs for students to lounge in while studying, the aerobics studio, locker rooms for both women and men, coaches' offices, and meeting space. The fitness center, containing a circuit of training stations, treadmills, elliptical machines, rowing machines, and free weights, averaged more than eight thousand student visits a month during its early period; those are "every student, every day" visits, as athletic teams have their own smaller workout space. (A side benefit is that no student will feel intimidated working out next to a defensive tackle.) The recreation center—essentially the long dreamed-about field house—includes four courts for basketball, volleyball, and tennis; a regulation two-hundred-meter track, and long jump, triple jump, and pole vault runways and pits, enabling the College to hold indoor track meets for the first time; and batting cages and other equipment for indoor baseball practice. One wonders what the athletes and Boles alumni, who had once tried to raise $50,000 for a dirt-floor field house, would make of the Scot Center.

CHAPTER 10

Ex Libris

Every campus has its distinctive building. It's the Texas Tower at the university in Austin or the Gothic Chapel at Duke in Durham, North Carolina. At the University of Alabama it's the football stadium. At Wooster it's Kauke Hall. But the true heart of any institution of higher education is its library. Major research universities have several libraries, but very few liberal arts colleges have three. Wooster does—three buildings and a state-of-the-art concept.

The College library began in 1870 with a handful of donated books in a single room of Old Main. Old Main got an official reading room in 1875, and the library expanded into a whole floor of a new wing in 1892. It got its own sanctuary for the first time in 1900, and in the nick of time, too, because the move saved the books from the great fire that destroyed Old Main. The library building was a gift from Henry Clay Frick, the Pittsburgh industrialist, in memory of his parents. On an exterior frieze are carved the disciplines of Literature, Science, Art, Religion, History, Philosophy, Law, and Architecture. The high-ceilinged neoclassical reading room is rimmed by intellectual salutes ranging, eclectically, from Biblical and ancient times into the nineteenth century. On one side: Newton, Saint Paul, Beethoven, Handel, Shakespeare, Cicero, Homer, Socrates, Plato, and Phidias. On the other side: Kant, Moses, Darwin, Copernicus, Raphael, Demosthenes, Angelo, Calvin, Lavoisier, and Milton. Over the years its sturdy tables were jammed with students, their books and jackets, evening after evening following dinner, until 9 o'clock or so, when many repaired to the Shack or the Union before women returned to their dorms. Remodeled for the art department when Andrews Library opened in 1962, it became a library again in 1997, now to house in a unified setting the College's extensive science collections, which in turn cleared space in Severance Hall, Scovel Hall, and Mateer Hall. But as is often the case, the remodeling ran into money problems, forcing Ted Bogner, president of the Bogner Construction Management Company, and Bill Snoddy, vice president for business and finance, to pull $300,000 from the budget. Rather than moving the building's essential mechanical equipment to a scheduled new extension behind the building, the planners placed it in an existing lower room that had been reserved for periodicals. To find new space for periodicals, they added mezzanines, under which went the periodicals and above which went study carrels. When they asked Donna Jacobs, the science librarian, what she might like to make the room special, she chose a globe. So the Bogner family created the globe, the first thing a visitor sees inside the building, and dedicated it to the memory of Jean "Bunny" Bogner, a graduate of the College and the late wife of Robert "Pete" Bogner, her classmate and the longtime president of the company. Ted Bogner, her nephew, said that of all the work his company has done at the College, this room is his favorite.

Andrews Library, it might be said, was conceived in a Cadillac belonging to Mabel Shields Andrews, the widow of Matthew Andrews, who had been board chairman of the mighty M. A. Hanna Company in Cleveland. She was the principal donor of the men's dormitory named for her late husband, which opened in 1954, and had become quite fond of Howard Lowry. As the story goes, Andrews and Lowry were riding in her chauffeur-driven limousine and stopped at the corner of Beall Avenue and University Street, where she casually inquired, "Howard, if I were to give the College a million dollars, what would you do with it?" He was said to be momentarily speechless but quickly recovered to tell her he would build a library, and on that very corner (where the student union stood). Soon the gift came—at that time the largest single gift in Wooster's history—and on December 7, 1960, ground was broken for Andrews Library. It was dedicated May 19, 1962, featuring an address by Henry R. Luce and the conferring of honorary degrees on Luce and the poet Robert Frost, who had read one of his works in chapel a day earlier.

But the more important time was the afternoon of September 18, 1962, the first day of scheduled classes, when the entire College—administrators, faculty, students, and library staff—turned out to move 125,000 volumes from the Frick Library, which had served the College for more than six decades, to its sibling next door. Mrs. Andrews, ninety-three years old, carried the first book, the Bible, which held accession number 1 in the nineteenth-century library and would now be number 158,965, as the first book accessioned in Andrews. Next, Lowry carried his choice, the first edition of *Jonson's Dictionary*. He was followed by a friend of Mrs. Andrews, Dr. Harry Sloane, who brought the *Life of Sir William Osler* by H. Cushing. Representing the Board of Trustees, Willis C. Behoteguy, who had once helped tote books from Old Main to Frick Library, carried the two books that (after the Bible) had been in the College libraries the longest, *Thanksgiving* by William Adams, and *The Life of Archibald Alexander* by J. W. Adams. Then came Lowry's friend and mentor Waldo H. Dunn, who had been chairman of the English department at Wooster and librarian of Scripps College in California: *The Life and Letters of Erasmus* by James Anthony Froude. And the final person honored in this initial group, a professor of English at the College for forty-two years and also a longtime head of the department, Frederick W. Moore. It hardly seems necessary to report that the book Freddy Moore carried was Herman Melville's *Moby-Dick*.

The second wave began with the library staff, the librarian, Maudie Nesbitt, and Librarian Emerita Elizabeth Bechtel, and a dozen others including secretary and custodian. The architect got his turn, then the College business manager, Art Palmer, and the Special Faculty Committee on the new library: Lowell Coolidge, carrying a facsimile of the first edition of Milton's *Paradise Lost* and a facsimile of Shakespeare's First Folio; Aileen Dunham, carrying the four published volumes of *The New Cambridge Modern History*; Clayton Ellsworth, carrying volume 6 of *The Dictionary of American Biography*, containing the article on Benjamin Franklin written by Ellsworth's former professor, Carl L. Becker; Myron Peyton, carrying *El Libro de Buen Amor* by Juan Ruiz, and its English translation. Finally, the president of the Student Senate, Dave Mortensen, carried the *Voice* and the *Index*.

Fanciful treatment completed, the serious campaign began. Maudie Nesbitt had drawn up a battle plan that included moving reference books earlier in the month and various special collections later by library staff. For this big day, however, the custodial staff built a wooden staircase that emerged from an east-facing first-floor window of Frick down a dozen steps to ground level whence the book carriers walked to the new building.

Working in two-hour shifts, some carrying dozens of volumes, wearing red, blue, yellow, and white tags, volunteers were directed in organized lines to the proper places in Andrews (Lowry, who made several trips wearing a red tag, mistakenly slipped into a blue line, where students ordered him out). Upon delivering their loads, they turned back to Frick, careful not to bump others still carrying books, for refills. The process was tiring but, as might be expected, cheerfully executed—students singing, reading titles aloud, reading snatches of the books they lugged. The effort began at 1:15 P.M. and ended about 9:00 P.M., when the movers queued up for ice cream bars and souvenir bookmarks. The next day at 8:00 A.M., Andrews opened for business. Its appearance inside and the forms of usage it renders have changed, but it continued to serve the College a half-century later.

The history of the third library began, in a way, during the 1947–48 academic year. Flo Kurtz, a senior from Canal Fulton, was in one of the two classes not required to undertake the developing Independent Study program; already planning her marriage to classmate Stan Gault, she decided against it. In 1980, when Stan became chief executive of Rubbermaid, Inc., and the family moved to Wooster, Flo grew increasingly involved with the College and wondered what she might have missed in I.S. So she decided to take it on, adding to her English major, and in March 1987 she completed her thesis, "The Influence of the Wesleyan Movement on William Wordsworth and George Eliot." Through the project, she gained respect for the many resources available in the library, but she was left short of working space for the copious material she was assembling. She spread the books and papers over every flat surface in her dining room on Christmas Run Avenue and enjoyed the view out the window into her backyard.

From that experience grew the Flo K. Gault Library for Independent Study, joined to the North side of Andrews Library, a $5.6 million facility, most of the funds from the Gault family. It was dedicated October 21, 1995. The Gault Library serves many purposes, but one in particular should be noted: It provided 350 individual carrels, each connecting to the internet, accommodation enough for every senior in the humanities and social sciences to work privately on I.S. (physical science majors mainly use Timken Science Library and laboratories). And almost every one offers a window view.

Construction of the Gault Library allowed for parallel updating in Andrews. Several floors of the building, by then more than three decades old, were renovated, and whole sections of books and journals were shifted, depending on how much students and faculty were using them. Space was created on two ground-level and below-ground floors for Special Collections—the College archives—directed by Denise Monbarren, with the assistance of Elaine Smith Snyder. Besides being the sine qua non for anyone interested in the history of the College, these archives are, according to Damon Hickey, Director Emeritus of Library Services, "better used by the faculty for teaching than any I've ever seen." For this, he credits Monbarren: "Denise not only organized it virtually from scratch, but she's also made the contacts with faculty for students to come in and use the material."

The Timken-Frick renovation, 1996–98, which allowed significant offloading of science material, was important because the libraries were filling up fast with books and journals. Together Andrews and Gault now house a collection of about 1 million items, including books, periodicals, microforms, recorded material, newspapers, and government publications. They provide seating for nearly eight hundred users (including the I.S. carrels). They offer classrooms and language laboratories. In 1966 Andrews joined the Federal Depository Library Program, thus serving as a selective depository for U.S. government publications; the two also house special collections including the Bell & Howell Black Culture Collection, the Library of American Civilization, and the Greenwood Science Fiction Collection. Most recently, the library system became even more an academic and cocurricular centerpiece. The first floor of Andrews Library is home to CoRE, for Collaborative Research Environment, and the ground level of Gault Library is home to APEX, the Advising, Planning, Experiential Learning Center, which offers one-stop advising and guidance. (Details about CoRE and APEX appear in chapter 21.)

The major physical changes, the Gault construction and Andrews renovation of 1993–95, took place more or less simultaneously with—and mutually reinforced—something increasingly important, a technological shift of momentous proportion: print to digital media. Hickey, the library director from 1991 until 2008, described that period as "the greatest change in libraries [worldwide], possibly forever, certainly in the history of the College. At least since Gutenberg." Wooster took its first steps toward library cooperation and technology as far back as 1971, when Andrews became a charter member of the Ohio College Library Center, an idea said to have been suggested by Howard Lowry, through which it shared catalogs and card-based interlibrary loans. Seven years later, it joined NEOMARL, for Northeast Ohio Major Academic and Research Libraries. The critical opening in technology came in 1990. Looking ahead, the Copeland administration abandoned card catalogs and installed an integrated online electronic system, costly for the time but an investment that kept the College ahead of its peers.

After two years of discussion, on June 30, 1995, Wooster joined Denison, Kenyon, Oberlin, and Ohio Wesleyan to form the high-status Five Colleges of Ohio. This group cooperates in a number of areas, its presidents meeting twice a year, its chief financial officers five times a year, its chief academic officers three times a year, and its environmental safety and health managers monthly. But the consortium began, using a Mellon Foundation grant, with a focus on libraries and technology, declaring: "Never again can our libraries stand completely alone in terms of library collections and other resources. We, therefore, reaffirm The Five Colleges of Ohio libraries' overall commitment to cooperation and mutual enrichment. We believe that any small loss of local control is well worth the many benefits we gain through our collaboration." They called their merged library system Consort. It then affiliated with OhioLINK, a statewide academic library consortium, which made all collections readily available to users throughout the state and allowed for a steady expansion of books, journals, and other databases. In a fine combination of twenty-first- and twentieth-century effectiveness, if students or faculty find a book or journal not available at their institution, they can type in their college bar code and make their requests electronically. The system decides what library can best fulfill it; within twenty-four hours that library puts the item in a bag, hands it to a driver, and it is delivered by truck within a day or two.

Obviously there are synergies. Given the increase in printed material, Frick served a useful sixty years, more or less, Andrews half that long (the number of books at Frick had increased by almost 15 percent just in the decade before Andrews opened). Gault might have served even less time but for the shift to digital media. Some faculty members resisted the movement for a while, partly because they were simply more comfortable with printed material themselves and partly because they were nowhere near as comfortable with digital media as their students were. That sense, of course, changed, but the College continued to add thousands of printed books and journals annually to its library shelves. The scale can be different: Hickey remembered that Wooster's library subscribed to about two thousand printed journals when he became director of libraries and about fifteen hundred when he retired; now students and faculty have electronic access to about fifteen thousand, at a cost lower than for a smaller number of subscriptions. And because the OhioLINK system is connected internationally, Wooster students can find out at a glance what might be available from a library in The Netherlands or Sweden. Hickey also observed with a smile that because Harvard, famous for its enormous library system, belongs to a New England consortium less efficient than OhioLINK, Wooster's students may have access to more material than Harvard's.

It has been well noted that recent I.S. projects—many comparable to graduate theses—are often far more sophisticated than the sometimes term-paper–like efforts of the earliest days. International electronic research availability is surely part of the reason. However, some faculty members worry that the relative ease can lead to a kind of strip-mining research, allowing students to sweep through so much material that they might not dig as deeply as they should. But then, reaching the appropriate median is what faculty-student I.S. advising is all about. It does seem clear that students today, with their laptop computers and other electronic devices, would hardly know how to work in the libraries of a half-century ago. And students from that era might feel like cavemen who had wandered into the twenty-first century.

CHAPTER 11

The Scots Tale

On a Sunday evening, Aug. 22, 1945, L. C. "Coach" Boles suffered a fatal stroke at his home, at the age of sixty-two. It was nothing less than a historic moment for Wooster athletics. Boles had come to Wooster in 1915 and for more than a decade coached the football, basketball, and baseball teams himself; four of his football teams were unbeaten. But the highlight of his coaching career came on a chilly November day in 1924 at the massive stone horseshoe in Columbus known as Ohio Stadium. There, a Wooster team boasting stars such as Hank Critchfield, Donald "Rosy" Starn, and Howard Smith played a 7–7 tie against Ohio State; never again did the Buckeyes fail to defeat a team from its home state. (The first time these teams played, in 1890, Wooster beat Ohio State, 64–0.) Over twenty-four years, until he gave up the football position in 1939, Boles-coached Wooster teams won 134 games, lost 50, and tied 19 and won four Ohio Athletic Conference championships. He continued to coach golf until 1945, spending as much time as possible on the course that the College named in his honor, the L. C. Boles Memorial Golf Course. He taught Sunday school and during World War II taught marksmanship to V-5 cadets. All this while, he also served as the College's athletic director, a post he held until his death. In his spare time, as Art Murray, one of his protégés, put it, "he was the greatest force for town-gown relations that [the College] ever had." Boles served as president of the Rotary Club; president of the YMCA; city council member; and a board member of the Auto Club, Masonic Lodge, and Board of Trade.

At a memorial for Coach Boles, the recently retired Prexy Wishart said that although two monuments, the stadium and the golf course, stood in honor of the coach, there was a "greater memorial in lives he had touched and strengthened and helped—that monument can never fade." Foremost among these, as Wishart noted, were the four coaches he had selected to work for him—Murray, E. M. "Mose" Hole, and Johnny Swigart, all Wooster graduates, and Carl Munson, whom Boles had found at Spring-field College in Massachusetts—and "the wholesome influence that they exerted on the thousands of young lives that they touched during their long careers."[1] When the College inaugurated its "W" Association Hall of Fame in the fall of 1967, Boles and his four hires—collectively they spent close to two centuries at Wooster—were charter members. Two others were also so designated: Kinley McMillan, class of 1886, who introduced football, a game he had learned at the Princeton Theological Seminary, to Wooster; and L. W. St. John, Wooster class of 1906, who served as Ohio State's athletic director for three decades.

The death of Coach Boles came at a low point for Wooster athletics. During World War II, trainees in the navy's V-12 program had turned some small colleges, like DePauw, into temporary football powerhouses. But Wooster's strenuous V-5 program, preparing navy flyers, attracted young men more for their intelligence than athletic prowess. Further, the cadets stayed at Wooster for only about three months, so a whole football or basketball team might turn over midseason. And of course there were almost no civilian athletes. In early August 1944, it was not clear whether there would even be a football season (swimming had been abandoned as an inter-collegiate sport during the war), but to sports fan Lowry's delight, Coach Boles managed to schedule five games, the only victory coming in the final game, against Oberlin. With the exception of Chuck Stocker, a freshman end, every player on that Wooster team was a V-5 cadet. Stocker soon entered the navy, but he came back to school in the fall of 1946 and played through the 1949 season—thus becoming the only athlete ever to play five seasons of football at Wooster. Mose Hole, determined to have a basketball team, started with six civilians and thirteen cadets, the roster

1. Regarding Hole's name: family records indicate that when the Hole family's beloved cat, Old Mose, died, the children thought that someone should carry on the name. Young Ernest's three brothers gave it to him, and he carried it to the end of his life.

changing as V-5 trainees rotated in and out; the final record was 3–12. During the fall of 1945, the navy took all its cadets away in midseason, and Wooster lost every football game for the only time in its history.

The postwar years were better. Returning veteran stars like Bill Shinn, Mynie Busack, and Jim Kennedy turned around the football team. In the 1947 season, Shinn kicked a fourth-quarter field goal to give Wooster a 16–13 victory over Muskingum, the other Presbyterian-related college in Ohio and then a bitter rival; Wooster was not to beat Muskingum again for thirty-one years. Earlier that fall, Kent State arrived at Severance Stadium for what its coaches thought would be a warm-up game. In the first quarter, Wooster scored twice, to lead 13–0, and the Scots held on for a grueling three periods to defeat the Golden Flashes, 13–6. In those days, Kent State and Akron University were major rivals in football and basketball; now those two former opponents play nationally televised games.

Hole assembled an Ohio Conference championship basketball team in 1946–47. One of its three stars was Don Swegan, who as a wartime navy trainee had played on a Harvard basketball team that earned an invitation to the NCAA tournament; not until 2011–12 did the Crimson receive another bid, and Harvard invited Swegan to the tournament as its guest. The other two were the rugged center Ralph "Fingers" Wagner, and Earl Shaw, a freshman with a deadly two-hand shot and flashy speed who over four years broke every Wooster scoring record. Six years later, Hole did it again, with a fleet group of juniors, led by Bob Voelkel, Jack Holt, and Ron Felty. After succeeding Boles in 1926, Hole coached for thirty-one years, through transition that would boggle the minds of contemporary fans. When Hole began his career, the teams lined up for a center jump after every successful basket, and there was no half-court time line or ten-second rule, so that teams could control the ball—and the clock—over the full court length; final scores in the teens were commonplace. As a much-in-demand after-dinner speaker, Hole liked to relate, in his languid, deep-throated style, how well he used his talent: one season, he maintained, his players didn't have much ability, but he did have one player who could spin the ball on his finger, so that's what Hole ordered him to do for most of the game against superior opponents. As the game changed, Hole adjusted, adopting what he called his "spray" offense—throw the ball at the basket as often as possible, on the assumption that some of the shots will go in. His defense, a full-court zone trap, could drive opponents crazy. In those years, playing schedules of fifteen to twenty games, Hole's Scots won 412 and lost 181 and three times won the Ohio Athletic Conference championship.

Typical of all coaches during his era at Wooster, Hole also coached tennis and as a full-time faculty member taught physical education classes and supervised intramurals. As the war ended, Hole succeeded Boles as athletic director—he kept all his other assignments—and the stalwarts who had worked for Boles continued to coach everything else. Swigart succeeded Boles as head football coach in 1939 and also coached baseball off and on before retiring in 1966. Munson led track and field, cross-country, and swimming, retiring in 1962. Murray, who also retired in 1962, coached baseball regularly and assisted in football and basketball, while also serving as the College's principal photographer for decades and often director of the news and sports information bureaus as well. It wasn't all peaches and cream, though, among these men who worked in close proximity for four decades. Hole and Munson, in particular, touched off sparks, and President Lowry more than once protected Munson from the athletic director. When Hole decided he had to replace Swigart as football coach in 1949, he gave him baseball as a consolation prize, probably hurting the feelings of both Swigart and Murray in the process.

If that chapter of Wooster athletics belonged mostly to the five men whose careers began around the time of World War I and ended a few years after World War II, the next chapter belonged to men, and women, who carried Wooster athletics competitively—and just as important, socially—into the twenty-first century. The generational shift began in 1949, when Hole hired as head football coach someone with no experience at any college, the Defiance High School coach, Phil Shipe. Shipe brought with him the single-wing, an offensive formation almost no one used anymore, and as his running-passing tailback, he recruited the basketball star Shaw. At that early point, Hole may have regretted his new hire. Watching from the press box, he winced every time his star was knocked down, but Shaw proved elusive and durable on the gridiron and survived to lead the Scot basketball team through the 1949–50 season. Shipe coached football for seventeen seasons—shifting to the T-formation quickly—compiling a record of 84 victories, 61 losses, and 6 ties, including an Ohio Conference co-championship in 1959, and also coached golf and wrestling. Shipe's principal disappointment was that his football teams played Muskingum

seventeen times and lost seventeen times. (The rivalry was hardly sweet-
ened in 1951 when Ohio chief justice Carl Weygandt, a Wooster trustee,
gave an overlong speech during halftime of the Homecoming game against
Muskingum, and the Muskies' coach, Ed Sherman, demanded—and
got—an unsportsmanlike conduct penalty against Wooster for delaying
the start of the second half.) When, before a joyous crowd at Severance
Stadium, Wooster did finally defeat Muskingum in 1978, Coach Tom Holl-
man presented the game ball to Shipe.

One of Shipe's many contributions to the College was to modify the
athletic teams' nickname. The name "Scots" sprang, as did so many other
unsung elements of Wooster's sports, from Art Murray. Early in the twentieth century, colleges began to give their teams nicknames, some pertinent—the Cornhuskers of Nebraska, the Hoosiers of Indiana—and some
more prosaic—the Wildcats of Kentucky, the Tigers of Missouri. For want of
something better, Wooster's teams were often identified as the Presbyterians,
although never officially, and sports writers even referred to Coach Boles's
gridiron powerhouses of the early 1920s as the Presbyterian Steamroller.
Probably around 1930 (precise date uncertain) Murray suggested to Boles
the name "Scots" for Wooster's teams, in recognition of the Presbyterian
tradition from Scotland. Boles liked it. As far as can be known, the *Voice*
was first to use the name when Wooster beat Bluffton in September 1931;
soon afterward students stringing for the *Plain Dealer* of Cleveland and the
Daily Record reported that the Scots had drubbed Ashland. Students took
to the name instantly, and sports-page headline writers loved its brevity.

So "Scots" it was, until the 1950s. The summer of 1950 Shipe spent
doing graduate work at the University of Pennsylvania in Philadelphia
and watched a collection of young underdogs—they were known as the
"Whiz Kids" and the "Fightin' Phils"—win the National League pennant.
After a losing season, and his judgment that his football team needed to
be more aggressive, he determined that the team should be called the
Fighting Scots. The name was carried on only in football until the 1960s,
when Al Van Wie, Hole's successor as athletic director, decided that it
should be applied to all the teams and then to the summer sports camps
he had created, which were now called Camp Fighting Scots. And if
Fighting Scots seemed a bit of a stretch for golf and tennis, so be it. For
the relatively new women's sports, the nickname seemed less of a fit. At
first, coaches of women's teams chose "Scotties." But in 1987, the Women's

Athletic Association changed the team's name officially to Lady Scots—it served as the women's varsity sports program grew to equality with the men's—then to just Scots in the new century.

It wasn't only the athletes, though, who remembered Shipe fondly. He was one of the few coaches who ever taught the required freshman seminar, in which, often, the instructor created his own curriculum—Shipe worked all summer on his programs—and his student evaluations were off the charts. Shipe and his wife, Pem (her maiden name was Pemberton), entertained the students at their home over cider and popcorn and discussed philosophic topics. In his retirement, he painted on panels of barn siding and gave his work away. "He was more than a coach," said Van Wie, who became his boss as athletic director. "He was a philosopher, an artist, a real mystic. He cared about people. During the late '60s and '70s, when all hell was breaking loose on campus, kids would line up outside his door, I'm not talking just about athletes, and wait to see him." Thanks to contributions from former students, a "Phil Shipe Memorial Walk" extends from Lowry Center to the Armington Physical Education Center.

During the Shipe years emerged a figure not widely known outside Wooster's immediate athletic community: Charles "Swede" McDermott, class of 1924, whose sports career consisted of serving as a football manager. McDermott, who built a successful playground-equipment company called Blazon, lived in Akron and scoured the city for young men with both the classroom intelligence and the playing-field ability to be successful at Wooster. He personally funded the education for upward of one hundred such students; the students never saw the money, which was channeled to the College mainly through McDermott's friend Racky Young, the dean of men. (Today's National Collegiate Athletic Association [NCAA], with its arcane governance rules, would perhaps not look kindly on such activity.) But it was not a secret: in October 1962, a Scot football program was dedicated "to Mac," listing at the time seventy-eight such young men, including four—Bill Evans, Dave Nelander, John Papp, and Dale Perry—who were dedicated enough to the College and successful enough in their careers to become trustees. How well did McDermott identify the young men? Besides having graduated, a number of these students became some of the greatest athletes Wooster saw in the 1950s and 1960s; afterward many became doctors, ministers, scientists, and business executives. One of the few nonathletes to be elected to Wooster's Athletic Hall of Fame, McDermott was enshrined, appropriately enough, in 1972, the same year as Young and Shipe.

Shipe's immediate successor as football coach was Jack Lengyel, whom Lowry personally approved after an interview at the Princeton Club in New York. Lengyel's first Wooster team, in 1966, lost eight of nine games, and his last team, in 1970, won eight of nine. His chief fame as a coach, however, came not on the gridiron but in the movies. When the football team and coaching staff at Marshall University in Huntington, West Virginia, were wiped out in a airplane crash that fall of 1970, and some major-college assistants thought rebuilding the program was too difficult, the little-known Lengyel called Marshall and talked himself into the job. Amazingly, the Thundering Herd he built from scratch won the second game they played the next year. This touching tale of death and rebirth was turned into a feel-good movie, *We Are Marshall,* in 2006, starring Matthew McConaughey as Lengyel. Scot football went through a series of up-and-down years after Lengyel, before Jim Barnes, who became coach in 1995, led the Scots to a 9–1 record and an NCAC co-championship in 1997. His successor was his offensive coordinator, Mike Schmitz, whose 2006 team won the conference title with a perfect 10–0 record. That team produced two Division III All-Americans, halfback Tony Sutton, and tackle Dick Drushal, grandson of the former president. The 1979 team included a three-time All-American, center Blake Moore, a fourth-generation Wooster graduate—his great-grandfather played on the 1890 Wooster team—who played for the Cincinnati Bengals in the 1982 Super Bowl.

While the football program veered erratically, basketball hardly missed a step. Hole's immediate successor, Jim Ewers, who had been both a football and basketball star at Wooster, left after three years to earn his PhD at Ohio State. Assuming Ewers would return, President Lowry persuaded Van Wie, who worried that he wasn't ready, to fill in for a year. Van Wie's self-assessment appeared valid. With Hole sitting in the narrow Severance Gym bleachers not far away, Van Wie's first team, 1961–62, won five games and lost eighteen. (The Scots played in Severance from 1913 until February 20, 1968, when they lost in overtime to Denison, 87–82.)

Ewers, however, did not return (he went on to teach at the University of Akron and the University of Utah), and despite Van Wie's inauspicious start,

Lowry said he had confidence in the young coach and insisted he continue in the job. It lasted twenty-one years. During that period, in which he also served as sometime tennis coach, Van Wie's basketball teams won 302 games and lost 216. The best of them, in the 1970–71 season, won twenty-three games, including nineteen in a row, and lost one during the regular season, and earned an NCAA tournament bid (during a period when colleges like Wooster, which did not award athletic scholarships, were matched against scholarship teams). The team was led by Tom Dinger, who scored more than twenty points in seventy-seven of the ninety-six games he played over four years, averaging nearly twenty-five points per game, the highest scorer in Wooster history. But the Scots, unbeaten in twelve Ohio Conference games that season, were barred from the conference tournament because the previous summer Van Wie had organized a pioneering basketball camp for teenagers. President Drushal protested furiously, arguing that since no rule had existed against such camps this amounted to ex post facto punishment, but the conference did not relent. Now hundreds of colleges, including a number in Ohio, operate similar camps in many sports.

Van Wie became athletic director in 1974, and administering the growing sports program led him to give up coaching in 1982. One of his two immediate successors was Lu David Wims, who won varsity letters in football, basketball, and track for four years, the only Wooster athlete ever to earn twelve letters. In 1987, Van Wie made one of the great hires in Scot athletic history, thirty-four-year-old Steve Moore, whom he had spotted years earlier as a savvy point guard at Wittenberg University. Soft-spoken off the court, yet a fierce competitor, Moore not only built a successful basketball program but also cemented extraordinary respect among Wooster's faculty. He checks closely his players' academic performances and has been known to hold them out of games if they miss classes. In twenty-five years at Wooster, through the 2011–12 season, Moore's teams won 595 games against 134 losses, a winning percentage of .817, and reached the Final Four of Division III three times; for the dozen years after 2000 Wooster compiled the best record of any team of any college of any size in the nation.

The only national championship won by a Wooster team came in 1975. Bob Nye, who tutored the golf team for thirty-two years, coached the Scots to a one-shot victory over Hampden-Sydney, when Mike McKeon dropped an eight-foot birdie putt on the final hole. McKeon's teammates

Daily Record publisher Ray Dix shakes hands with board chairman Arthur Holly Compton as President Lowry and Prexy Wishart look on (1944)

Above left: Bob Wilson, board chairman and donor of Wooster Inn; below left: Cary Wagner, board chairman from 1964 to end of Lowry era; above: Two board chairmen, Bill Pocock (left) and Stan Gault (center) with President Henry Copeland (1987)

Left: V-5 cadets marching between classes near Memorial Chapel (circa 1942–44)

Below: Bill Syrios, popular proprietor of the Shack (1946)

Veterans' housing, the "units," behind Scovel Hall, Bever Street in background (1959)

Above: The first Homecoming queen, Olivia dePastina, presented flowers by Student Senate president Art Palmer (1946); above right: Good-night kisses at 11:59 P.M. on the steps of Holden Hall (1947); right: A formal dance on the basketball court at Severance Gymnasium (1949); below: Girls dancing around the maypole on Color Day (1950)

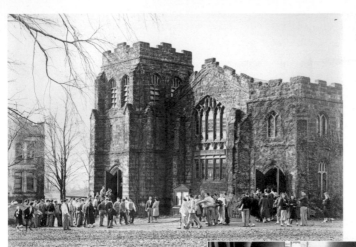

Left: Students outside Memorial Chapel (1950)

Right: Lowry addressing opening convocation inside Memorial Chapel (1960)

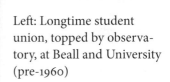

Left: Longtime student union, topped by observatory, at Beall and University (pre-1960)

Right: Students watch the Student Union (TUB) being moved around the corner to clear room for Andrews Library (1960)

Above left: Students carrying books down temporary stairs from Frick Library to the new Andrews Library (1962); above: Freddy Moore, carrying his beloved *Moby-Dick* to Andrews Library, escorted by Dean of Men Racky Young (1962)

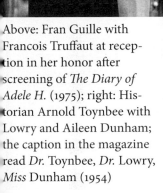

Above: Fran Guille with Francois Truffaut at reception in her honor after screening of *The Diary of Adele H.* (1975); right: Historian Arnold Toynbee with Lowry and Aileen Dunham; the caption in the magazine read *Dr.* Toynbee, *Dr.* Lowry, *Miss* Dunham (1954)

Right: Chemist Bill Kieffer at the blackboard (1975)

Far right: Mathematician Melcher Fobes at his desk

Ted Williams, chemist, mentor, "conscience"

Professor of English Ray McCall biking to campus

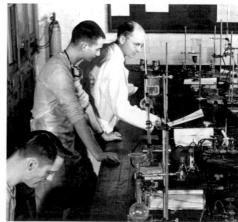

Chemist John Chittum with students in the lab (1969)

Medical Director Vi Startzman, with Wooster surgeon Robert Wright (1959)

Clare Adel Schreiber with children at the nursery school she directed for many years (circa 1977)

Dorothy and Garber Drushal (circa 1968)

The provocative McGaw Chapel

Above: Archaeologist Bob Smith studying effects from Pella dig (1967); right: Historian of religion Gordon Tait, leading the movement to "religious studies"

were Mike Schneider, who led Wooster with a three-round score of 225, Greg Nye (the coach's son), Steve Bamberger, and Rodger Loesch.[2] Tim Pettorini, who coached baseball for thirty-one years (as of 2012) has come close, losing twice in the national championship game, once in twelve innings. His Wooster teams (through 2012) won 1,002 games, losing 376, for a winning percentage of .726. After years in which tennis had been coached as a second effort by Hole and Van Wie, then as almost an afterthought by a football coach, Hayden Schilling, a professor of history and avid tennis player, persuaded Van Wie to give him the varsity assignment in 1980. In more than thirty years Schilling's squads compiled a winning percentage of over .600; the 1985 championship team was led by Bob Savitt, who was the son of a Wimbledon champion and who became a College trustee.

The most unusual of Wooster athletic teams—whether or not fans were even aware of it—was the College of Wooster Sailing Club. Formed in 1955 by a few interested students who paid for their own equipment and got no help from the College—except the use of one of the old units behind Scovel Hall to do their maintenance—the team sailed from Charles Mill Lake near Mansfield and competed over the next decade in the Midwest Collegiate Sailing Association, against teams from Michigan State, Purdue, Notre Dame, and Ohio State, among others, winning more than its share of cups and trophies.

Thirty-seven words, Title IX of the Education Amendments of 1972, introduced by Representative Patsy Mink of Hawaii, and signed by Richard Nixon on June 23, 1972: "No person in the United States shall, on the basis of sex, be excluded from participation in, be denied the benefits of, or be subjected to discrimination under any educational program or activity receiving Federal financial assistance."

Title IX was the most important piece of federal legislation concerning collegiate athletics ever approved. At first few understood its ramifications—for example, would Alabama have to share its football profits with the women's tennis team? Answer: yes. And it had opponents on both sides.

---

2. Regarding academics and athletics at Wooster: the players on this team posted a collective 3.73 GPA during the 1975 spring quarter. Nye became the golf coach at Penn State; McKeon a judge; Schneider an anesthesiologist; Loesch a CPA; Bamberger invented a laser optics system to measure distance, as in fairway to green on a golf course.

Many female athletic leaders fought the prospective changes, fearing that the Association of Intercollegiate Athletics for Women (AIAW), which had nurtured and governed college women's sports for years, would be driven out of business by the male-ruled NCAA; it was. Almost needless to say, the law also had to overcome fierce opposition from diehard men, who feared that their precious football receipts might have to support volleyball for students they believed better suited to be short-skirted cheerleaders. Ultimately, though, the NCAA's television revenue and visibility helped build women's athletics at all levels. In 1971, the year before Title IX became law, 310,000 American girls and women participated in interscholastic and intercollegiate sports; in 2012, 3,373,000 participated, about eleven times as many. It seemed a clear break from the days, which lasted into the '60s, when females played six-girl basketball, each team fielding three on offense and three on defense, who could not pass midcourt, so as not to damage their dainty bodies running on a ninety-foot court.

Before Title IX, thanks largely to the efforts of Maria "Doc" Sexton—one of the founders of the AIAW—beginning in 1965 Wooster offered women intercollegiate competition in field hockey and in 1967, volleyball. When the physical education budget did not cover women's tennis, Sexton asked the varsity coaches to contribute $8.33 from each of their budgets and they all agreed; with the $100 collected, Wooster women inaugurated intercollegiate tennis in 1970. The year after Title IX became law, they began varsity competition in basketball and swimming and diving; the next year brought lacrosse. Softball became a varsity sport in 1979 (fast-pitch softball in 2000), track and field and cross-country both in 1981, soccer in 1985, and golf in 2010. By 2012, well over two hundred women, approaching one-quarter of the women's enrollment, competed in varsity athletics, and the College supported eleven women's teams, compared to ten for men.[3]

Historically, though, most of the women's physical-education faculty members spent their careers mainly teaching phys ed and mentoring intramural players, struggling to gain time at the various facilities, grasping for budget crumbs as they saw it. The oldest was Kathleen Lowrie, a PhD

3. Wooster's women's sports include basketball, cross-country, field hockey, golf, lacrosse, soccer, softball, swimming and diving, tennis, track and field, and volleyball. Its men's sports are baseball, basketball, cross-country, football, golf, lacrosse, soccer, swimming and diving, tennis, and track and field.

who came to Wooster in 1921 (the same year as Carl Munson arrived from Springfield) and directed women's physical education until she retired, in 1952. Ginny Hunt, who spent fourteen years at the College, may have been the only female athletic director in the nation while Bob Bruce took leave in 1972–73. Nan Nichols, who joined the faculty in 1962, coached basketball for twenty-two years, including a championship tie in the first year of the NCAC, and swimming for its first seven official years—until then, the only "coach" the women had was a male varsity swimmer. In 2010 she was elected to the Ohio Basketball Hall of Fame. Brenda Meese, who came to Wooster in 1989, became assistant director of the combined athletic department in 2004. It should not be surprising that ninety-one men were admitted to the "W" Association Hall of Fame before the first women, the 1985 inductees: Vi Startzman and Hunt from the faculty and Annie Baird Frick, class of 1974, the first of the outstanding modern athletes. Sexton, Nichols, and Meese are all now part of the Hall, along with fifty-two female athletes of the modern (some even pre–Title IX) era. In 1992, the first year in which the gender totals were even, Sarah MacDougall, Marion Mason Strandh, and Melinda Weaver were enshrined along with three men. In the twenty-first century, Amanda Artman became a four-time All-American in field hockey, Beth Hemminger a multiple All-American in lacrosse, Kayla Heising in swimming, and Katie Wieferich in track and field; swimmer Elizabeth Roesch was the 2005 national champion in the one-kilometer freestyle.

In a coincidental but not unrelated occurrence, the North Coast Athletic Conference was founded the year after Title IX passed. "It doesn't sound like a new idea today," Van Wie, one of the NCAC founders, said years later, "but it was a new idea at the time. There would be a single structure. Men and women with equal power. When it came to a conference vote, the male athletic director had one vote, the female athletic director had another vote. There would be championships, for men's basketball, for women's basketball, right down the line." More than gender equality, however, brought about the NCAC. For more than fifty years Wooster had been a member of the Ohio Athletic Conference, along with such schools as Mount Union, Muskingum, Capital, Heidelberg, Baldwin-Wallace, and Otterbein. But it began to discomfort administrators at Wooster, among others, that some of those institutions appeared to be increasing their emphasis on sports—overemphasis, it was occasionally called. And though it was never admitted publicly, one could fairly observe that certain members of the old Ohio Conference thought their academic standards were higher than those of some other members. So under the leadership of Wooster's Henry Copeland and Kenyon's President Phil Jordan a group of academic and athletic administrators held a series of furtive organizing meetings, in places like a motel in Cambridge, Ohio, to consider a new affiliation, intending to become something of an Ivy League of small midwestern colleges.

At its inception, the NCAC consisted of the Ohio Five, the academic stalwarts Denison, Kenyon, Oberlin, Ohio Wesleyan, and Wooster, plus Cleveland's Case Western Reserve, Allegheny in Pennsylvania, and Earlham in Indiana.[4] One standard for admission was that each college possess a Phi Beta Kappa chapter, something many in the Ohio Conference lacked. Wittenberg became the first addition—its president pleaded to join the NCAC as a signal of its academic ambition—then Hiram and Indiana's DePauw and Wabash were admitted; after several years Earlham decided to withdraw. Only Wabash faced serious opposition; as an all-male school it couldn't uphold one of the founding principles—gender equality.

While the competitors themselves changed significantly, the road to modern athletic and recreation facilities—Armington Physical Education Center, Timken Gymnasium, Scot Center—was, to understate a cliché, long and tortuous. The College's nineteenth-century gym, between what became Galpin Hall and Taylor Hall, gave way in 1915 to Severance Gymnasium, was turned into a service center, and is now a parking lot. Everyone knew, at least by the end of World War II, that Severance—a cramped arena with a stressed floor, hosting dances, concerts, performances, and convocations along with basketball games—should be replaced sooner rather than later. And everyone knew the College needed a field house to give athletic teams indoor practice space and students a little room to work out. Not long after Coach Boles's death, several of his former athletes started a fund to build a field house in his memory; they collected $19,000, but President Lowry said the structure would cost

4. Carnegie Mellon in Pittsburgh planned to become a member but declined to participate because of anxiety about travel expenses. Case Western Reserve withdrew to join the University Athletic Association, with such other institutions as Washington University in St. Louis, the University of Chicago, and New York University.

about $100,000, and the campaign slowly fizzled. (The consolation prize was to affix Coach's name to the L. C. Boles Memorial Golf Course.)

In early 1946, Mose Hole, the new athletic director, wrote the campus architect with notes on what a first-class physical education plant and field house should contain. "One of the main points to remember," Hole cautioned, "is to have plenty of showers and toilet facilities. The locker rooms should be pleasant, well-lighted and with air conditioning." The specs included a basketball court; a twenty-five-yard swimming pool; a boxing ring; four handball courts; coaches' offices; classrooms; and two locker rooms, one for the varsity, one for visitors, each accommodating fifty men—with no mention of any such space for women. By that spring, Lowry informed the architect that although the idea of a field house was included in the earlier specifications, "Wooster's needs will be served best by a gymnasium rather than a fieldhouse." At a June 1961 "W" Association party, the College exhibited drawings for a $2.8 million four-building complex with separate men's and women's gyms, swimming pool, field house, handball courts, rifle and archery ranges, training rooms, and classrooms. Fall 1963 brought a sixteen-page proposal for remodeling Severance Gym and adding a major new structure. It recommended using the downstairs alternate gym at Severance (the "cage") for a dance studio and the main gym for tennis practice and gymnastics. A new facility would include a varsity basketball gymnasium seating twenty-five hundred and would also be available for dances and convocations; a second gym for fencing, weight-training, and fitness activities; a twenty-five-yard swimming pool; and various locker rooms and offices. A field house could be added, "primarily designed to provide indoor space for outdoor activities during inclement weather," but might be made big enough for indoor track. The proposal conceded, however, that the field house might not be necessary. "The fieldhouse was always the second priority," remembered Van Wie. "Something else always jumped in front of it."

Upon Hole's retirement in 1964, Bob Bruce (class of 1939), who had directed plebe physical education at West Point, took over as athletic director, and the next year Lowry assigned him and Van Wie, the basketball coach, to calculate the needs for a new facility and to meet with architects. With the support of important trustees, they quickly disposed of the idea that a new gym would be built for men and Severance remodeled for women and their limited varsity sports. A more critical issue was its location, which some trustees wanted to be unobtrusive. Planners considered three sites—near the Wooster Inn, slightly removed from the main campus; in Galpin Park, closer to the men's dorms; or more central, between the prospective student center (Lowry) and Babcock Hall. The compromise: a central location but farther east. A problem existed: the last two holes of the golf course lay on the rolling turf adjoining Wayne Avenue. The solution: the two golf holes were rebuilt east of Palmer Street: a ditch was dug so that nearly all of the main structure was unobtrusively below grade, and the excavated soil was used to level the nearby land to create three new playing fields for recreation and intramurals, soccer, and baseball. By eschewing permanent seats in the main gym, fold-out bleachers could provide seating for thirty-four hundred, and with the bleachers folded up, a second gym would become available for basketball and volleyball and a mezzanine for baseball batting cages. The building could also fit in a wrestling room, fitness rooms, and storage space.

That left one problem—how to pay for it. The Timken Foundation contributed $750,000, which along with smaller gifts and some borrowing took care of construction, and the basketball team played its first season at Timken Gym in 1968–69. But the College lacked the funds for what else it needed—a swimming pool, locker rooms for men and women, a training room, and administrative offices. The financial shortfall for what was called "Phase II" of the physical education center was about $1.6 million, so the College decided reluctantly to borrow some of the funds, which meant public bidding. Just as with construction of three dorms several years earlier, a Canton firm came in low, then ran out of money midway; once again, the Bogner company stepped in to finish the job. While the Board of Trustees pondered the cost, Buck Smith, the chief development officer, got a call from George Armington, chairman of the Buildings and Grounds Committee, asking if it would all right if he came to Wooster to visit with President Drushal and Smith. At the president's home, Armington said, "Would you mind if [my wife] Helen and I gave the $1.6 million?" Drushal said he wouldn't mind, and he accepted the donor's wish that the gift be anonymous. Phase II was completed in the summer of 1973, and that fall the board decided to name it the Armington Physical Education Center—not mentioning the contribution, only in honor of Armington's work as committee chairman. One dream remained unfulfilled, a field house; that dream would not come true until 2012, nearly forty years later.

CHAPTER 12

A Chapel for Its Time

It rises from a little dale, startlingly light, its flat roof sprouting oddly angled corner panels that might be called turrets, were they not so sleekly modern. It stands central to the campus, just off Quinby Quadrangle, tucked between stately Kauke Hall and Taylor Hall. It is a religious sanctuary, yet so much more, symbolizing a momentous change in College history. It is the McGaw Chapel, and it is certainly the most provocative physical structure ever at Wooster.

McGaw Chapel is nearly a half-century old, a lifespan not much shorter than the revered edifice it replaced, yet it still maintains an aura of newness. It in no way resembles Memorial Chapel, which looked like everyone thinks a church is supposed to look, dark facade, covered with ivy. Built in 1902, the Romanesque Memorial Chapel meant to generations of students required attendance, segregated seating for boys and girls, faculty ensconced on stage, the Rock outside a convenient gathering place, the public University Street populated with smokers not allowed to indulge on campus. But President Lowry and the Board of Trustees knew by the early 1960s that it had outlived its best days and needed to be replaced or at least renovated.

By the fall of 1964, the Board of Trustees Buildings and Grounds Committee had agreed that a new chapel, bigger than the nine-hundred-seat Memorial, should be constructed. At a meeting of the board in early December 1964, an impassioned Lowry described his own vision for a new chapel. After exalting the faith for which the College stood, the president said: "A chapel expressing such a faith will have about it the signs of openness and aspiration as well as the marks of memory. It will have ancient and eternal Christian symbols as well as the suggestion of questions unresolved. . . . It will project a great deal of what a decent thoughtful college student wants to find in a relevant faith. . . . Above all, it will suggest that all life is sacred." Turning to the practical, he continued: "One of the problems for the architect is securing a building that will accommodate daily chapel and other uses to which the present building has long been put. . . . There are commonsense bounds of decor to be observed, of course. Some things go better in a gymnasium or at a college union."

Lowry seemed, though, to hedge his bet. He suggested that some early planners "felt that the new building has been too much tied to the past rather than to an imaginative future, the architect's freedom being thus curtailed. . . . I believe our alumni, for all their gracious memories of the past, are even more interested in the future and the young people yet to come here. In that future we all have to live. It has far horizons, of which this building—if inspired—can speak, with dignity, imagination, and Christian excitement."

Over the next couple of years, a flurry of correspondence ensued, primarily about how to raise the funds. The board also established a Chapel Working Committee, consisting of Lowry; Dean Garber Drushal; Buck Smith, the vice president for development; Rod Williams, secretary of the College; Art Palmer, the business manager; two professors of art, Arn Lewis and George Olson; a professor of music, the organist Jack Carruth; the minister of Westminster Presbyterian Church, Bev Asbury; five trustees, Cary Wagner, Lucy Notestein, Carol Dix, Wilson Compton, and Reverend Alex Meakin; plus the chapel's longtime custodian Andrew "Red" Weaver; and, at Lowry's request, a prominent Wooster physician, Robert Wright. This advisory committee soon discovered that, given the parameters it was establishing—including a budget probably inadequate for the building's required services—a number of architects were declining invitations to participate. Although one Cleveland architectural firm finally did agree, the relationship soon became rocky. In November 1966, the advisory committee, which had been negotiating with the Cleveland firm, decided to terminate the relationship; in December, the Buildings and Grounds Committee reversed that decision; in January 1967, the advisory committee once more refused to work with the firm; soon it was gone, apparently a mutual decision by which it either dropped out or was fired by the College. By spring, a new firm had been engaged; it laid out a schedule that might produce a completed chapel within two or three years. In the meantime, since the student body had grown too large for Memorial Chapel, and students were still required to attend chapel regularly, the overflow was shunted next door, to Scott Auditorium of Taylor Hall; listening there by closed circuit did not increase students' attention to the programs or decrease the complications of taking attendance.

But at least the principal funding had materialized. Through membership on the board of McCormick Theological Seminary in Chicago, Lowry was an acquaintance of Foster McGaw, whose immense fortune came from a hospital-supply business. Although McGaw had never been to Wooster, his father was a nineteenth-century alumnus of the College, and in the spring of 1966, Lowry asked him for a $1 million gift in memory of his father. Not until the middle of the week before reunions in June 1966, the Centennial Weekend, did the College receive an answer. McGaw called Buck Smith from his summer home in Michigan to say, "You've got your million dollars." Then he interrupted the telephone conversation, "Oh, Mary [Mrs. McGaw] is saying something." Back on the line, he advised, "Don't forget the [chapel's] bride's room." At the reunion, Lowry could announce the McGaw gift and the successful completion of the Centennial Campaign. And McGaw Chapel (unlike Memorial) has a "bride's room."

Even with much of the money at hand, the indecision with architects was not the only roadblock. As late as 1968, the planning committee and Board of Trustees were considering a site west of Beall Avenue, somewhere between Andrews Library and Bissman Hall. But the strong religious sentiment still existing within the board, and the influential Department of Religion, made certain that the chapel would stand in a central place on campus. Before that, however, Howard Lowry, who loved Memorial Chapel—he was not alone in the College community—had decided that it might be saved, expanded for the larger student body or at least rebuilt for religious services. (If the church were to have stood, an alternative would have been a large convocation center elsewhere on campus.) At the June 1967 meeting of the Board of Trustees, in the Tartan Room of the Wooster Inn—the last board meeting of Lowry's life—an extraordinary scene occurred. Lowry presented the case for restoring Memorial Chapel. Cary Wagner, the then-new chairman of the board, presented the case for tearing it down and building a new chapel. It was not an argument, rather a shocking public disagreement between two smart and determined men.

No one present had witnessed a clash like this before. Within a month, Lowry was dead and the issue soon resolved.[1]

In any case, Lowry, no engineer, was wrong about saving Memorial Chapel. The building was falling apart. Inside, the balcony sagged, the floor rolled unevenly, and the radiators interrupted speakers and singers with clangs. Outside, the principal culprits were the romantic vines covering the structure from ground to roof. If they thought about it at all, most people thought Memorial Chapel was built of solid limestone. It was not. The inside walls were red clay tile, plastered over with a four-inch limestone veneer, which meant that the building had essentially no insulation. The vines, which had been crawling up and down the sides of the building for a half-century or so, were locking moisture against the outside walls. As the moisture froze and thawed in Ohio winters, it was ripping the walls from outside; the building was disintegrating.

Memorial Chapel, "conceived at the beginning of the twentieth century, spoke to the times it was created . . . a kind of Victorian cocoon," wrote Clare Adel Schreiber in a 1969 alumni magazine tribute both to the old and the new. McGaw Chapel, so unlike Memorial in appearance, "makes sense when one considers the fractured turmoil of man's present world placed against the conscious and unconscious longing to find in the Christian faith a workable answer to his dilemma. . . . [Yet it] will continue to be a place of secular community as well as of worship, continuing that tradition of its predecessor." In short, McGaw was to be a product of its time, both the specific Wooster context and the political and social life of the United States. At the institution itself, Lowry was gone, a new president was finding his way, and the financial picture was unnerving—an endowment around $10 million and debt nearly that large, so given the prospective demands on the chapel, the budget considered for its construction was about half the size of what it should have been. (See chapter 13 for more details about the finances.)

1. According to the Blackwood biography subsequent to this board meeting one of Lowry's final acts before leaving for San Francisco was to dictate a three-page memo, "Notes on the Site of a New Chapel," in which he "explained his reasons for thinking that the old chapel should be removed and the new one built at the same place on the quadrangle." James R. Blackwood, *Howard Lowry: A Life in Education* (Wooster, Ohio: The College of Wooster, 1975), 316.

At least as unsettling was the national picture, the struggle for the civil rights of black Americans, increasing protests against the war in Vietnam, a growing drug culture, and a sexual revolution unmatched since the 1920s. All of these movements had breached college campuses nationally, and although Wooster's was by no means at the forefront, its students—and its faculty—could hardly remain untouched. "You have to go back to the times when it was planned in order to understand McGaw," said Lewis, the art historian. "Revolution was affecting society. The building committee paid attention to students concerned about the decade's social and political change. We sensed that the campus community wanted a chapel which was not a traditional sanctuary. . . . One architect we considered talked to us about velvet ropes and chandeliers—not at all what the students had in mind." Whether students knew exactly what they wanted, they seemed sure that they wanted something different—a building that represented Christianity in a changing world.

After the chapel planning committee renewed its consideration of architects and interviewed four firms, it settled on a modernist with deep ties to New York City and the Ivy League, a professional of national reputation. Enter Victor Christ-Janer. He graduated with honors from Yale, taught at Yale and Columbia, served as chief graphic designer for Nelson Rockefeller at the U.S. Office of Inter-American Affairs, and helped remake his adopted hometown of New Canaan, Connecticut, from a village of traditional Colonial-style homes into what was called "an incubator for distinctive Modernist dwellings" (including his own home). In an admiring obituary upon his death at the age of ninety-two in 2008, the *New York Times* said: "Mr. Christ-Janer's style was sleek and contemporary, and he worked mostly in glass and concrete. He designed buildings on a human scale, without aspiring to monumentality."

If McGaw Chapel was the most provocative structure at the College, Christ-Janer was surely the most provocative architect. Among those most closely involved in his relations with Wooster, he has been dismissed as "a fraud" by one highly placed administrator and accused of "selling a bill of goods" by another. He is said to have seduced College authorities, especially a professor or two in the Department of Religion, with his presentation connecting the chapel to early Christianity. "He was masterful," said Ted Bogner, who witnessed the presentation and whose company constructed the building. "The entire idea of McGaw Chapel as he sold it was an extension of the Roman catacombs. . . . McGaw was to be completely buried. . . . The only things sticking up, above the ground, were the turrets. . . . You walked into one of those turrets, you went down, and descended like you were going into the catacombs. The reason the interior of that building is so stark is because the people are the excitement in the building, not the walls and not the furnishings. He just spellbound everybody." Then the pièce de résistance. "At the very last part of his presentation, someone asked him, 'Mr. Christ-Janer, what are we going to make this out of?' He waved his arms a little bit in the air, and he said, 'Oh, I don't care. You can make it out of feathers if you want to.' People were just awestruck."

Then there is a different take on the story, from Professor Lewis, an art historian not easily seduced.

> Christ-Janer listened to the campus community and then shared ways in which representation could reflect contemporary campus thought and priorities. . . . The interior, analogous to a womb, would be a communal space of reassurance and strength. From this space would grow the towers, expressive of transcendence, aspirations, and energy. . . . [He agreed] that McGaw, though different, should be "compatible" with surrounding buildings. Aggregate stone would recall the brick of its neighbors, the white was related to the cream, and the towers were variations on the towers of Kauke. He produced a lively, unified design, certainly one of the more compelling buildings on campus.

But tastes are always changing. Planners then "failed to understand that hard oak benches and cinder-block walls, victories for one generation, would become incomprehensible to another," Lewis observed, noting that Christ-Janer's "social philosophy was more contemporary than his sense of acoustics."

But what of the "catacombs" and the "womb"? Why does the building stand out as it does when its architectural raison d'être was that it be buried deep into the ground once occupied by Memorial Chapel? That part of the story began after workmen had unleashed their backhoes on the quadrangle turf. One day a backhoe operator yelled to Harry Ditch, Bogner's onsite construction superintendent, that he had struck something hard about eighteen feet below grade. Ditch and his team soon determined that they had hit solid, dense sandstone, which was clearly not going to give way to a backhoe. Ditch (a Wooster graduate and onetime football captain) called his boss, Pete Bogner. Bogner's on-scene confirmation set off a series of conferences among the highest officials of the College. "We knew there was rock there, but we didn't know it would be as hard as it was," said Ted Bogner, Pete's nephew who succeeded him as president of the company.

In the twenty-first century, the rock could be cracked, relatively easily, through a process called hydraulic fracturing (commonly known as "fracking"), but neither the knowledge nor the equipment was available at the time. Dynamite would work. But this was 1969, when political unrest was sweeping across college campuses (students with guns took over the student union at Cornell University that year) and rumors circulated that bands of radicals were journeying from one college to another, hoping to incite trouble. Garber Drushal, one year into his official presidency, did not want explosives on his campus. So the digging would stop where the sandstone lay.[2] The chapel would drop underground to the sandstone. The rest of the structure—about sixteen feet, as it happened—would stand above ground. To the public, the College announced that dynamite would not be used because it might damage Kauke or Taylor halls—unlikely but possible.

So the College was caught between a rock and a hard place. Without the chapel's major concept, its construction was now being done on the fly, or, as Ted Bogner observed, "The whole thing goes to hell in a handcart." Although Christ-Janer had not contemplated the adjustments, he never bothered to come to Wooster during the actual building process; he had an architectural representative present but did not inspect conditions himself. For his part, Pete Bogner, said, "Of all the projects I've ever worked on, that was the craziest design of anything we ever built." Just the projects at Wooster? "Anywhere. Crazier than anything anywhere."

One consequential change (aside from the lost catacombs) came with the turrets. Conceived as entrances to the underground sanctuary, they now became nothing more than storage sheds for the building's mechanicals. As entrances, the turrets had been designed with sloping surfaces,

2. Scovel, Taylor, Timken Library, and Kauke have steps to their first-floor entrances. It is surmised that when they were constructed early in the twentieth century, and basements were hand-dug, builders simply stopped when they hit the same shale, thus requiring the first floor to be raised.

but it turned out that the flashing (sheet metal installed to prevent water from penetrating a structure where angled corners met) was inadequate for the new purpose, and water could leak inside the building. Pete Bogner also recalled that it was once considered that the roof, which would have been at ground level, could be flooded and frozen in winter for ice skating. This is one of several chapel memories that cannot be confirmed, but it may help explain why the concrete roof deck was poured above the roof membrane. As a result of the roof deck, water coming through the deck could travel to another part of the membrane and then leak into the building, so that one could seldom be certain where the deck leaks were. (It was even suggested that because the roof carried so much weight, it might actually move, since expansion and contraction caused by temperature fluctuation can be a problem in Ohio.) Originally, too, the building walls could be simply poured concrete with no architectural feature, since they would be underground. Now, much of the walls would be above ground, and the more decorative material, hurriedly ordered, was porous, so with inadequate flashing in Ohio's rain and snow, moisture dripped down, penetrated the block, ran through the steel innards, and dropped inside the building. Leaks were occasionally so bad that custodians maneuvered about two dozen Rubbermaid Brute trash cans inside the building to catch dripping water when the building was not being used.

Over several years, at one Board of Trustees meeting after another, the chairman of the Buildings and Grounds Committee would stand and solemnly report that new measures were being undertaken to stop the roof from leaking. By the fall of 1995, a consulting firm reported to the committee that fixing the roof would require significant effort. First, major work would be needed to clean and recaulk expansion joints and stress cracks on the roof deck, the roof turrets, and the side walls, and to redesign and replace the improper flashing. Then waterproof coatings could be applied to the roof and exterior walls. To do all this, the board agreed to borrow $350,000 from the trustee-designated endowment, to be repaid over a ten-year warranty period. The work stopped the leaks—although some complained that the coating made the chapel look like a sugar cube.

Among the elements of the Chapel, which honors many faiths inside and serves as an events site much of the time, is the presence of a cross that dominates the primary entrance, greeting visitors as they descend stairs to the auditorium. It stands a startling thirty-five feet high and fourteen feet across, with both vertical and horizontal arms three feet thick. The decision to install the cross occurred sometime after the building's completion. It is not clear, even from board minutes, how the decision was reached or who pushed for the installation; it is widely thought, however, that some influential board members and perhaps some administrators believed that whatever other uses the chapel was put to, it should be understood as a Christian church, and the cross would represent that. Some explanation about the cross and the circumstances surrounding it can be found in a 2002 letter to President Stan Hales from Lewis:

In the late 1960s students and faculty seemed to accept the new chapel as a statement of Wooster's view of Christianity in a changing world. The campus community approved of housing the sacred and the secular under one roof. Though the majority of the campus understood its unchurchlike appearance, the planning committee requested that a small bronze cross be embedded in the outside wall near the main entrance. However, some trustees were apparently unsatisfied by this modest designation. Shortly after the building was completed, a large cross was erected in front of it. The planning committee was not notified of this decision. Shortly after the cross was completed, students painted it black.... A few days later, the cross was sandblasted; students did not act again.

The dedication ceremony for the Chapel was scheduled for October 23, 1971, a festive Homecoming weekend. The McGaws were introduced to the College in a charmingly informal manner; they were first treated to breakfast and tours with some of its most accomplished students, one day with Jay Yutzey, who went on to an academic career at The Ohio State University, and Beverly Kimble, daughter of a Presbyterian minister, Homecoming queen, and already recipient of a Rotary Foundation Fellowship; a second day with Darcey Johnston, double major in history and religion, Phi Beta Kappa, and cheerleader, and Jim DeRose, football star and a leader in the Wooster Christian Fellowship.[3]

3. The McGaws said they were so impressed with Wooster students, these and others, that they later contributed $1.6 million more to help complete Lowry Center.

Nothing about the Chapel is easy, of course. On this most celebratory occasion, events were transpiring a few hundred yards away at Severance Stadium, events that signified in their own way how the Chapel seemed to fit the tenor of the times. These unfolded in two parts. One directly concerned the football team (which beat Kenyon that afternoon, 13–12). The black players issued a Black Ultimatum and planned to boycott the Homecoming game to protest perceived racism within the coaching staff. During a flurry of tense meetings that week, Jim DeRose, a white student and acknowledged campus leader, announced that he would refuse to play in support of the boycott. Then he decided that loyalty to the team required that he play, but he asked for and received permission to read a statement to the crowd from the field before the game. His expression of personal anguish induced anger on both sides.

The larger event was an organized protest by black students and white supporters to charge the College with racism. Before the game, the group lined the gridiron, goal line to goal line, carrying signs complaining about racism. Then protesters repaired to bleachers on the opposite side of the field from the grandstand, where they spent the game with their backs turned to the action. (See chapter 7 for further details on diversity and racial issues at the College.) When this plan became known a few days earlier, one white senior, Betsy Bruhn, declared her support by resigning from the Homecoming court. Kimble, the Homecoming queen, and others met with President Drushal to assess their responsibility. They came up with a message that Kimble read to the assembled alumni and parents at halftime: "We would like to express our sincere appreciation and gratitude for the honor of being here today. In recognition of the present polarization on our campus, we on the Homecoming Court stand before you as a group symbolizing unity with diversity, with the hope that by doing so we will be expressing our feeling that much more can be accomplished in unity with diversity, rather than in polarization. Polarization without cooperation is a dead end. Unity with diversity holds promise."

The McGaws never saw these protests and, as far as anyone recalls, never knew about them. The Chapel was packed to overflowing for the dedication ceremony that Saturday morning, addressed by Edward Lindaman, a Presbyterian minister and president of Whitworth College in Spokane, Washington. And for more than four decades it has not just maintained its striking visual image at the center of campus but has also served its intended purpose as a site for convocations, lectures, concerts—even religious services. It no longer, however, looks like a sugar cube. Shortly after the turn of the twenty-first century, the building was repainted a light almond, and tall shrubs were planted to shield it from the weather, which reduced complaints about the chapel's appearance to the lowest level ever. To this day, some wish the McGaw Chapel would just go away. Still, it can be said that a feeling of comfort about it, if something less than universal admiration, has slipped featherlike into the Wooster psyche.

PART 3

Renewal, Growth, Ambition

CHAPTER 13

The Worst of Times . . . and Revival

It is probable that the years 1967–70 constituted the worst times for The College of Wooster since Old Main burned down in December 1901, leading Louis Holden to cry out memorably to Andrew Carnegie, "Yesterday I was president of a college. Today I am president of a hole in the ground." Unlike in 1901, however, when Wooster's very existence appeared threatened, the tribulations of these later years, falling, ironically, just after the College's centennial celebration, certainly would not doom it—and the troubles were so carefully masked by the Board of Trustees that hardly anyone else, not faculty, not staff, not students, not alumni, understood how parlous the times were.

The single most stunning event of those years occurred on the Fourth of July 1967. Howard Lowry, sixty-five years old, was stricken with a heart attack while in San Francisco, dead almost instantly. The news shocked the Wooster campus, and for its leaders was a bit unnerving. Leaders learned fairly quickly that Lowry had died at the apartment of his woman friend, Gretchen Harmon, a twenty-seven-year-old graduate of Wooster High School, now a dean at Mills College in Oakland, whom he apparently hoped to marry. But these leaders worried about circumstances they didn't know, which they feared might be scandalous. James Blackwood's biography of Lowry supplies details: "As they sat and talked into the morning of the Fourth of July, Howard moved uneasily, got up and said, 'I'm cold,' started for the door but struck the wall, hit it with his hand once, twice, as if attempting to break through. . . . Howard's heart had failed. He died before the ambulance reached the hospital." Buck Smith, vice president for development and a Lowry confidant, and his wife, Joni, who, coincidentally, had been attending a meeting of the American Alumni Council in San Francisco, accompanied the body back to Wooster, where Lowry's memory was honored July 7 in Memorial Chapel. As Harmon sat in the family pew, the Reverend George Buttrick, preacher-scholar, pastor of Harvard's Memorial Church, great friend of Lowry, offered only the faintest allusion to the period before the president's death, which, since it was not known about, continued to be somewhat troubling to his closest friends: "It should be said among us that to the last moment of his life this glow of friendship remained both worthy and true."

The College was suddenly stripped of its charismatic leader at a very dangerous time—charismatic leaders can inspire followers to great triumphs, but they can leave a yawning chasm when they depart. No one doubted that an era had ended, but the Board of Trustees had business to attend to quickly. In an emergency meeting July 12, it took the obvious step of designating Drushal, Lowry's chosen deputy, as acting president. For Drushal, this was an unenviable responsibility. Obviously, he had to steady the College community, faculty, students, and alumni, although he knew he would receive their support. As vice president for academic affairs and chairman of academic committees, he knew a lot about the faculty and the curriculum. But there was a great deal he didn't know. It was not quite the same as Harry Truman entering the presidency not having been told by Franklin D. Roosevelt that the United States was building an atomic bomb and was almost ready to drop it on Japan, but still, Lowry was in many ways a lone ranger, sharing little information with even his closest associates and keeping relatively few records to guide the board or administration. The Board of Trustees included a number of businessmen and ministers not well informed about higher education, many of them Lowry pals not actively involved with the College, and he, not the chairman, unquestionably ran the meetings. Curt Taylor, Lowry's longtime secretary and secretary of the board, kept copious notes, but even he could not be fully aware of what the president maintained in his agile and encompassing mind.

As Drushal began, the campus was also not as quiescent as Lowry was accustomed to and would have liked. The few black students were raising their voices. The students—and faculty—who detested the Vietnam War were saying so loudly (the Tet Offensive, which broke national confidence over whether the war could be "won," began about the same time as the second semester in early 1968). In addition, Drushal held another public responsibility: president of the Wooster City Council, which benefited the College in town-gown relations but detracted from the increased time he had to spend in his new position. His shock was perhaps greater when he first learned details about the College's financial straits. Although Smith was helping to attract major donors, fund-raising was almost pure Lowry: he was known to say with an encouraging smile that he had "a check in my pocket," but no one ever saw such checks; in retrospect, it could be surmised that if they had existed, the donors might have stepped forward to confirm them. (It was even thought that Lowry sometimes mislaid or forgot to cash checks written to the College.) When Drushal showed up for work July 5, he found that loans for the three ill-starred mid-1960s dormitories were still being paid. And three major buildings—the student union, which had just been named Lowry Center; Mateer Hall, the biology building; and the unnamed physical education center—were under construction, less than half finished. The estimated cost to complete them was $4 million, of which about $700,000 was in hand. Although some suggested that construction be halted, campus leaders dismissed the idea as a public act of desperation. So Drushal; Hans Jenny, his vice president for finance and business; and the chairman of the board's Finance Committee, Bob Critchfield, drove the hour on winding Route 5 to Akron to negotiate a bank loan, of necessity unsecured.

Critchfield's role here cannot be underestimated. Senior partner of Wooster's largest law firm, influential civic leader, prominent sportsman (his Gay Acres Farm just east of the city housed Demon Hanover, the nation's most famous trotter), and director of national corporations, he was respected widely, not least in the canyons of Wall Street. The bankers at First National of Akron didn't know the acting president or the college economist, but they knew the Wooster lawyer, who assured them that the College was in good hands. One of Critchfield's friends was Gustave Levy, the legendary chief of Goldman Sachs, and the two frequently lunched on Critchfield's trips to New York. It cannot be established with certainty, but two people in a position to know believed that Levy called executives at First National, verifying Critchfield's bona fides and thus easing the path to the loan. The $4 million loan was granted so the buildings could be completed. But the College's longer-term financial status remained troubled.

In the immediate term, there was the issue of finding a new president. At what turned out to be his final meeting with the board, in June 1967,

Lowry had announced his intention to retire after the following year. At an emergency meeting after his death, the board quickly created a search committee (called the Nominating Committee) to seek Lowry's successor. It consisted of eight trustees and eight faculty members, plus an advisory committee of students. The trustee committee was extremely senior, chaired by Bill Pocock, vice chairman of the board, with the board chairman, Cary Wagner, as the official secretary. The other trustees were George E. Armington, Juliet Stroh Blanchard, John W. Dodds, Dan Funk (the College lawyer), Dean Hopkins, and John H. Weeks. The eight faculty representatives were Paul Christianson, English; Fred Cropp (the acting dean), geology; Clayton Ellsworth, history; Bill Kieffer, chemistry; Arn Lewis, art history; Win Logan, speech; Helen Kaslo Osgood, history; Gordon Tait, religion. The students were Margaret Wanty, chairman; David Hicks, cochairman; Susanne McQueen, Patty Richards, Phil Brown, Marvin Shie, and David Wehrie.

Over several months, the search committees examined roughly a hundred presidential possibilities, none of them except for Drushal connected to the College. Throughout the search, a determined group of professors sought another scholar in the Lowry mode. (Ironically, some of the students opposed Drushal because he seemed to represent a continuation of the straitlaced Lowry era.) What the faculty did not know—what almost no one except a few leading trustees did—was the difficult state of College finances. These trustees worried that action could not long be delayed, and they were uncomfortable about the learning curve of an outsider. During the trying months after Lowry's death, Drushal had shown himself a capable steward of the campus, an adept delegator, and an articulate leader—and the trustees seemed to want him officially in place as soon as possible.

The denouement came at a meeting in the Sheraton Hotel at the Cleveland Hopkins Airport, both trustee and faculty committees, led by Bill Pocock. Four of the faculty members—Christianson, Kieffer, Lewis, and Tait—made it clear that while they liked Drushal and respected his performance, they wanted to continue the search, because, as Tait said, "the candidates that had been brought in were not exciting, we wanted to continue looking for what we thought might be the appropriate person for the job." In short, another Lowry intellectually but with different style and direction. The professors appeared to have found their choice in a Cornell University vice president, Steven Muller, but the trustees seemed uninterested. (A year later, Muller won plaudits when he took de facto charge at Cornell during protests in which black students took over the student center and brought guns on campus; he went on to a distinguished career as president of Johns Hopkins University.)

Decades later, Lewis and Christianson, two of the holdouts, remembered identically what ensued—still with some amusement and a touch of awe. "I'll never forget this," said Lewis. "Bill Pocock stood up, and he took off his jacket, and he rolled up his sleeves, and he said, 'I'm going to do a Pocock on you.' And he began to nudge us and persuade us and mildly threaten us in one way or another, and eventually he made it clear that there was only one choice, and that was Garber." As Christenson recalled, Pocock addressed and characterized each of the four in turn: "It was revealing, and humiliating, and distressing—and exhilarating at some level. He recognized where we were coming from and why we were saying this." Pocock spoke of too much idealism, and of not seeing the full picture. Then he played his trump, "without spilling all the beans," Christianson said: "the crisis of the College's finances." The four holdouts clearly had not known. And they shortly agreed to choose Drushal. And shortly after that, Tait, as representative of the quartet, visited Drushal in his office, explained their position, and pledged the faculty's support. On April 9, 1968, the board announced that it had unanimously selected Drushal to be the College's seventh president.

Garber Drushal differed from Howard Lowry in a plethora of ways. He was born to a Brethren minister and his wife in Lost Creek, Kentucky, apparently an appropriate name for what was described in a Drushal family history as "a region of moonshine and violence." He graduated from both the Moody Bible Institute in Chicago and the Brethren-affiliated Ashland College (where he was elected class president and "Ideal Man"). While ridding himself of an Appalachian accent, he developed an interest in language training, which propelled him toward a PhD in speech at Ohio State. At the age of thirty, he became the youngest person elected moderator of the national Brethren Church, and he later became president of its missionary board. In his first academic posting, at Capital University in Columbus—interrupted by service in naval intelligence during World War II—he confirmed the connection of a lifetime with Bill Craig, Wooster alumnus and graduate-school friend. Craig returned to Wooster in 1944 and in 1946, upon the retirement of his mentor, Delbert C. Lean, and succeeded Lean as the College's theater instructor and entrepreneur. To fill an opening for a speech and debate professor, Craig recruited Drushal, who liked the idea of working with Craig and liked the idea of Independent Study. Garber and his wife, Dorothy—a most enthusiastic and popular addition to the campus—and their two children (later four) also became head residents at Kenarden Lodge.

Combining his interests in speech and politics, Drushal completed his doctorate at Ohio State in 1950 with a dissertation, "The Speeches of Louis Dembitz Brandeis, 1908–16." By 1952 Lowry tapped him to join Bob Bonthius of the religion department and sociologist James Davis in preparing a report funded by the Carnegie Foundation for the Advancement of Teaching, which became a book, *The Independent Study Program in the United States.* In 1959, with politics increasingly important to him (he once considered a run for the state legislature), Drushal was elected president of Wooster's City Council. Four years later he changed his faculty appointment from speech to political science. Shortly afterward, when chemist Clark Bricker did not work out as dean and left to teach at the University of Kansas, Lowry offered the place to Drushal. A bit taken aback, Drushal hesitated, but upon the urging of his friend Craig, he took the job. In 1966, Lowry's reorganization made Drushal vice president for academic affairs; a year later, with the president's death, he was the Board's logical choice for acting president. After the search and Drushal's official designation, some potential difficulties were dispatched quickly. A gracious man, Drushal had little trouble winning over even skeptical faculty, who, especially as word got around about the College's problems, were predisposed to be helpful. He maintained the Galpin Hall structure that had been put into place under Lowry. Having learned to respect his skill and energy, Drushal promoted the geologist Fred Cropp, his successor as dean, to the academic vice presidency. Hans Jenny remained vice president for finance and business and Buck Smith vice president for development.

The toughest immediate task was still dealing with finances. Although the major building support had been negotiated, the College was reduced to using thirty-day rollover loans to pay its bills during the "dry" periods of August and December–January as it waited for tuition payments. Further, although the endowment was then a minuscule $6 million or so, all the available revenue—even sizable bequests such as one from the Birt Babcock estate—that should logically have gone into endowment went straight to the operating budget. As Smith remembered, "If [funds] were not nailed down by restriction to endowment, it was free money. Hans looked for wherever there was money, not violating any legal requirements, but is there any loose change around." Clearly some major bills needed paying, yet it was awkward—the College had just come off its ten-year Centennial Campaign, which only in its last moments edged over the $20 million goal.

Still, a new Chapel, a physical education facility, and a student union, needing millions more to complete, were growing on borrowed money. Trustees realized it was time to step up. At a special meeting in December, they approved a $700,000 line of credit with the Wayne County National Bank to help toward construction of Mateer Hall and a $2.5 million line of credit from an Akron bank to help toward the estimated $3.5 million cost of Lowry Center. The 1967–68 budget projected a $310,000 loss, made up by moving funds from the reserve fund and throwing in a Ford Foundation payment. For the longer range, what Buck Smith and his development team came up with was the Essential Extras Campaign, promoted as a way to finish what the Centennial Campaign had begun. How that campaign moved to its rapid conclusion, and how the notes were repaid demonstrated Smith's unending search for—and skill in persuading—friends capable of a major gift. The initial strike came from the Timken Foundation, which offered nearly $1 million to complete the first gymnasium Wooster had built since 1913 (named the Timken Gymnasium). The campaign raised more than $7 million, topping its $5.5 million goal, providing enough funds to complete construction of the important new buildings and pay off long- and short-term debt.

The board made significant decisions in the ensuing period. By the end of the 1968–69 academic year, it had revised its committee system and arranged clearer lines of communication between the committees and appropriate administrators. For the first time, it also allowed faculty and student observers at board meetings. In October 1969, the board took upon itself responsibility for investment activities by establishing its first investment committee, whose goal was to increase endowment yield by 10 percent; by the following June it could report that yield had increased 19 percent. In the fall of 1971, the board hired Walter Wiley as an in-house investment manager and adopted a formula for endowment payout. It dealt with the nerve-wracking annual fluctuations in repair and rehabilitation of campus facilities through a plant reserve and set a regular charge to the operating budget to stabilize maintenance funding. Trustees now seemed confident about the College's long-range financial structure, but they realized only years later that they had made one critical error. In the early 1970s, with debts cleared up, endowment performing well, and increased enrollment helping balance the budget, Wooster gambled that it could improve its admissions standing by holding the line on tuition while its competitors were raising theirs. Unfortunately, in the mid- and late '70s inflation rocketed, as did interest rates, while endowment income and gifts dropped. The combination was understood to have cost the College several million dollars and ravaged the budget, sending finances into a renewed downward spiral that took another decade to control.

Important to all of this was Hans Jenny. From the time in the early 1960s that Lowry had recruited the young economist to help prepare a Ford Foundation request, the president had relied increasingly on him, which led to his 1966 appointment as Wooster's first vice president for finance and business. Swiss-born and educated, Jenny had been at the College since 1949 and was sui generis on the faculty. He regularly clashed with his economics colleagues—he was known, among other things, to hold informal tutorials for students he deemed promising but who he believed were not pushed hard enough by others in the department. During his time as vice president, from 1966 to his retirement in 1982, Jenny was a source of both respect and frustration to the administration and the board. Said his friend and vice presidential colleague Buck Smith, "Hans was a kind of roll-of-the-dice kind of guy." Fascinated by the stock market, he participated eagerly as the board's Investment Committee began to extend the endowment into equities. And it was his idea that the fines students paid for missing chapel be turned into an investment pot that students themselves managed both for experience and profit—a successful resource that became known officially as the Jenny Fund. All the while, Jenny's imaginative efforts to manage college finances were attracting national attention. He wrote articles and books on the subject and was regularly invited to consult with other institutions and to speak to organizations of financial officers.

"In [Hans's] mind, the College was forever going bankrupt," Henry Copeland remembered years later. Jenny was wrong about that, but he was right that the financial holes existed, and he didn't mind borrowing money as needed. "Hans believed in deficit financing," Smith said. "Going into debt [was] an investment in the future." This view required an attitudinal change within the Board of Trustees from its historic conservative approach to "make the economy work for us." It clearly caused tension, opposition from members such as Carl Weiss, an accountant from Cleveland, and Dan Funk, the College lawyer; but Bob Critchfield, as chairman of the Finance Committee, usually supported Jenny's view, and the College continued to roll over its debt.

Part of the Jenny mystique, too, was his personal life, shared with a male partner, a high school teacher. Doug Drushal, Garber Drushal's son who became a prominent Wooster lawyer, remembered that when he was a young teenager, his family would visit the two of them in their renovated old red-brick house in Rowsburg, about ten miles from Wooster. "Here you have the vice president of the College living with his gay partner, more or less openly, although I'm sure it was somewhat closeted in that era," said Drushal. "As a child, as far as I knew, it was just two guys living together. It never was an issue of discussion at all. But it had to be obvious to prominent people in the College community and in the greater community. I think that's an interesting feature of the College's history, that there was that toler-ance there." In 1982, Jenny retired as vice president, and he and his partner built a desert house in Arizona, where they lived until his death in 1998.

Growing the College was a critical part of the financial strategy de-vised by Jenny, Drushal, and Cropp. This marked a dramatic change from Lowry's thousand-student ideal, where everyone was expected to and did greet each other as they strolled across campus. In the 1960s, Wooster had already grown to about twelve hundred, which Lowry considered a maxi-mum, and, Smith remembered, "He would shake his head and say, 'I didn't come here to preside over the death of a small college.'" He worried that it "would lose the personal touch, everybody knowing one another." But the new administration's theory was that more students meant more revenue, as long as costs were controlled, and debts, both operations and capital, could be paid off. By 1969 enrollment approached fourteen hundred, and as Drushal's presidency neared its close in the mid-1970s, with audits by Wooster residents included, the number almost touched two thousand. Along with the trustees' financial efforts, this tactic essentially worked—the College began to run modest surpluses—until the administration and Board of Trustees made their hold-the-line tuition decision in the mid-1970s.

Through all these years, controlling costs meant, among other things, that the size of the faculty would not grow commensurate with enroll-ment. Thus, into the 1970s, a number of professors were teaching courses of 60 to 100 students or more, even up to 160 in rare instances. One could certainly lecture to 100 students—however limiting this was to class discussion—but grading papers and essays became a serious burden, even an "all-nighter" on occasion; some turned to multiple-choice tests to ease the load. Some of the students admitted to increase numbers inevitably failed to meet usual Wooster standards. Some administrators contended that this represented, "giving these students a chance"; these students required, though, a new program to help them catch up. Nonetheless, the number of dropouts increased, and the circumstances also damaged the morale of faculty, which found itself dealing with less attentive and capable students. Melcher Fobes, in mathematics, and Fran Guille, in French, were openly disturbed, and Copeland, a dean then, remembered Ray McCall of the English department lamenting, "How can we pretend to offer BAs to students who have never read one of Shakespeare's plays?"

Students were also frustrated. They were unhappy in part because of their deteriorating living conditions. Eating was often crowded and uncomfortable. Double rooms in dorms became triples, and study halls and study lounges became bedrooms. Because the College lacked dormitory space, it began buying small houses, up to two dozen along Beall Avenue and on side streets. But student unrest during these years could be attributed to many causes, by no means all of them resulting from local conditions. Antiwar protests on campuses across the nation, which had revved up in the mid-1960s, continued into the mid-1970s, until the United States withdrew its troops from Vietnam in 1973 and ended its longtime commitment in 1975. Nor was it just the war. White students signed on to support the cause of civil rights for black Americans. "Unrest" was not an inappropriate word as Wooster students, and administrators—like their compatriots on almost every campus—wrestled with relatively new challenges: serious use of illicit drugs and long-standing challenges largely ignored: overuse of alcohol and careless sex.

Suddenly, warm-hearted tradition seemed less important to students: freshmen wearing beanies didn't seem cute anymore; nor did the idea of anointing a Color Day queen—the first one had been crowned in 1911—while her classmates danced around a maypole. So dismissive of nostalgia had the era become that the *Index,* the yearbook that many alumni counted on for memories of their college days, nearly died. In a plaintive yet firm note to their fellow students at the front of the 1971 *Index,* the coeditors, Lora Dennis and Cate Howard, wrote: "We do not want this introduction to be a defense, justification, or plea for our book. . . . Nor do we wish to grumble about the 'long hard hours' of work that the responsibility entails. . . . Suddenly our senior year the *Index* arrived at a 'do or die' situation. . . . . You are about to lose a necessary and meaningful tradition. To continue tradition for its own sake is senseless, but to reject a positive tradition solely because it is traditional is equally as stupid." The *Index* did survive, and although it seldom reached the near-professional style of the 1940s and early '50s, it improved noticeably over the years, so that it continued to bank memories for alumni who nurtured them.

Changing student attitudes did not go unnoticed at Galpin Hall and a number of rules were modified. Rules about smoking were replaced by rules about drugs in the 1968–69 *Scots Key;* in that handbook there is no mention of a tobacco policy. (By 1992 smoking was permitted only in designated areas; by 2004, smoking was banned in all buildings except the Underground or at sports events and outside within twenty-five feet of any door; by 2006, all buildings were tobacco free, including smokeless tobacco.) At a college where men and women did not even eat together until 1956, coed housing became an issue. In 1972, when Babcock Hall was designated an international program house in which both women and men deserved to participate, it ipso facto became a coed dormitory; that met with disapproval from some trustees, but coed housing was on the way. (See chapter 9 for details on coed housing.)

Student administration changed. Before Doris Coster arrived as dean of women in 1968, four short-term deans followed the 1960 retirement of the strong-willed Marjorie Golder, who had protected the honor of Wooster's girls, as she saw it, during a stern fourteen-year regime. Coster joined the dean of men, Racky Young, football star of the 1920s, Presbyterian minister, respected member of the religion faculty, and trusted friend of Howard Lowry, who had held the position since Lowry arrived in 1944 (except for a two-year leave). Upon Young's retirement in 1970, the deanships were merged under Coster—women and men were now considered one unit. When she left in 1975 to become dean at her alma mater, Barnard College, she was succeeded as dean of students by Ken Plusquellec, a Wooster graduate also trained as a minister, who served twenty-six years as a valued advisor to three presidents, with a firm yet understanding view of Wooster students. He was succeeded by Kurt

Holmes, who dealt imaginatively with the problems of a different era and a new generation of college students, many of whom had come to believe that comfort and entertainment were their birthright.

By the late 1960s, students were bristling at many rules, including chapel attendance. Although segregated gender seating had finally ended in the 1950s, students were still required to attend at least three of four weekly sessions, with fines for excessive absences. One of the stated reasons for chapel attendance was to hear announcements of meetings and events—Dean Bill Taeusch seemed puzzled by titters in the audience when he once read a note that Miss G. R. Lee would give a modern dance performance at a Canton theater—but new techniques like photocopying had eliminated that need. In 1969 seniors were excused from required chapel, and the next year formal chapel was replaced by an optional convocation series; that, too, eventually dwindled away. About the same time, the rule that students must attend a church of their choice at least eight times a semester disappeared.

Possibly to assuage some trustees' anxiety about collapsing standards, the College created a Student Code of Conduct that acknowledged both its founding principles and certain individual rights, while requiring students to accept personal and community responsibilities. Enforcement of the Code and dominion over other student issues was handed to a new tripartite body, composed of administrators, faculty, and students, called Campus Council. The birth of the Code was not easy. It was, Dean Coster remembered, "a rather remarkable document, written and rewritten dozens of times before the Executive Staff was willing to take it to the trustees.... hammered out in many, many late night sessions." At its institution in 1969, Campus Council was specifically tasked with setting rules affecting student life and extracurricular activities, including chartering student organizations and making decisions on their budgets. It could also make recommendations concerning student affairs to the president and the Board of Trustees. Over the years, the influence of Campus Council waxed and waned—in 1982 Council voted to dissolve itself when a majority of its members decided it had no meaningful influence, but they reconsidered—and the council continued to exercise authority in a number of ways.

Amid so much cultural turmoil, it was perhaps inevitable that Wooster, like many other colleges and universities, was caught up in a fervor for academic change. In what was described as the largest revision since 1956—the year Freshman Seminar was instituted—the College announced plans for a sharply different curriculum, which would begin in the 1969–70 academic year. Academic Vice President Cropp hastened to claim that the new plan was not a sudden attempt by the faculty to get into the "game of change so popular in America today" but rather the culmination of almost four years of "thought, discussion, debate." For starters, the College adjusted its calendar from two semesters to a quarter system. For new students, the path got easier. Once Wooster had required two years of study in a foreign language; now it asked for a single quarter. The first two quarters of the freshman year need not be included in the 2.0 grade point average required for graduation, and only a 1.5 was needed for a student to remain in good standing after the first year. First-year seminar was reduced from a full year to a single quarter, and rather than any single theme for all students, faculty members could simply teach their specialties in each. It was to be graded merely Satisfactory/Unsatisfactory. Students would now carry only three courses per term to "allow [the student] time for student academic growth as he devotes his energy to fewer courses in any one term of study." In acknowledgment of minority issues, the curriculum would offer courses in African history; the economic problems of the ghetto; and African American poetry, drama, and fiction.

An alumni magazine article by Ray McCall of the English department and the historian Jim Hodges—by any measure two of the College's most rigorous scholar-teachers—defended the softening in the first-year seminar. In it Hodges said a very great deal about the academic culture of the moment: "This is the faculty's effort to respond to a changing world and to a different kind of student. . . . One of the reasons I think the faculty will adapt to a less and less structured curriculum is the inability not only of this faculty but of all faculties to make really sound generalizations at this time about contemporary society." The "less structured curriculum" remained more or less intact for much of the next decade.

From the stunning moment of Lowry's death, through the unsettling late 1960s and into the '70s, Wooster traversed a rocky path, but Drushal, popular and steady, smoothed it. Still, even at a small college in Ohio, worldly events have a way of intruding. At the Pentagon in Northern Virginia, in downtown Wooster, in jungles eight thousand miles away, and on a campus knoll fifty miles away, events out of the College's control threatened to tear the campus community apart. They also established Garber Drushal as its undoubted leader.

CHAPTER 14

The World Intrudes

From a parochial perspective, the College's first years under Garber Drushal were traumatic enough, as it struggled to recover from the shock of Lowry's death and to right its financial ship. But this campus, half a square mile in a small town in the Midwest, did not exist in a hermetically sealed dome. As much as at any time in its recent history, with the exception of World War II, Wooster was forced to adjust to stunning events and cultural changes in which it had little say. The American escalation of the Vietnam War had begun in 1965, but North Vietnam's Tet offensive in early 1968, although eventually halted by United States and South Vietnamese forces, encouraged furious domestic protest against the war. In the winter of 1968, the youth-fueled presidential campaign of Minnesota senator Gene McCarthy led to the virtual abdication of President Lyndon Johnson, and before the summer was over, there were bitter demonstrations at the Democratic National Convention in Chicago. Within two spring months the Reverend Martin Luther King Jr. and Senator Robert Kennedy had been murdered. Overseas, the Prague Spring in Czechoslovakia had been obliterated by Soviet tanks, reminding Americans vividly of the Cold War, and students in France and Germany were revolting in ways American students were loath to dare. Music, dance, and film were setting new moral standards for American young people. And many had decided that they couldn't trust anyone over thirty.

If anyone thought the College could remain unaffected by such events, a poignant answer came on November 2, 1965. That afternoon, Norman Morrison, a member of Wooster's class of 1956 who had studied for the Presbyterian ministry before becoming a Quaker, drove from his home in Baltimore to Washington, D.C. His wife, Anne, had gone to pick up their two older children at school, so Norman took their nine-month-old daughter, Emily, whom he was caring for, with him. Near dusk, in a parking lot outside the Pentagon, Morrison laid his baby down, poured kerosene over his body, lit a match, and set himself on fire. Workers leaving for home ran to his side, but in thirty seconds he was dead; his daughter was unharmed. Morrison's self-immolation shocked the nation and the world. When days went by without any official reaction from the College, a *Voice* columnist pleaded, "I don't want to force anybody to condemn or condone out loud. I do want a Christian institution to act like one. . . . Can't we even have two minutes of silent recognition for a former Wooster student who died for what he believed?" Lowry, nearing the end of his presidency and uncomfortable with political action, finally responded in chapel a few days later, mentioning that one alumnus had said he hoped Morrison's death would not hurt the College's fund drive, and that he Lowry had "chewed him out." Then the president concluded mildly, "I assume . . . you will join me in a few moments of prayer for those who have died young."

A generous obituary in the alumni magazine, followed by a note about establishing an education fund for the Morrison children, set off what might have been the angriest exchange of letters ever seen in the magazine. "Mr. Morrison, by his action, debased the very principles that made this country the greatest citadel of freedom," wrote one alumnus, and another wrote, "I am proud that our Christian country and our nation's men are fighting in Vietnam." When another suggested that any letter in the alumni magazine "personally criticizing another Woosterian was inappropriate," the editor, Estella Goodhart King, responded that she regretted publishing the vitriol. When, many years later, Robert McNamara, who had been secretary of defense during the Vietnam War, authored his mea culpa memoir, he wrote, "Morrison's death was a tragedy not only for his family but also for me and the country. It was an outcry against the killing that was destroying the lives of so many Vietnamese and American youth."

Two years after Morrison's death—Drushal was now acting president—a group of undergraduates brought the antiwar movement home in a protest that demonstrated how hardened sentiments had become in the community. Four students—Lily Hom, eighteen; William Barrie, nineteen; Phillip Pink, eighteen; and Allen Easley, eighteen (who became a law school dean)—went to the Wayne County draft board to "ask questions." When they refused to leave, the board secretary called the building owner, who pressed trespassing charges. The reluctant prosecutor was Ed Eberhart, graduate of the College and son of a faculty member. The defense counsel was Kent Weeks, College graduate and faculty member. The presiding judge, William H. H. Wertz, whose wife had attended the College, was a local lawyer substituting for the vacationing municipal court judge. All ninety-six seats in the courtroom were filled, nearly all by students and faculty, and many others stood through the hearing that lasted most of the day. Hom was tried first; she pleaded innocent and was found guilty. The three men were tried together and found guilty. Wertz declared: "Disturbance is not the issue. It is not the question of a protest movement. It is a simple case of trespassing." With that, he fined each of the four $50 and sentenced them to jail—eliciting gasps in the courtroom—for the three days remaining until Christmas vacation began at noon Friday. During those nights, faculty and administrators joined students in vigils outside the jail. Several times, occupants of passing cars or persons in a parking lot across the street from the jail hurled eggs at those on the vigil; no one was arrested.

The *Daily Record* editorialized that the episode damaged neither the College nor the town, but it clearly became a lively local issue. Various letters to the editor supported the students, but the other side was represented by letters including this from a rural Wayne Countian who said, "A grimy little nest of pink adolescents are flourishing under our collective noses on our hallowed college campus." After Christmas vacation, the four students answered questions in chapel and in the *Voice* wrote a scathing critique about dank, unsanitary conditions in the jail. They charged that the cell doors were controlled electronically, so that in case of fire prisoners would be trapped inside. City Solicitor Eberhart agreed that the jail was not fireproof and that inmates might die of heat before the doors could be opened. Officials noted that a bond issue to build a new jail had been defeated three times, by progressively larger margins. (A bond issue was passed and a new justice center constructed years later.)

As anger appeared to grow, on February 1, 1968, Acting President Drushal stated the institution's official position in a wry but firm open letter addressed "To the Students of The College of Wooster." It began:

For a long time certain fundamental principles regarding individual liberty and campus rights have been rather taken for granted here at

The College of Wooster. Hence it has been thought unnecessary to make any kind of statement in defense of them. It is quite apparent that on many campuses across the country where the students do not have your degree of insight and commitment that there has been a wide variety of types of abridgement of individual freedom by those who mistakenly assume liberty to be absolute for each individual. . . . . [T]he College merely emphasizes by this letter that it will not tolerate infringement of the right of movement, assembly, and free discussion, no matter what morality may be invoked in support of such infringement.

Although campuses nationwide continued to simmer with antiwar protest, President Nixon's decision to invade Cambodia in the spring of 1970—followed by the shocking killing of four students at Kent State University, less than fifty miles from Wooster—touched off a national conflagration. The trauma was as heartfelt at Wooster as anywhere else, but perhaps because of the kind of place it is, Wooster did not erupt as many other schools did. For that, the College could thank students who displayed sensibility in their hurt, a number of thoughtful faculty, and President Drushal, of whom it could be said this was his finest hour.

For that fateful day, Monday, May 4, 1970, students and faculty had previously scheduled an evening march to Wooster's Public Square to protest the Cambodian invasion. In mid-afternoon, news arrived from Kent about the killings by National Guardsman whom Ohio governor James Rhodes had called to duty.[1] Despite the anger this caused, the march—probably the largest ever within the city by College students—remained calm. The *Voice* estimated that between six hundred and seven hundred students, faculty, and administrators participated, plus a number of townspeople. They gathered behind Lowry Center and, undeterred by a rain shower, set out quietly down Beall Avenue to East Liberty Street, continuing through the business district to the Square. A rally followed,

1. As an illustration of Wooster students' concern, the *Voice* sent two reporters, Kerry Stroup and Lou Young, to Kent State to observe a campus that had already seen several days of mass demonstrations leading to the National Guard patrols. Thus they were present that May 4 and witnessed the events that led to the killing of four students. Their minute-by-minute chronology appeared in the paper's May 8, 1970, issue.

including folk singing, speeches by faculty and students, and a turning in of draft cards by several students. About sixty police from Wooster and neighboring communities watched over the event, protectively, and some were said to have unobtrusively flashed the peace sign to the marchers.

On the return trip, the mood was almost jubilant, the marchers talkative, singing. Back on campus, a few students spent the entire night in a vigil on the grass near the gymnasium. Some were on the telephone to friends at Kent and Oberlin; Vi Startzman allowed them to use a room and a phone in the basement of Hygeia Hall. But a large group moved into the Lowry Pit for talk, some of it angry, an uncertain agenda that threatened to turn an ordered protest into something dangerous. A handful of faculty members and administrators, including fellow historians recruited by Acting Dean Henry Copeland, joined the group, hoping to keep the lid on. For a while it was a close call. Copeland remembered a few students removing a portrait of Howard Lowry from the wall and taking it he knew not where; he was relieved when a couple of hours later they brought it back untouched and rehung it.

One turning point came when Ken McHargh, a respected senior and president of the Black Students Association, took the microphone and essentially harangued the nearly all-white crowd: You whites are spoiled, he said in effect. You don't understand what pain and trouble really are. Looking back years later, McHargh—who became a federal magistrate judge—said that on the one hand, Kent State showed "government suppressing, in an unfair way, students doing nothing wrong but exercising their rights." But on the other hand, he worried that the evening at Lowry Center was "more capitalizing on emotion than dealing with the realities of the situation we were facing and what was important." McHargh remembered saying, "We needed to think about serious things, and be serious about what's important, and how to effectuate change in a way that has some long-term ability to make a difference, and to make sense. . . . Some of the things that were being talked about, to me, had no relationship to anything constructive, no relationship to anything other than taking an opportunity to raise mayhem, as opposed to doing something with thought behind it."

Still, some students were loudly demanding Drushal's presence. Memories fade, obviously, especially concerning a time filled with turmoil like this, but about something quite important that occurred Monday evening, three leading figures are in agreement. Sensing the budding unrest as the sky darkened, the art historian Arn Lewis and the philosopher Ron Hustwit visited the president at his home, where he greeted them in his living room.

> Lewis: Garber, to his credit, was willing to listen. He said to us, "Well, what should I say?' We went through what we thought would be honest and what the students would understand and respond to.
> Hustwit: [We] worried that Garber had a different impression of what was going on, that . . . he did not need to read the riot act. He gave . . . a really fine talk. It was very empathetic. He talked about his father as a minister in Kentucky. . . . He mentioned the loss of his daughter [in an automobile accident a year earlier]. He had people on his side. The message was, this is going to be all right, that there was a lot of tension, but that reasonable people with good intentions can manage this.

Doug Drushal wrote in a memoir about his father: The administration "debated the wisdom of the president's personal presence in such a situation. Over some objections, he went to Lowry Center near midnight and started a dialogue. He never told the students that their protest was out of place, but rather attempted to channel it through effective means. The immediate crisis passed and the next day he and other GLCA [Great Lakes College Association] presidents telegraphed President Nixon, admonishing him for the invasion and pointing out its effects on college campuses." The message to Nixon said in part: "We implore you to consider the incalculable danger of an unprecedented alienation of America's youth and to take immediate action to demonstrate your determination to end the war quickly."

Beyond what President Drushal said, it was also what he did. We will not close Wooster, he declared, as so many other colleges did, but we do not intend to go on as if nothing had happened.[2] He urged faculty to step away from their syllabi and encouraged students to vent about the killings at Kent State—about how terrible they thought the world was; faculty did,

---

2. Nationally, students struck at least 279 colleges and universities, and administrators closed 14 following protests, including Miami, Ohio State, and Kent State. After seven hours of clashes between an estimated three thousand students and police and National Guard troops in Athens May 15, Ohio University closed for the summer.

and students did. On May 6, in another open letter "To the Students of The College of Wooster," the president wrote, "I would like to meet with small *ad hoc* groups to discuss these issues. . . . Please keep the groups small enough to meet at my home. If you don't belong to an organization, feel free to get together with others so that we may discuss the issues. . . . [M]y trip to Washington . . . will occur on May 12. I hope the views of one person, speaking at least in part for one community, will be important to the democratic process. I covet your prayers and support in this venture."

Given the uprisings on so many other campuses, Wooster's students could be painted, according to one prominent historian, "as intensely conservative." Yet the frenzied events on campus that Tuesday, May 5, demonstrated that Wooster students were incensed and active, just not violent. In the afternoon, about five hundred students and faculty assembled on the slope north of Lowry Center "to voice their own demands and opinions." Wind and a light rain drove the gathering inside where, the *Voice* reported, "discussions grew increasingly heated. . . . After an hour of bickering, name-calling and argument, the students split on the issue—150 walking to Galpin with a list of demands, while the others remained in Lowry Center to discuss their response." Then, that evening, about seventy strike leaders from colleges around the state—Denison, Hiram, Kenyon, Oberlin, Muskingum, Ohio State, and Kent State, among others—arrived to gather in the Lean Lecture Room of Wishart Hall (used with permission of speech department chairman Bill Craig) to plan cooperation and plot strategy. One of the plans they agreed on was to hold a rally at the state capitol in Columbus on the following Friday. But Thursday Wooster students announced that they would not participate, citing "convincing evidence of participation . . . by groups not committed to the non-violent aims." About five thousand students and others did gather at the statehouse without violence, and the next day a peaceful protest rally attracted about a hundred thousand in Washington.

Understanding that alumni and other friends of the College might be disturbed by the foment they were hearing about from afar, alumni magazine editor King skillfully assembled a section she called, "The First Week in May." It included contributions from a dozen faculty members and two students, introduced by Drushal, who offered three points: "(1) There was a strong desire all along the way on the part of administration, faculty, and students to keep the dialogue going, to keep lines of communication open, and to continue what had been characteristic of the year, namely, a free and open discussion of a wide variety of topics . . . (2) There was a strong desire on the part of all concerned to keep the College open. . . . (3) It must be mentioned again, as it must be continuously kept before us, the College must provide a forum for the discussion of ideas." Bob Smith, the archaeologist and professor of religion, observed: "The greater informality, individualism and activism now evidenced on the campus represent no threat to the existence or identity of the College; rather, they express in fresh ways Wooster's traditional dedication to the enrichment of human life. If the upheaval is less intense than at many colleges and university, it is in part because the College has never lost its concern for both the individual and society."

After the stunning first week in May, the next action in this tumultuous spring was genuinely Wooster. Rather than violence, or pointless kicking and screaming, Wooster students, led by senior Alan Unger, aided by supportive faculty—among them John Hondros, Arn Lewis, Kent Weeks, John Pierson, Paul Christianson—and President Drushal, who negotiated with foundations for financial support, planned a pair of summer conferences, which they dubbed "Participation '70." The goal was to provide training for active political effort at all levels of government. The sessions were introduced by an advertisement in the Sunday *New York Times* asking, "Are You Tired of Demonstrating? Try the Politics of Participation—Join Us." Two senators, Birch Bayh, the Indiana Democrat, and Bill Saxbe, the Ohio Republican (who later briefly served as Nixon's attorney general), signed on as honorary chairmen. Scores of inquiries came from about thirty states. The two-week session beginning in late June featured programs titled "The Techniques of the Electoral Process," "Polling and Data Analysis," and "Large Interest Groups and the New Constituency" and talks by representatives of both political parties and the columnist Robert Novak; it attracted about a hundred young people. But a second session was abandoned because both foundation funding and registrations seemed too slim. It was a foreshadowing of dwindling interest among students, because by autumn political protest both at Wooster and nationwide had all but ceased.

CHAPTER 15

The Word Is Quality

In all the history of The College of Wooster, only two presidents served longer than Henry Copeland—Charles Wishart, twenty-five years from 1919 to 1944, and Howard Lowry, twenty-three years from 1944 to 1967. Copeland was forty-one years old and had been at the College eleven years when, in 1977, he accepted a job that he had not foreseen. He left it gracefully eighteen years later. "It's hard work," he said, cheerfully enough, yet zeroing in on elements of a president's job not widely understood by others. "I'm not complaining, but, boy, I went to the office every Sunday afternoon, every Sunday night, every night of the week except for Fridays and Saturdays. And your Saturdays are planned. You go to the football game, you've got an alumni group on campus, during a campaign you're out on the road four days a week. It's fun in the sense that you do something every day, but I honestly wanted to teach and go back to France." Besides all that, his wife, Lolly—a paragon of college First Ladies—encouraged his decision to leave the position. "She said, 'you should get out before they kick you out,'" Copeland remembered.

His predecessor, Garber Drushal, had come to the presidency a decade earlier at a critical time in the College's history: the unexpected death of Lowry, dangerous financial circumstances, growing student unrest. But he had steadied the institution and grown to love the job, to the point that he was hinting to a few trustees that the bylaw requiring administrators to retire at sixty-five might be waived. As it happened, the issue settled itself. Drushal had suffered a mild heart attack in 1972, and as his projected retirement age approached, he appeared increasingly weary. So it was less than shocking when he required open-heart surgery in 1976 to repair a defective valve, and soon afterward, he underwent prostate surgery as well. Thus, his retirement in 1977 was assured. It was a fond departure. He was honored at many parties, and he and Dorothy were rewarded with a going-away trip to Bavaria. He delivered the commencement address that spring and received an honorary Doctor of Humane Letters degree from the College (and an honorary degree from Wittenberg as well). The board endowed the J. Garber Drushal Distinguished Visiting Professorship, and the students dedicated the *Index* to him, quoting from his 1973 opening convocation address, this man who had been raised a Brethren minister's son in rural Kentucky: "So that when you leave here . . . you will have developed an affection, not just for the place, but for people, for ideas, and for life itself. . . . Then you have become a Scot by affection."

Planning for the transition, the board appointed a presidential search committee in October 1975, chaired by Alex Meakin, a Presbyterian minister from Parma, Ohio. Conscious of the openness understood to be important in the restless late 1960s and '70s, the board declared that its official search committee of trustees was to be aided by advisory committees of alumni, faculty, and students, and, unlike quieter searches, this one would be "advertised in certain professional journals" and "carried out in full compliance with the principles of Equal Employment Opportunity for all persons," as well as "personnel channels of the United Presbyterian Church." The collection of interested parties was sweeping. Besides Meakin, trustees were Mary Coleman, Carol Dix, Stan Gault, Don Noble, Bill Pocock, and Tim Smucker. John W. Dodds, now an emeritus member of the board, was designated an official consultant. The Alumni Advisory Committee was chaired by John C. Johnston Jr., a prominent Wooster lawyer, and included Dennis Barnes, Bob Bone, Nancy Braund Boruch, Jim Clarke, Dave Dowd, Erma Wooding Foley, Dwight "Pete" Hanna, Margo Drury Irvin, Lee Eberhardt Limbird, Margaret S. Ronaldson, Carl Toensmeier, Norm Wiebusch, and Lu David Wims. (Johnston, Boruch, Clarke, Hanna, and Limbird all later became trustees.) The faculty elected a committee chaired by the economist Bill Baird. It included Henry Copeland, history (then also dean of the faculty); Melcher Fobes, mathematics; Dave Guldin, sociology; Vivian Holliday, classics; Ray McCall, English; Dick Reimer, economics; and Ted Williams, chemistry. The student committee consisted of two juniors, Mark

Schmiedl and Thomas Shupe; five sophomores, Richard Harrison, Sandra Hopfengardner, Robert Klemens, James Ogan, and Vickie Zurcher; and one freshman, Lucille Teichert.

The search began with two possible internal candidates, Vice President for Academic Affairs Fred Cropp and Vice President for Development Buck Smith, both alumni of the College. It was widely thought that Cropp, a geologist and the president's chief deputy, was Drushal's favorite to succeed him. Copeland, then a new dean, credits Cropp with introducing him to administration. "Fred was a good administrator because he anticipated," Copeland said. "He was always two weeks ahead of everybody else. And more importantly, he had an understanding that you didn't just make a decision, but you had to put in place some institutional arrangement to see that it was done." Much appreciated for his hard work, Cropp had nonetheless drawn the ire of some faculty members for what they perceived as micromanaging. Sadly, he had also sometimes seemed preoccupied, as his wife, Helen, a College classmate and mother of his four children, fought and eventually lost a painful battle with cancer. Smith, who had been particularly close to Lowry and was his choice as the first person to hold the title vice president for development, had produced sterling financial numbers, had established strong contacts with major donors, and was already building a national reputation as a fund-raising authority among liberal arts colleges. Some trustees thought his record had earned him the chance to lead. But his formal education had ended with a master's degree in public administration, not a doctorate, which did not match the trustee-approved job description; worse, his lack of scholarly experience was anathema to faculty members whose respect for Drushal's performance during difficult times did not gainsay their only grudging acceptance of his appointment upon Lowry's death.

Nothing much happened until the spring of 1976, when the advisory committees were selected and all the committees began meeting. Although the net was to be cast wide, a difference from later searches was that the committee hired no non-affiliated outside consultant to provide professional advice. Baird, the faculty chairman, remembered that one of his colleagues wrote him a detailed memo outlining the skills required of a new president, which, Baird noticed, "exactly described him." After the usual screening process, the committees agreed to bring four candidates to campus to meet students and staff and to make presentations to the faculty, but, as one committee member put it, "Each of them blew it, that's all I can say." One (who went on to a college presidency elsewhere) defended the Vietnam War, from which the United States had recently extricated itself and which was exceedingly unpopular with much of the faculty. Another, a university professor of religion, was genial to the point that he appeared to think it would be fun to be a college president for a while.

It seemed a tad surprising that Copeland had been elected to the search committee by his peers, since he was then serving as dean of the faculty—temporarily, he thought, and even hoped. A French historian, Copeland was preparing to take a second research leave in Paris for the 1977–78 academic year. "My children had loved France when we had been there before, we were all signed up, school, apartment, the whole nine yards." Given the committee's unfinished task, "I thought we were going to start the search over, "Copeland said, assuming he would be away during much of the remainder of the process. Not long after the inconclusive campus interviews, though, board chairman Pocock met with him and, as Copeland remembered it, "He said, 'You know, we've been talking, Henry, and if you're willing to be a candidate for the position, we'd like you to be. The faculty committee supports you. And the trustee committee. So you just don't want to fall on your face.'"

The first issue for Copeland, of course, was to discuss the opportunity with Lolly, and she was not overjoyed. Having seen how hard he had worked as a dean, she understood the prospective load and time away from family, but she would be supportive. Like the other candidates, Copeland had to give an obligatory lecture to the faculty. He postulated that the world had changed around the turn of the twentieth century from the modern era to a postmodern era, citing among other things the influences of Einstein, Picasso, and Freud. In the subsequent question-and-answer session, one faculty member contended that not all that much had changed, which allowed Copeland to retort that the condition of women had certainly changed through the century—a winning argument to much of the faculty. The positive response was rapid at every level—the exalted mathematician Melcher Fobes sent off a note, "I think the College will be fortunate to have you to lead, cajole, persuade, and kick it (as the need may be) into being what it has the potential to become and remain"—and less than a month later the trustees elected him to the presidency. He had to tell his children that they wouldn't be going back to France, but the

Copeland family treated itself to a six-week trip to London as a consolation prize, and he became president July 1, 1977.

Henry Copeland, son of a physician, grew up in Griffin, Georgia, and
went to college at Baylor University in Waco, Texas. Planning to follow
his father's career, he entered Cornell (now Weill Cornell) Medical College in New York City; midway through that first year he married Laura
Harper, known to all as Lolly, whom he had met during school days in
Griffin. A year of hearing about neurobiology research shattered his
interest in a lifetime of medicine, so he returned to Baylor for a year of
French and Russian as preparation for graduate school. Then it was off to
Ithaca, New York, on a Woodrow Wilson Fellowship to study European
history at Cornell, where he taught for a year while completing his PhD.
One of his friends there, Dick Graham, a Latin American historian who
had graduated from Wooster in 1956, suggested Copeland consider a job
opening at his alma mater. That was 1966, the year Aileen Dunham, the
longtime head of the history department, was retiring; Dunham and her
successor as chair, Clayton Ellsworth, hired Copeland. He joined a highly
regarded department anchored by Bob Walcott, the much-respected
English historian, and the redoubtable Helen Kaslo Osgood and Dan
Calhoun, and which had recently taken on two young Vanderbilt-trained
southerners, Jim Hodges and Hayden Schilling. Copeland taught the basic
Western Civilization course and as a European historian fell heir to some
of Dunham's specialties, classes in nineteenth- and twentieth-century
Europe and the French Revolution. Three years later he was named an
associate dean, and in 1974 he became dean of the faculty.

Copeland inherited the leadership of a College that faced difficulties
both financial and academic. Under the Drushal-Jenny-Smith triumvi-
rate, Wooster had largely overcome the budget and capital dangers of
the mid- and late 1960s; then the ill-fated decision not to raise tuition
in the early '70s, just before double-digit inflation unsettled the entire
national economy, plunging the College budget into deficit again. And
the endowment remained at a pathetic $15 million, which produced too
little annual revenue. Academically, there were a number of troubling
issues. A somewhat less restrictive curriculum—although in the context
of similar movement at many other educational institutions—endangered
the College's long-term integrity. The growth of enrollment to near two

thousand had certainly increased revenue but had required the admission of some students who might not ordinarily have met Wooster's standards. And the faculty, which had not grown in proportion with the larger enrollment, was, in a word, tired.

To the new president's eye, the College faced two momentous challenges—first, to restore the academic standards that the financial crisis and cultural inroads had threatened and second, to build the financial strength needed to maintain and enrich those standards, primarily through a vastly increased endowment. "What I talked about when I interviewed with the faculty committee, when I interviewed with the trustees," Copeland recalled, "was the word 'quality.' Wooster had gone through a terrible time, and we had to limit the size of the student body, we had to get rooms for everybody, we had to bring our physical facilities up to standard, all of the things that I had felt, sitting in the dean's office, had been in jeopardy." He was aware as well that as the baby boom generation faded, there would be fewer students in the pipeline, and public universities and community colleges had expanded after World War II to absorb most of them. But "there was room in the universe of higher education for an expensive, high-quality education. And we had to be among the best. That was kind of a platform."

It was the kind of platform Howard Lowry would have appreciated. Occasionally, though, Copeland's exalted view of liberal arts in general and Wooster in particular proved, Lowry-like, too much for his audience, and the new president had to fall back on his wry sense of humor. A case in point was his inaugural address, titled "A Place Apart": "In my judgment, Wooster should strive to remain an autonomous center of ideas, values, and standards which, while rooted in the present, transcends in its concerns the here and now; which, rather than reflecting the world, challenges it; which, rather than assuming all of the tasks that require doing, assumes one and does that one superbly; which, rather than accepting the inevitable, creates a tension between what is and what could be; which, rather than being a mirror of society, remains *a place apart* with its own character and purpose."

Five years later, in a convocation address he called "The Heavenly City Revisited," Copeland referenced his inaugural and some of the responses it attracted:

It has been attacked by everyone from those who saw it standing in the way of open visitation to those who saw it restricting Tuesday night parties. . . . [It] has also been attacked in public forums as elitist, fascist, authoritarian, racist, and sexist . . . What was "A Place Apart"? Well, of course, it was never a place at all, but rather a dream that Wooster might retain the freedom to define itself as a particular kind of academic institution rather than deriving its identity from some other sphere of human activity—be it an industry, a training institute, a caterer to trendy consumers, a service station for society, a church for divine worship or even a hospital for the mentally ill. "A Place Apart" reflected my own view of the College as an association of scholars in which students were members of the association, not simply outcomes of a production line.

The trustees had not doubted Copeland's intellectual strength, but he had relatively little experience in dealing with the institution's financial affairs. His first teacher in the ways of the budget was Hans Jenny, the vice president for finance and business, and that instruction might be less than transparent. "Hans befriended me as a young faculty member," said Copeland, who smiled as he recalled their relationship. "He was a very interesting man. But he [could be] terribly frustrating. He was forever having a new idea, a new way of keeping the books, a new concept for the capital charge. So [sometimes] the figures from last year were not compatible with this year's figures." When the imaginative but idiosyncratic Jenny retired in 1982, Copeland took a deep breath as he searched for a successor: "I didn't want anybody picking fights with the faculty, picking fights with George Ingram [chairman of the board's Finance Committee]." Jenny's deputy, Bill Snoddy, directed the office for a year while Copeland ran a national search, telling the president he would not apply for the job. "I've been at the College for almost thirty years, and I love what I'm doing," he said at the time. Copeland knew he could trust Snoddy. "You couldn't always believe Hans's figures," he said, "but I could always go down to Bill and get the straight scoop on whatever I needed to know." After three candidates were invited to campus but none was offered the job, Copeland walked into Snoddy's office and offered him the position. "I was confident Bill was exactly what the College needed," Copeland said. "He struck me as a terribly honest, thoughtful, humane scorekeeper, widely trusted by the staff."

So Snoddy became the successor to the cosmopolitan economist Jenny. Bill Snoddy had grown up on a dairy farm near Wooster; married his high school sweetheart, JoAnn, the year after their graduation (they soon had three children); and spent three adult years on the farm until he decided he didn't want to milk cows seven days a week for the rest of his life. He took a job at a general store, grinding feed, driving a truck, delivering fertilizer and cement blocks, shoveling coal down farmhouse chutes. And he enrolled in evening classes (his parents helped with the tuition) at Ashland College, taking accounting and business courses; discovering he enjoyed the additional formal education, he took courses for about three years—not long enough or varied enough to earn him a degree. Noticing a newspaper ad for an accounting job at an unnamed "educational institution," he applied, was interviewed, and was offered $350 a month to start at Wooster in 1959. Not only was this less than he was making at the general store, but he also had to abandon the blue jeans and flannel shirts he usually wore to work; it was a "major expenditure" for JoAnn and Bill to buy him a suit, sport coats, and ties. But they decided it was an "excellent opportunity."

Snoddy began as assistant treasurer in what was almost a quill-pen office, in which Kermit Yoder, the treasurer, would spend half a day signing monthly checks. When the College acquired its first computer in 1964, Snoddy directed the business office punch-card operation and wrote programs for both the payroll department and the registrar. When Yoder died unexpectedly in 1972, Snoddy was elected treasurer of the College, and he recalled years later the "humbling moment" when board members gave him a standing ovation. Jenny, he said, "was a tremendous mentor. He challenged me to do things that I thought I was not prepared or trained to do." Snoddy also learned unimagined skills from George Ingram, a brilliant New York investor who as chairman of the board's Finance Committee created an audit committee and monitored investments and the budget with a practiced eye. Snoddy began to work closely with Copeland even while Copeland was dean. Snoddy said that as president, "Henry was just very knowledgeable and astute with regard to financial matters and the College's budget. He had an analytical mind that would always look ahead of the decision at hand to predict what the end result would be." When Snoddy joined the College, its operating budget was $2.3 million; when he retired forty years later, in 1999, the budget he managed was more than $44 million, and endowment was nearly twenty times higher.

To reach that endowment required a long, difficult journey under any circumstances, and even before he officially took office in 1977, Copeland hit a bump, more like a boulder, in the road. Although as dean he dealt with budget issues, he had almost no experience in one of a president's chief jobs, fund-raising. That seemed all right, though, since Buck Smith was vice president for development. Smith, who had returned to Wooster at Lowry's urging in 1962, had been chiefly responsible for restructuring its fund-raising. He had rescued the Centennial Campaign, directed the Essential Extras drive, and built rapport with major donors. In the course of his successful performance at Wooster, and in advising other liberal arts colleges, Smith had achieved a national reputation. One of those institutions, Chapman College in Orange, California, facing a severe financial crisis, saw Smith as the answer; after declining the Chapman presidency at first, he acceded. In May 1977, less than two months after Copeland had been appointed, and nearly two months before he took office, Smith went to the president-designate and told him he was leaving. Unexpectedly, the underpinning of Wooster's fund-raising efforts was removed.

Smith's departure stunned Copeland, who would now have to learn about fund-raising on the job. "I was focused on raising money in terms of how you spent your year. At the beginning of the year you sketched out, okay, we're going to make these eight trips, and we're going here and here and here." Recalling the effort, partly with a smile, partly with a shudder, Copeland said, "Most of my psychic energy went into development. When you wake up in the morning: 'Whom may I have lunch with today? Should I call Mrs. Critchfield, or should I go to Cleveland to see Jo Morris? Should I go to Canton [home of the Timken Foundation]?' You spend incredible, intense days. Florida sounds [easy], but you see four people in a day and have dinner with Marian Nixon [who ultimately endowed two faculty chairs]."

But Copeland knew, and board chairman Pocock knew "that we had a college we couldn't afford. We had a college with I.S., we had a college with a leave program, we had a college with a first-year seminar. We had ambitions in various ways. But we did not have the financial underpinning to support that kind of Howard Lowry–ideal program. So Bill made it very plain to me at the beginning, and I certainly agreed with him, that time for building the financial base, for the endowment, is short, and rather than go out and create new academic programs, or try to restore Wooster-in-India, that we had to build the endowment."

Ah, but how would the new administration fill the large vice presidential void left by Smith's departure (Smith recalled that Pocock was so angered by his leaving that Pocock wouldn't speak to him for several years if they crossed paths at national meetings). The College conducted two national searches to replace Smith, and Copeland made offers to two people. Both declined, perhaps for a variety of reasons—Wooster was not offering enough money, the neophyte president was too young and inexperienced, and probably most of all because its $15 million endowment was minuscule compared to those of other ambitious liberal arts colleges. The development officer who kept the program operating was Grace Tompos, who had already performed the same tasks for much of two years—albeit with Smith's guidance—a period when he lived in Arizona because his wife, Joni, needed a dry climate to recover her health. But Tompos was not interested in the travel and strain required for the top job. The office also had a relatively new grants writer, Sally Patton, who had graduated in 1967—a star actress in College plays—and had lived in Europe and earned a master's degree from the University of Illinois before returning to Wooster to assist one of her mentors, art historian Arn Lewis, on a community arts project. She worked part-time writing grant proposals for the College until she was offered a job in Boston, at which time Smith quickly hired her to run the alumni fund, while she also continued to work on grants.

Having failed to find a new chief development officer, and having watched Patton perform adeptly at every task given her, Copeland decided to offer her the vice presidency. "I presented the idea to Bill Pocock, and he said, 'Well, it's like taking a young pitcher out of the bullpen and putting him in the seventh game of the World Series.'" But Pocock agreed that here was a person with proven ability and energy and a willingness to work very hard; besides if it didn't work out, they could always make a change. Patton was thirty-four years old. There was a little quiet muttering on the board about sending a girl out to do a man's job, and one trustee questioned the propriety of sending a young, attractive, unmarried woman on fund-raising trips with the president. Worries aside, the appointment did work out very well indeed—and Patton retired as vice president for development in 2011 after thirty-two years during which she led three comprehensive campaigns and raised tens of millions of dollars for the College.

It is also probable that Sally Patton knew more graduates of The College of Wooster than anyone else who ever lived. "Sally's natural grace and gift for friendship made her expert at getting to know each wave of Wooster alumni as they emerged into their adult lives," said Mary Neagoy, class of 1983, who served as president of the Alumni Association and became a prominent trustee. "She knew everyone on campus, of course, and she knew hundreds of Wooster people in cities and towns all over the country. Sally weaved these relationships together for the benefit of the College—she could tell you what your favorite professors were doing these days. She kept many far-flung alumni feeling like they hadn't lost touch."

Losing Buck Smith on the eve of his presidency was a challenge to overcome, and it was followed by the kind of disaster they don't tell you about in presidential interviews. The second semester of Copeland's first presidential year had just begun when the College dealt with what the governor, Jim Rhodes, called the "greatest disaster in Ohio history," a Midwest blizzard powered by eighty-miles-per-hour winds that hit January 26, 1978, and continued for two days. Wooster mayor Roy Stype declared a state of emergency, urging businesses to remain closed and people to stay home. Roads in and out of the city were blocked. Statewide, at least thirty-one people died in the storm, and more than thirty-five hundred National Guardsmen and volunteers worked to dig the state out. The College closed for two days.

Clearing the snow was one kind of problem; restructuring the academic program was another; this task occupied the attention of Copeland and the faculty over much of his term. In the never-ending discussion of the value of a liberal arts college in an ever-changing world, it is enlightening to note Copeland's early characterization, in an interview with the *Voice*, September 22, 1978, as he began his second presidential year:

> I think the liberal arts are a tradition with a future. The matter of vocationalism tends to go in cycles, and seems to me to be terribly shortsighted. The more rapidly the world changes, the more vital and necessary will be liberal education, the cultivation of one's general capacity for understanding the world. It's shortsighted to prepare for what appears to be the "best seller" at the moment. . . . And I'm not thinking in dollars and cents terms, I'm thinking in terms of human satisfaction. In coming to a liberal arts college, you bet on the long run.

These thoughts echoed what Copeland's intellectual precursor had written thirty-three years before, in his "Adventure in Education": "We believe,

moreover, that all liberal arts education is a continuing education. It offers increase and renewal till the very end of life. . . . A liberal education,
with such a content and a method, is clearly a vocational asset. We have
too long apologized for its so-called impracticality, and it is high time
we stopped doing so."

As Copeland and the faculty well knew, a number of colleges had
instituted an undergraduate business administration degree—hardly the
stuff of liberal arts—resulting from their anxiety about losing job-oriented
students (and, more likely, their parents). When some Wooster trustees
raised that possibility, the administration examined the issue, and the
result was a compromise that has served the College well over three decades: a business economics degree, earned through the Department of
Economics, with all the appropriate intellectual standards, supplemented
by a measure of business pragmatism. That compromise came about as
part of the efforts led by the new president and his first vice president for
academic affairs, the economist Bill Baird, to stiffen the entire academic
program. Using a foundation grant and at a modest cost of $3,000 to
$5,000 each, they instituted an evaluation of every department by a panel
of visitors, usually two successful alumni who had been majors from those
departments along with a university academic. Each panel spent about
three days on campus, interviewing faculty and examining a departmental
self-study, then made recommendations. Three or four departments were
evaluated each year, and the reports, which the administration and one
or more trustees studied, led to modifications in many departments. The
business economics degree grew from one such evaluation, in which the
two alumni were Bill Longbrake, a scholarly banker who later became
chairman of the Finance Committee of the Board of Trustees, and Jim
Wilson, who later became chairman of the board. (Wilson credits his
participation with renewing his ties to the College after he had had little
connection over many years following his graduation.)

An important element in the academic renaissance was the arrival in
1982 of an outsider with a fresh view as vice president for academic affairs.
Baird, who had agreed somewhat reluctantly to take on the responsibility
of aiding the new president in achieving his academic goals, planned to
step aside after five years. As Copeland considered leading candidates,
two of his most trusted confidants, the chemist Ted Williams and the
historian Hayden Schilling who were members of the search committee,

insisted the decision was really quite simple: it had to be Don Harward, dean of the Honors College at the University of Delaware. Harward had been a scholarship undergraduate at Maryville College in Tennessee, a small Presbyterian college where he said Wooster was looked upon as "the Princeton of Presbyterian colleges." After earning a PhD in philosophy at the University of Maryland and teaching at several institutions, he was asked to found the Honors College at Delaware, starting from scratch recruiting faculty and students. So he understood something about recruiting when he arrived at Wooster, where the admissions department was struggling. He remembered his first board meeting, at which the admissions report, a good deal less than positive, was met with silence. Ignoring the admissions officer, the vice chairman of the board, Stan Gault, turned to Harward and said, "You're new." Yes, the fledging vice president conceded. "What are you going to do about it?" That, Harward remembered, "was the first thing Stan ever said to me."

One of the first things he did was to steal Schilling from the history department to become dean of admissions. Besides making staff changes, Harward and Schilling unleashed the faculty and sports coaches, wanting them "fully engaged, fully involved, taking responsibility for the admissions effort," which included, among other things, almost endless hours of telephone calls to prospective students. Harward, Schilling, and Copeland developed Wooster's merit scholarship program, bringing hundreds of high school students to campus for faculty presentations and for examinations. The exams surprised the teenagers: these were not multiple choice like the SAT or ACT but required essays on attractive topics prepared by faculty. Many of the prospects, even those who did not win scholarships, chose to attend Wooster. "It uses your faculty resources in ways that are ultimately telling," Copeland said. "It was well thought out and well executed. And Don's energy executed it." To cut down on freshman attrition, Harward enlisted Yvonne Williams, who had organized the black studies program, to rebuild the seminars for first-year students, moving from the conventional series to a thematically organized program with visiting lecturers and related seminars. This meant, Harward said, "not only lectures but plays, films, a theme with a variety of engaging elements, and courses that picked up the theme but expressed it in [a professor's] own disciplinary way—in effect the theme as a center to the wheel, and every spoke, every course, a connection to that theme."

As an intermediate step from first year to I.S., Harward instituted sophomore seminars to introduce students to interdisciplinary research and leadership seminars that brought visitors to campus to allow students to spend time with successful professionals and business executives. Always a fierce proponent of affirmative action, he worked on an early retirement plan for white male faculty, which would create slots for women and minorities. Sometimes when Harward faced an acute affirmative action problem, he would close his office and go to Ted Williams's home on College Avenue, where they would sit on the front porch and talk through the issues. Although the '60s are usually remembered as the high point of student activism, racial matters continued to be a difficult challenge. A campaign to divest the stock of companies doing business in apartheid South Africa aroused students in 1986, and two years later anger concerning local conditions led to the occupation of Galpin Hall. Respectful negotiations diffused both circumstances (see chapter 7).

After seven years at Wooster, the inevitable occurred, and Harward was recruited to the presidency of the well-regarded Bates College in Maine, where he would serve eighteen productive years. His memories of the College remained fond. "I think I learned everything at Wooster," he said. "Henry provided sufficient space, he always was encouraging, always was supportive, a wonderful mentor. And what I learned had so much to do with the qualities of the people"—he named a sampling: Schilling, Susan and Dick Figge in German, Yvonne and Ted Williams, Larry Stewart in English. Copeland's view of the Harward tenure is similar. As the College worked to retain what worked best from the 1969 curriculum modifications and revise the rest, Copeland said, "Don carried the ball. His drive, the critical eye he brought to Wooster from his experiences at Delaware, and his willingness to insist on high standards made the difference, and he deserves much of the credit for the changes." When Copeland retired in 1995, some at the College looked longingly to Lewiston, Maine, but that was a ship that had already passed by.

The focus always was to toughen the curriculum. The option of meeting the foreign language requirement by a single cultural area studies course was eliminated. A number of off-campus programs, usually abroad, and managed elsewhere, were phased out; some were so ill conceived and badly executed that students returned to Wooster during the term because the programs were a waste of time. Some majors were strengthened; for example, urban studies, which had begun on an experimental basis and was now revised to require a solid core of courses in economics, political science, and sociology, thus becoming one of the more difficult majors. A few majors were eliminated, including social welfare and physical education. And a dozen new majors were created—among them anthropology, molecular biology, Chinese, theater, black studies, and women's studies. Notably, in 1987 the College returned to the semester calendar from the quarter calendar that had been set up in 1969. This made a special difference in I.S.: the time devoted to I.S., in general three quarters, or thirty weeks, became three semesters, or forty-five weeks. And to the relief of the faculty, the student body was gradually trimmed back to a more academically capable sixteen hundred.

A critical element of the Copeland presidency was its guidance and support from an invigorated Board of Trustees, a process that had begun under Drushal, led by activist chairmen, first Bill Pocock, then Stan Gault. Although no one could doubt the power exerted by and the effort expended by the Board of Trustees in recent years, it was not always so. Legal control of the College, which the board accepted from the Presbyterian Church in 1968, is one thing; who is actually calling the shots is another. It could hardly be said that chairmen of the Board of Trustees during the Lowry era were anything but strong, accomplished men. Arthur Compton, who chaired the board from 1940 to 1953, was a Nobel laureate and chancellor of Washington University in St. Louis. Bob Wilson, the chairman from 1953 to 1964, was chief executive officer of Standard Oil of Indiana and a member of the Atomic Energy Commission. Cary Wagner, the chairman from 1964 to 1970, was a renowned scientist and successful businessman. These men also had things in common besides accomplishments: they had been undergraduates together at the College, Compton graduating in 1913, Wilson in 1914, and Wagner in 1915. They shared a love for the College—Buck Smith said that Wilson's widow once told him tearily, "Bob loved Wooster more than he loved me." And they shared a long friendship with Lowry, who had been almost a member of the Compton family since college days and considered Arthur his best friend. Because these busy men trusted Lowry, they were quite comfortable letting him run the College, even to the point of setting the agenda for the board and essentially presiding over its meetings.

The boards Lowry assembled—and he was almost always the recruiter—were sprinkled with big names. Besides such internationally known scientist/administrators as Compton and Wilson, they included Charles Kettering, "Boss Ket," who had invented the automobile self-starter and was vice chairman of General Motors; Harry Luce, who founded *Time* magazine and built its empire; Carl Weygandt, chief justice of the Supreme Court of Ohio; and Ben Fairless, the nationally famous president of U.S. Steel. Some of these men and other well-known figures on the board did participate actively in College affairs, and some did not. Fairless, for example, was not recorded as having attended a single meeting, and as many as one-third of the trustees might not bother to attend any given board meeting. It was not then, and it is not now, uncommon for a chief executive of a college, or of a business, to build a board committed to his goals and his success, and Wooster's was no exception. This was Lowry's board, but as over the years he appeared increasingly tired, the tenor of the board changed.

Upon Wilson's death in 1964, Wagner, a tough-minded chemical engineer, became chairman, and one of the board's most revered members, Cleveland lawyer Dean Hopkins, became vice chairman. The number of trustees with financial experience in business and industry rose to about a dozen, and the board began to take on a more assertive role. Wagner brought structure to the meetings and visited the campus regularly, sometimes startling the staff as he wandered unannounced into administrative offices. As agendas focused more on financial issues, Lowry, who was not only wearing down but also was often bored by money matters, participated much less.

Wagner appeared to have identified a prospective successor when he appointed Bill Pocock as chairman of the search committee that selected Drushal, a committee Pocock led with particular savvy. (See chapter 13 for details of the search and Pocock's role.) So it was a logical step in 1970 when Wagner retired and Pocock stepped in as chairman. Although this was, after all, a volunteer group, it did not take long for Pocock, building on his predecessor's momentum, to refit the board into the policy-making unit it continued to be over the next decades. Many decisions were financial. The board established a "plant reserve" to smooth fluctuating repair costs; it loosened restrictions on use of endowment revenue; it authorized a long-term line of credit to eliminate the need for short-term rollover notes. Detailed material provided to members in advance of meetings, called "attachments," allowed for more enlightened discussion. Then there was a procedural modification that came about almost serendipitously. Until the mid-1970s, the board had limited its members neither by number of terms served nor by age. In 1976, John W. Dodds, a friend of Lowry and longtime member, told his colleagues that at the age of seventy-two he felt it proper to give up his seat to a younger person. Two other, older trustees immediately joined him. Thus, a "tradition" of serving until that age was established; only later did the board formalize in its bylaws that trustees became "Emeritus Life Members" at this age or after fifteen years of service.

Pocock, who was to serve seventeen years as chairman, from 1970 to 1987, knew how things were supposed to work; that's what he did for a living. A graduate in Wooster's class of 1938, he had been chief executive officer of Booz, Allen Applied Research, serving as a consultant to the Pentagon, NASA, and the Republic of Vietnam, among others; at the time he took over as chair of the Wooster board, he became a senior vice president of the parent company, Booz, Allen & Hamilton, Inc. Copeland recalled early advice from his predecessor Drushal. "Garber said, 'You can rely on Bill Pocock. He never tells you what to do, but he has opinions that are worth listening to.'" Pocock chaired the board through Copeland's first decade as president and regularly flew his own plane from his home in suburban Chicago to Wooster. According to Copeland: "Bill would come into the office at ten o'clock and say, I'd like to see the following people. I'd say fine. Once in a while I'd say, there's a problem you should know about. He'd go off and visit with all the vice presidents and deans and probably drop in on a few faculty, and then at the end of the day he'd come back and report on what he felt was going on and what I ought to know." Copeland remembered that when Jim Wilson became chairman of the board and asked for suggestions, "I gave him the Bill Pocock model. A month before every board meeting, spend a day on campus, and then be sure you follow up after the board meeting with your presence. . . . Stan Gault did it a different way [because he lived in Wooster], and he was well-informed."

By the end of Copeland's presidency, momentous challenges had been overcome, his twin goals essentially achieved. The Board of Trustees under Stan Gault and well-organized committees was functioning smoothly. (Gault's role is discussed in greater detail in chapter 17.) The College's endowment, which had risen from $15 million to $150 million, and its financial state generally were understood to be more solid than they had ever been. And its academic strength, bulwarked by a faculty more diverse, younger, and more scholarly, had been stabilized. Art historian Lewis reflected a consensus among faculty and trustees: "At heart, Henry was a scholar. Henry respected intelligence. He was very, very good to the faculty, almost too good. . . . He bent over backwards to make the faculty feel that it counted . . . and at a small school that is extremely important." Copeland's decision to give the College nearly two years' notice of his retirement as president appeared to ensure a comfortable transition. There was widespread hope that a new leader, not previously associated with Wooster, would build on a solid foundation with fresh ideas.

But as Scottish poet Robert Burns once wrote:

The best laid schemes o' mice an' men
Gang aft a-gley.
An' lea'e us nought but grief an' pain,
For promised joy.

CHAPTER 16

Searching for a President

Henry Copeland had led a renaissance of the College, but after fifteen years, he was ready to let go. He told Stan Gault, the board chairman, three years in advance. Since Copeland would be a relatively young fifty-nine in 1995, when he planned to retire from the post, his resignation would come as a surprise, so Gault insisted that the president make his decision public as soon as possible.

The sense of the Board of Trustees—and of the College community in general—was that here was an excellent opportunity to bring a fresh face to the institution. No outsider had become president since 1919, when the College reached out to Wishart, the Presbyterian minister from Chicago. His successor, Lowry, was an alumnus, former faculty member, and trustee. Lowry's successor was his deputy, Drushal. And although the search committee had brought several outside candidates to campus the last time, it settled on Copeland, a dean, as the new president. The likelihood of looking for someone unconnected with the College was increased now because no one on campus seemed an obvious choice. The vice president for academic affairs, Stan Hales, had been at Wooster only three years, was never an official candidate, and was not seriously considered.

Gault appointed the vice chairman of the board, Jack Dowd, a Wooster alumnus and Cleveland lawyer, to chair a search committee; Dowd added seven trustees and invited the faculty to select eight of its number. The trustees were Ed Andrew, Marge Carlson, Jim Clarke, John Compton, Steve Minter, Bob Tignor, Jim Wilson, and Dowd. The faculty representatives were Lori Bettison-Varga, geology; Dick Bromund, chemistry; Tom Falkner, classics; Susan Figge, German; Madonna Hettinger, history; Ron

Hustwit, philosophy; Yvonne Williams, political science and black studies, and Mark Wilson, geology, whom the faculty chose as its chairman. It is notable that this faculty contingent, elected by peers, was an all-star team, including some of its brightest young lights and some of its most respected older scholar-teachers.

The search failed. Its ultimate failure is usually ascribed to a clash between the eventual choice and some trustees, but it is also worth observing how strong a role campus politics—in this, Wooster is not unique in higher education—played in the process. It appears that a number of other senior faculty members had campaigned quietly for places on the search committee, and they were disappointed, perhaps even a tad bitter, when "kids" like Bettison-Varga, Wilson, and Hettinger, the last not even tenured at the time, were selected by their peers. Several faculty members on the committee, especially the younger ones, felt under siege from the first day. Wilson, highly regarded though barely a decade into his career at the College, faced the task of reporting the ups and downs of the search to faculty meetings and found contumely heaped upon him. One colleague wept at a meeting as she listened to those open taunts. Looking back as a senior faculty member, Wilson said, "These were the worse days of my life. This was the nadir of my experience at Wooster."

One of the committee's first tasks was to gain professional assistance, a consultant, or headhunter, specializing in academic searches. After interviewing several possibilities, Dowd settled on John Phillips, diminutive, stocky, a touch disheveled, well connected in higher education, a former chief of the National Association of Independent Colleges and Universities, who knew dozens of college presidents and was known to relax with many of them over a cigar and a cocktail or two. Henry Copeland knew Phillips casually from lobbying trips to Washington with other presidents, and he was prepared to assist the consultant when Phillips made his first visit to campus. Copeland remembered that they spent a half-hour in his office, chatting amiably, "and he asked me one question. Could I get him tickets to a Cleveland Indians game?" Copeland answered that he could not; the conversation left him with a sinking feeling about the search, but he knew it was not his business to interfere.

Over some months, Phillips brought forward scores of candidates, and after sorting through 150 or so, and bringing 12 of them to Cleveland for private interviews, the committee decided, as was standard, to invite three to campus, for a presentation to faculty and interviews with students, faculty, and administrators. One, perhaps the most surprising, was a congressman from the South, a second the dean of liberal arts from a Big Ten university, both of whom eliminated themselves. The congressman, who was charming and created some excitement, troubled the faculty, not because he lacked academic credentials—he was Phi Beta Kappa and held a law degree—but because he seemed to think it necessary to brag about how many books he had read, possibly to compensate for lack of a PhD. The dean, favored enough that leaders of the search committee flew to his campus for an additional interview, turned off the faculty and almost everyone else on campus with a style that seemed abrasive and fussy—and because he was, as everyone who met him remembered, boring. In fact, his supporters warned him in advance of his college presentation, suggesting he add a little zing. Then, as one said, "it was boring." (He eventually became president of two different colleges.)

The third candidate seemed the likeliest prospect. He was George Davis—and he carried a big handicap in the minds of some: he was a graduate of The College of Wooster. In 1990 Henry Copeland had invited Davis, a prominent professor of geology at the University of Arizona, to become vice president of academic affairs at Wooster, but at the same time he was offered the presidency of the University of Vermont, which he accepted; the Wooster position went to Stan Hales. Davis's tenure at Vermont lasted only about a year, for reasons that are in dispute. He carried out cutbacks that angered some of the faculty there, but those cutbacks may have been forced upon him by the governing board. As a Wooster undergraduate, Davis had been not only an honor student but also a star athlete, and his wife, Merrily Siepert Davis, one class behind him at the College, was, among other things, a member of the Color Day court. Many senior faculty who had known Davis since his student days supported him strongly. Part of the opposition to his candidacy came from uncomfortable tales that reached the College via Vermont colleagues. But the strongest opposition, ironically, appeared to stem from his outspoken faith in Wooster. As he talked about how much he and Merrily loved the College, some faculty—especially the younger—recoiled. They wondered if he wanted to return the College to his days of the 1960s. As he spoke fondly of chapel experiences, they wondered if he hoped to return to required chapel or somehow to church control— misunderstandings, no doubt, but at a tense time issues nonetheless.

When acrimony on campus made it obvious that the candidacy of Davis, the only survivor from the original three, was also possibly doomed, it became a flashpoint. In early February 1995, Hustwit, the well-respected philosopher, resigned from the search committee in frustration, writing to his colleagues, "I will not participate in the stupidities that are about to follow. There is no possibility of a rational solution to the mess we have created." Praising the Davis candidacy, he continued: "My argument for Davis rests on the strength of the person—and his character and integrity. . . . Junior faculty are worried that Davis will listen to the senior faculty and not to them because of his being an alumnus of the College. While this is an understandable worry, I do not see that result coming from Davis's character nor from his position as a Wooster graduate." Ten days later, he added "a parting admonition" to "either back out of the mess by appointing Davis or restart the search."

The search committee did not accept that advice. Now, although Henry Copeland had given the College more than adequate notice to find a successor—did that give the searchers a false confidence?—his retirement was closing in. Dowd decided that no one who had been in the original pool should now be considered—damaged goods. Not to worry, said Phillips, the consultant; he knew of other viable candidates. This was one of the several mysteries concerning Phillips: if other good candidates were available, why had the committee not heard about them before? The question might have been answered when a standout quickly surfaced: Susanne Woods, vice president for academic affairs at Franklin & Marshall College in Lancaster, Pennsylvania. Woods, it appeared, had declined to be part of the original Wooster search—it cannot be confirmed, but some think it was because she was on the short list for the presidency of nearby Kenyon College—but now she agreed to participate. Not only was she the chief academic officer of a respected liberal arts college, but also her scholarly credentials and administrative experience were impressive: she held a PhD from Columbia University, was a professor of English literature, and had served as director of Graduate Studies and associate dean of the faculty at Brown University, where she founded the Women Writers Project. It was appealing as well that she was not merely an outsider to Wooster but also a woman, potentially the first woman president in the College's history. Invited to the campus, in short order she won over almost everyone and wowed her prospective colleagues in the English department.

On March 1, 1995, the search committee voted, 15–2, to advance the names of both Woods and Davis to the Executive Committee of the board, "with priority given to Susanne Woods." When Dowd informed Davis of the vote, Davis asked to withdraw his name. Five days later, Hustwit, now in an open letter to the entire faculty, stated his reasons for leaving the committee: "I fear that these flawed procedures have led us to an end which was not the result of a fully informed, representative, or rational decision-making process. I am making these statements primarily for my own sake. I feel better having said them." Two days after that, the Executive Committee approved the Woods nomination. In April, the full board acted, and Woods accepted the offer. She would succeed Henry Copeland July 1, 1995.

The rest of this story lies in even more puzzlement, dispute in what occurred over the next couple of months and conflicted memories among those involved. The one piece of important information that no one appears to dispute is that Susanne Woods had a close relationship with a professor of English at Denison University, Anne Shaver. In the 1994–95 Denison faculty directory, Shaver listed Susanne Woods as her partner. It is hard to believe, for someone coming to this many years later, that such relationship was not considered or at least known at the time to the many intelligent people involved in the search. To ask Woods directly about her relationship with Shaver might have been questionable or even illegal. It is stunning that Phillips either did not know about the relationship, which suggests incompetence, or did not tell the Wooster committee he was serving, which suggests unethical behavior. Those on the search committee agreed that any potential ramification of the relationship was never discussed in its meetings. Trustees indicated that they did not know. At the same time, one faculty member of the search committee said flatly, "We knew." A number of leaders in the women's studies program knew as well, because they were familiar with Shaver's work at Denison, but the faculty's sense was that any such discussion seemed unnecessary.

Beyond that, Woods made her social position clear during interviews at Wooster, according to faculty who spoke with her. "She said, 'I am single by choice,'" one professor reported. "She made it as clear as she could." Mark Wilson, their chairman, related a sidelight on faculty attitudes. During the decision process, Lori Bettison-Varga, also on the search committee and his friend and geology colleague, came to his office and hesitantly asked if he knew that Woods was possibly lesbian. Wilson replied that he hadn't known, but he expressed puzzlement. What difference did that make? Bettison-Varga, so tense about raising this question, then hearing this response, burst into tears of relief.

In the first weeks after the Woods selection was announced, rumors abounded. It is pointless to repeat any of these, but it must be noted that questions—cowardly, anonymous—were being raised in letters and electronically. The most common difficulty cited—it seems not just insulting on several levels but quaint in the twenty-first century—was that some alumni and donors would not be pleased with the appointment. Serious discussion was now taking place among leaders of the Board of Trustees, and finally they decided that the situation seemed untenable, which led to negotiations between the board and Woods. On June 29—two days before she was to take office—at a conference call meeting of the Executive Committee of the board, Chairman Gault explained that an agreement "terminating her appointment" had been reached eight days earlier. According to the minutes, "Mr. Gault stressed that in reaching her decision, Dr. Woods had been guided by a conviction that a clear sense of mutual purpose and trust between a President of a College and a Board of Trustees is essential and had concluded that she would serve both her own interests and those of Wooster by withdrawing, and he expressed his concurrence with her assessment." Gault stated that a severance package with Woods, to be paid over twenty-four months, had been agreed to, as well as a confidentiality requirement restricting any further statements by both Woods and the board. The Executive Committee approved the agreement and recommended that the full board accept Stan Hales as acting president, effective August 1, 1995. Gault said he would appoint a new search committee, again chaired by Dowd, with the intent that a new president be selected by early 1996. (Mark Wilson immediately told Dowd he would decline to take any part in the next search.)

These negotiations and the denouement remained guarded all through the spring and did not become public until a deliberately mild announcement came the day before Woods was to take office. As an example of how guarded, consider the experience of Hales, the College's second highest-ranking administrator:

I just remember, by maybe June, by then I'd heard less from her than I thought I might. She had not been on campus. . . . The next clear memory I have was of a day in [late] June. I was in my office in Galpin, Henry [Copeland] came in to me and said . . . "Stan Gault's here and we'd like a chance to talk to you a bit." . . . I expected the two of us were going to walk into his office together and talk with Stan Gault.

But I walked in, and he closed the door after me and didn't come in. . . . The only thought I had in mind was that I was about to be fired. . . . But Stan Gault sat me down and said, "I suppose you've been wondering about Susanne Woods and why you've not heard too much from her in recent weeks." I said, "Yes, I guess I've been a little curious about that. . . ." Stan said, "Well, you should know, she's not going to be coming. . . . She has decided to withdraw from the presidency. And we need to talk to you about being acting president while we do a second search. . . . I said, well, boy, this is a bit of a surprise."

Hales discussed the offer with his wife, Diane, that evening and confirmed his acceptance—which led to twelve years as president of the College.

Although the announcement of the Woods withdrawal occurred during the summer, it hit hard with the faculty, especially women. Jenna Hayward, a leader in the English department, said, simply, "We felt betrayed." Susan Figge, one of the founders of the women's studies program and then dean of the faculty, remembered that Deb Hilty, daughter of a prominent Presbyterian minister, tenured professor of English, and at that time also secretary of the College and of the Board of Trustees, came into her office, and, "We wept together. We wept. We were so angry. We were so angry." Memories now are bitter at several levels. Woods is thought to have felt ill treated by the College. (Because of the confidentiality agreement, she cannot address the issues.) Some committee members insist she had told them she knew little or nothing about Wooster before being brought into the search, which they found disingenuous, considering that she had a friend at Denison.

At first, the decision attracted little attention off campus except for area newspapers. But on August 4, 1995, the *Chronicle of Higher Education,* which considers itself the *Wall Street Journal* of higher education, published a major story that made Wooster a subject of national attention. It was headlined, "Public Job, Private Life, Wooster's President-to-Be Bows Out Amid Talk of Relationship with a Woman." The story quoted Wooster faculty women who reported themselves "shocked and dismayed," as one put it, by the outcome. It also quoted an anonymous source saying that when trustees hired Woods, "they did not know, or did not fully understand the nature of her relationship with Anne Shaver. Colleagues say Ms. Woods is a very private person who does not describe herself as a lesbian or discuss her sexual orientation. But Ms. Shaver . . . does identify herself as a lesbian. . . . The two have attended campus functions together at Denison. They own property together and some of Ms. Woods's colleagues [at Franklin & Marshall] describe them as partners." Although noting that some in higher education thought Wooster could suffer "negative publicity," the *Chronicle* story also offered an explanation: "Others suggest, however, that no college's trustees would have been entirely comfortable with a situation so delicately nuanced and potentially difficult, as Ms. Woods's."

The question will always remain, of course, of what effect the Susanne Woods episode had on the College. From a twenty-first-century vantage point, the entire affair seems anachronistic; many successful college presidents today are openly gay or lesbian. Still, it should surprise no one to hear that long after the event, there continued to be disagreement. Woods renewed a productive career at other institutions, although she never received a presidency. A number of faculty believe that the episode continued to quietly punish the College over the years—that they found in recruiting that Wooster was losing professorial prospects skeptical of the institutional image publicly portrayed. Others, however, although obviously disappointed by the attention, believe that in the context of its long history this episode seems less significant than it appeared at the time. Setting aside the unknowable, Stan Hales's presidency produced the largest capital campaign in the College's history, a dozen new or renovated buildings, and new academic programs. And the subsequent presidency of Grant Cornwell built success and optimism from the start, increased respect for the institution, strengthened the student body, and established a footprint to the world. This is to say, in the long view, the College bounced back, learned lessons, and prospered.

CHAPTER 17

The Legacy of a Hometown Boy

In examining the trajectory of The College of Wooster since the middle of the twentieth century, a handful of names stand out, starting, of course, with Howard Lowry. But if Lowry provided the intellectual force that began Wooster's ascendance to the highest echelons of liberal arts colleges, Stan Gault's impact on the institution is virtually immeasurable—both as a financial contributor and as a strategic advisor to presidents and the longtime leader of the Board of Trustees. One has only to wander the campus to make an initial judgment: Look to the Gault Alumni Center, the Gault Family Admissions Center, the Gault Manor residence hall, the Gault Recital Hall, the Gault Recreation Center in the Scot Center, and of course the Flo K. Gault Library for Independent Study, named in honor of Stan's wife of more than sixty years. Each of these facilities was constructed with a principal gift from Stan and Flo Gault, but that barely begins to describe this local-boy-makes-good story.

Stan Gault grew up in Wooster, on College Avenue a short walk from campus and one block from the Compton family home. His father was one of the founders of a little company that made toy balloons, which became the Wooster Rubber Company, then Rubbermaid, Inc., but he sold his interest prematurely and during the Depression was essentially broke. So Stan helped to support the family—mowing yards, trimming gardens, shoveling snow, starting and maintaining furnaces, washing kitchen floors on Saturday afternoons, carrying the longest paper route in town, working odd jobs for the city of Wooster and the Ohio Agricultural Experiment Station. He enlisted in the Army Air Corps upon graduation from Wooster High School in 1943 at the age of seventeen, but the Air

Corps required him to wait until he was eighteen, so he had time for one year at the College up the street, where a small scholarship helped with tuition and jobs at Babcock and Holden paid for room and board. In 1944 Gault became a gunner with one of the early squadrons of the B-29 Superfortress in the South Pacific. Discharged in early 1946, he was back in college by summer and accelerated his course load to finish with the class of 1948. The next year, he and classmate Flo Kurtz were married. As a senior, Gault was president of his class, president of the Geology Club (his major), and president of his Seventh Section, admittedly a "rough and tough" section even by the standards of hard-bitten war veterans who did not always follow Wooster's old-fashioned rules of decorum.

One day that year, Stan walked in on the section's regular poker game and noticed a suspicious newcomer. "He's a snoop, he's a snitch, get him out of here," he told friends. Sure enough, Stan was soon summoned to the office of Dean of Men Racky Young and as leader of the section was threatened with expulsion. A few days later,

> We were walking down to the Shack. And just as we passed the Rock, here comes Howard Lowry, big black coat on, full-length, big black hat on. We said, "Good morning, President Lowry." . . . And he said, "Stan, is there gambling going on in Seventh Section?" And I said, "Not any more." . . . He said, "Thank you." Then I turned around and went down to the Shack. I made a telephone call when I got there. I said, "I want everything that appeared to be about gambling out of that building in the next hour. Tables and all the things like that."

So Stan Gault did not get expelled from The College of Wooster.

Upon graduation he passed up a geology fellowship at the University of Pittsburgh and after a brief stint at Republic Steel began as a sales trainee with General Electric. From selling GE toasters in Akron and managing advertising and sales promotion in Cleveland, he sailed up the corporate ladder, one supervisory job after another, leading operations at the major facility in Louisville, until in 1978 he became senior vice president of GE's Industrial Products and Components Sector at headquarters in Connecticut. Gault was clearly on the short list for the top job at GE, but the chairman who had been his primary supporter retired early, and a different chairman made a different choice. Already a director at Rubbermaid, he was brought home by Don Noble, who was retiring as the company's CEO, to become chairman of the board and chief executive officer. Building on Noble's base, Gault created new product lines while selling off unproductive ones, bought companies whose products he admired, visited plants all over the world every year, extended the company's sales outlets from 60,000 to more than 125,000, and persuaded consumers that Rubbermaid products did not fail, which among other things allowed the company to charge more than others did for a similar product. The stock price (adjusted for splits) that had been less than $2 a share in 1980 was more than $50 a share when he retired in 1991; a $1,000 purchase in 1980 was worth $25,567 on March 31, 1991.

A director of Goodyear Tire & Rubber in Akron, Gault was persuaded to accept the CEO's mantle there, and at the age of sixty-five set off energetically to put the famous but now struggling tire maker back on its feet. (Here, Flo laid down the law. They weren't moving to Akron, and he was too old to drive the thirty-five miles on winding, two-lane roads back and forth each day, tired as he would be. So he took on a driver, which enabled him to call Goodyear sites all over the world for two hours every day.) Goodyear had just suffered its first loss in fifty-eight years, owed $1 million a day in interest, and was near bankruptcy; Gault introduced new products, paid down debt, and even changed the color of its iconic blimp (which, not coincidentally, cruised over the Wooster campus on the day Gault received an honorary degree in 1993). Gault spent five years running Goodyear, in what, as they say in the business world, was a classic turnaround job. He also accepted appointments from Presidents Nixon, Reagan, and Bush and collected a bevy of business achievement awards. He immersed himself in endless eleemosynary pursuits, most of them in the Wooster and Wayne County community. For instance, the new Wooster High School campus, opened in 1994, contains the state-of-the-art $5 million Gault Family Fitness Center, and Stan's old Beall Avenue elementary school, abandoned by the school board, was remodeled into the Gault Family Learning Center to serve a variety of needs for families near the poverty line. Still, he gave primary attention to his college alma mater. After serving regularly as a class agent, then an alumni trustee, he rejoined the Board of Trustees in 1972 and became vice chairman under Bill Pocock. He chaired two major fund-raising campaigns and in 1988 succeeded Pocock as board chairman, a position he held until he assumed emeritus status in 2000.

Gault exerted consequential influence as chairman, but in no area quite as much as development. The chief development officer, Sally Patton, had earlier mentors: Henry Copeland, Grace Tompos, Bill Pocock. But for much of her career, Patton worked with Gault, as he chaired two campaigns and was the actively involved honorary chairman of a third, and she is unstinting in her admiration. "The thing about Stan, for anyone who knows him, he's a hometown boy at heart. He grew up in Wooster, he loves Wooster, and he loves being able to make things happen for people who have not been as fortunate or as hard-working as he is." And she saw another component. "For someone who has had as many people doing his bidding as he has had most of his working life, he is remarkably attentive to details, and the importance of details. In dealing with people, there is no way to be too hands-on, to do too much, or care too much. Stan absolutely gets that, to his core." Similarly, Copeland remembered how much Gault helped him as well as Patton in development. Besides the mentoring, "he was always ready to write another letter," Copeland said. And he signed thousands of letters to prospective contributors and spoke at dozens of meetings.

The College set a goal of raising $50 million during the 1980s. It began with the Campaign for Wooster, from 1979—the newly minted vice president's first year on the job—to 1984; in what amounted to the College's first ever comprehensive campaign, it reached out to all alumni to raise funds for endowment, buildings, and operations. The four development professionals—Patton; Tompos; and two directors of development, Frank Knorr and Howard Strauch—separated the country into sixty-five areas, with about three hundred to five hundred people each, and recruited leaders for each. All but three of those leaders made the trip to campus for a spirited weekend training session. Dean Hopkins, a longtime trustee and an authority on estate planning, joined with Tompos for a planned-giving seminar; Pocock and Patton talked about solicitation. They role-played everything, how to arrange for an appointment, how to discuss the College's needs, how to ask for money. "Remember," Patton cautioned, "after you've made the 'ask,' the person who speaks first loses." Given the tiny professional staff and its inexperience for such an effort, the enthusiastic and tireless response of volunteers was crucial. Patton soon knew without doubt how much so many alumni cared about their College.

The Campaign for Wooster goal was $32 million, and the result was an over-the-top $36 million, enough to renovate Scovel Hall and Taylor

Hall and several residence halls and to endow chairs in history, geology, religious studies, and French; it also added endowment funds for faculty research and scholarships. By the end of the decade, the $50 million goal was comfortably topped; the College had raised $65 million, enough to fund Scheide Music Center, build Luce Hall, and retrofit the Frick Library into an arts center. The endowment, which had totaled about $15 million when Copeland became president and $19 million when the decade began had reached an almost undreamed-of $75 million—aided by a rising stock market and surviving the 1987 market crash.

Next came Wooster's Campaign for the 1990s, again led by Gault and Patton and coinciding with the final years of the Copeland presidency; the goal was twice that of the previous campaign, or $65 million. At its conclusion in mid-1996, it had exceeded its target by more than $10 million, through gifts and pledges from nearly ten thousand individuals (almost all of them alumni), foundations, and corporations. The Flo K. Gault Library for Independent Study rose from this campaign, thanks largely to the Gault family's $5.25 million contribution, then the largest single gift ever received by the College. A dozen other gifts of more than $1 million each helped convert Severance Gymnasium into the Ebert Art Center, convert the Frick Library from an art center to a science library, and renew and expand Severance Chemistry for a second time. Among the contributions to endowment were no fewer than three in honor of Copeland, who had retired as president a year earlier: the Henry Jefferson Copeland Campus Minister position; the Henry J. and Laura H. Copeland Chair of European History; and the Henry Copeland Fund for Independent Study, which provided research and travel assistance for I.S. seniors, something even Howard Lowry could hardly have hoped for.

Ambition (and inflation) led to Wooster's first campaign of the twenty-first century, the culmination of Patton's three decades in charge of development. This time a campaign was to have a name that reflected the College's unique academic characteristic: "Independent Minds: The Campaign for Wooster." Once again the planners, chaired now by veteran trustee and experienced businessman Jim Clarke, established a goal—$122 million—nearly twice that of the previous campaign, which had ended only four years earlier. When this effort closed in 2007, coinciding with the end of the Hales presidency, it had collected about $147 million, also nearly twice that raised only a decade earlier. The $50 million in capital funds produced an astonishing building boom—a full-scale renovation of Kauke Hall; a new academic building, Morgan Hall; two new dormitories, Bornheutter Hall and Gault Manor; the Longbrake Student Wellness Center, and the Gault Admissions Center. The nearly $57 million poured into endowment funded seven new professorial chairs—in black studies, classics, economics, Spanish, and theater, plus two visiting positions to aid the faculty leave program; seventy-eight different scholarships, and twenty-seven special funds to support lectures, music, and the arts. Over seven years, the campaign attracted nearly fourteen thousand donors, among them twenty-one (including couples) who contributed more than $1 million each. Together, members of the Board of Trustees gave more than $1 million specifically to honor the retiring president by endowing the R. Stanton Hales President's Discretionary Fund. As the campaign closed (just before the Great Recession of 2008), Wooster's endowment was $278 million, about eighteen times higher than it had been when Patton became vice president.

One casualty of the campaign was the field house, for what seemed the umpteenth time. There was a reason. The keystone contribution, $9 million, came from the Walton Foundation—Stan Gault had served many years on the Wal-Mart Board of Directors, and Henry Copeland was a longtime friend of Rob Walton, chairman of the company board and a former Wooster student and trustee—but the foundation laid down three conditions: First, $1 million should go toward endowed scholarships; second, the $8 million remaining must be matched; third, the money could not go for a field house; every high school wants a new gym, its executives said. The Walton gift and its match, totaling $16 million, were earmarked to renovate Kauke, which Patton recalled as "the most successful project I've ever done." When the total price for the work became $18 million, including the Old Main Café, the remaining funds came from the sale of inscribed bricks on a wall outside the coffee shop, at prices ranging from a few dollars to a few hundred dollars. The project was well oversubscribed.

Every college and university hopes for someone who can make what development officers call the "transforming gift." (The first one occurred when a Puritan named John Harvard gave a few books to a school in Cambridge, Massachusetts.) A century ago, such a gift might have been in the hundreds of thousands of dollars; today it is more likely to be in the hundreds of millions. No such single gift came from Stan Gault or anyone else at Wooster. But Gault's contributions over the years, both the literal dollars from his accounts and the contributions he shepherded, come as close as Wooster has known—and that is without accounting for his influence in other, frequently unheralded ways. It is not merely the several buildings bearing his name that leave their mark on the College. It is not even the facilities that bear the Rubbermaid name—among them the Student Development Center; how might Rubbermaid have been influenced to make such a contribution? Influence? The Burton D. Morgan Foundation, whose namesake patron had no connection to Wooster until Gault joined its board in the 1980s, contributed $8 million. (Another College trustee, Wooster businessman Dick Seaman, was also an influential member of the Morgan Foundation board.) The Timken Foundation, the philanthropic arm of a company on whose board Gault served, funded the gymnasium as well as the renovation of the College's old library into a science library. There was the Walton Foundation gift. And Bob Ebert, a childhood friend of Gault's and once perhaps the largest individual shareholder in Rubbermaid, funded the Ebert Art Center.

As the ubiquity of the name on campus suggests, when Stan Gault saw a need, he simply set out to satisfy it—sometimes with a fillip. For years, College applicants had to find their ways into crowded Galpin Hall and wait in small spaces for interviews, while various members of the admissions staff were strung in different offices around campus. At the extraordinary gala in his honor in 2000, as he moved to emeritus status on the Board of Trustees, Gault announced to the audience that he had a surprise: he and his wife Flo would give the campus the Gault Admissions Center. He wanted it friendly, so it was built to look like a home, complete with front porch. He wanted it comfortable, so the restrooms are unusually roomy. And he wanted it to make a statement, so it was constructed at the corner of College and Pine, the southern edge of the new campus mall, as a bookend to Kauke Hall at the northern end, even to the point of its octagonal notched tower, added to mimic those of Kauke.

Beyond the big campaigns, behind the scenes, Gault was instrumental in countless decisions, from the mundane to the critical. The sight of overflowing garbage containers outside Kenarden Lodge angered him enough to demand action. So, with his son Steve Gault as the trustee chairman of the Buildings and Grounds Committee and Beau Mastrine, director of campus grounds, leading, Wooster became one of the most impeccably maintained campuses in the nation. The sight of McGaw Chapel looking, as some said, like a sugar cube led Gault to quietly pay for painting and shrubbery around the building. He chose Jim Wilson to be his successor as chairman of the board. Gault's style as chairman could be casual yet firm. He would make certain to visit the president's office about once a month, just to chat. He also took the board's committee structure particularly seriously, making sure it functioned properly.

Ted Bogner, president of the company that has supervised almost every major building element at the College for decades, offered another knowledgeable take on Gault's contributions. Discussing the institution's planning, he observed that the process that culminated in the late twentieth and early twenty-first century building boom had been led by Henry Copeland, president for eighteen years; Bill Snoddy, then vice president for finance and business; Patton; and Gault. "An awful lot of planning that went into this was not done by the [official] campus planners. It was really done by a bunch of locals," Bogner said. "Most of these good ideas came from Stan Gault. He knew what he wanted to do. That's the reason this was so successful, because obviously it takes money. So [in many ways] the 'campus planner' was also the CEO of Rubbermaid and Goodyear. There was no campus master plan other than what was in his head." There are a number of colleges and universities in this country that bear the name of someone who made the transforming gift, including such famous institutions as Stanford, Vanderbilt, Tulane, and Duke. Wooster won't change its name, but the name of Gault will be, like Lowry, forever an integral part of its history.

CHAPTER 18

In the Long Run, We'll Be Fine

Stan Hales inherited a tough task. He was following the presidency of Henry Copeland—which had been a success in every measurable way—but not following it directly; rather, it had been an academic year of curiosity about who Copeland's successor might be, then a spring fraught with anger and anxiety about the failed transition. During what could hardly be termed a summer holiday, gossip and rumor took hold, and not merely among faculty. Even students, who might not have fathomed undercurrents of the issue, sensed something was unsettling as they returned to school. Faced with his unexpected responsibilities, Hales spent the summer pondering his first official appearance as interim president, standing at the lectern in McGaw Chapel, August 29, 1995, for the opening convocation of the 1995–96 academic year. "I sensed that there was this overriding concern on campus that the College was in a state of emergency. . . . But Henry had done such a superb job that the College was in a position of strength. . . . [So besides] doing the regular parts of the job . . . I had this [other] obligation to calm down this sense of emergency in the community, reassure people that the College was going to be OK."

Hales came up with what he likes to call his "crazy monkey" speech, officially titled, "In Case of Emergency." After evaluating emergencies large and maybe not so large, he noted that Wooster had suffered through one real emergency, when Old Main burned down, and had survived and prospered.

In early July of this year, about the time that Wooster began to experience a new crisis, a friend of mine sent to me an aphorism meant as consolation, "Life, she is a crazy monkey face." . . . I believe I know its meaning for us. . . . Crises can arise, and then shift and change like the frantic and plastic face of a crazy monkey. They may be true emergencies, or they may be something less. But we should remember . . . that we are intelligent people, able to analyze problems and construct creative solutions even in difficult circumstances.

Not long into his interim year, Hales told trustee Jack Dowd, chairing the renewed search, that he would be an open candidate for the presidency. The committee was reconstituted with most of the same trustees, but with four (instead of eight) new faculty representatives and, now, two student members and two non-academic staffers.[1] The faculty members were Dick Figge, professor of German; Joanne Frye, professor of English; Hank Kreuzman, associate professor of philosophy; Arn Lewis, professor of art. The staffers were Pam Allison, an office manager, and Gary Thompson, director of human resources. The students were Benjamin "Jamie" Christensen and Andrea "Andi" Reinhart, both seniors. This time the College chose as its consultant John Chandler, the distinguished retired president of Williams College. A friend and colleague to numerous leaders of higher education, Chandler assembled another list of more than a hundred possibilities, including a few candidates who applied personally in response to public advertisements. Once more, the committee narrowed the list to a dozen or so who were interviewed in person, after which five were reinterviewed and three invited to campus.

One was a provost at a leading midwestern college. A second was a liberal arts dean from a major university, young, smart, and attractive, who impressed the faculty and charmed the students. The other was Hales, who, understandably, described his position as awkward: "Being an internal candidate is infinitely harder than being an external candidate." Why? "You're so much more exposed. If you're an external candidate, you come to campus, you come fresh, you've not heard any of the conversations that have preceded your visit, you do your talk, and your meetings, and you go home. . . . Whereas if you're an internal candidate, try or not, you hear

1. Some of the description of this search is personal, because I was a trustee member of this second search committee, although not of the first one. The other trustees were the same, except Clarke did not participate.

the things people say and are thinking about you as a candidate, both before and after your visit. You pick up things . . . [laughing] the student newspaper carries everyone's reaction to your visit."

At its critical final meeting, the committee was confident about both of its two final choices, the liberal arts dean and the acting president, but split evenly. Hales was well liked on campus and much appreciated for his steady performance during the traumatic period following the first search, qualities that appeared to turn the decision in his favor. The College had been burned in its earlier determination to choose an outsider—an important memory to some trustees—and here was a known quantity, someone who had demonstrated that he could guide the campus during difficult times. So the search committee, then the Executive Committee of the board, and then the Board of Trustees, on March 7, 1996, voted to remove the "interim" tag from Stan Hales's presidency.

Hales was a native Californian who had attended Pomona College and entered the mathematics doctorate program at Harvard in the fall of 1964. In the middle of his third year, Pomona invited him back to fill a math instructional position, and while teaching full time he completed his Harvard PhD dissertation in graph theory (the broader field is combinatorics). In only his sixth year at Pomona, he was offered a newly created associate dean position; thus, Hales, who had envisioned a career as a professor in a liberal arts college, took a new route as a college administrator. Upon his return to California to teach in 1967, he married Diane Moore, whom he had first encountered on an adjoining badminton court when he was seventeen and she eleven. Let it be understood: this was not hook-up-a-net-between-two-trees-after-a-backyard-cookout badminton. This was a competitive sport played among a dedicated coterie in the United States and with nationalistic fervor in places like Indonesia and Singapore; since 1992 it has been an Olympic sport. This couple was dedicated. Stan, rangy and competitive, won the national eighteen-and-under championship twice, then won the national men's championship twice. Diane, tiny and competitive, had her first child in 1969 and two years later won the national women's championship, so the two were national badminton champions at the same time.

After his championship career ended, Hales remained an international leader in the sport, even many years later when he became a leader at Wooster. In 1985 he was elected president of the U.S. Badminton Federation, then to the council of the International Badminton Federation; he also umpired international matches. During Hales's early years as vice president for academic affairs, he traveled to Asia three times a year and spent a week at a time in Europe. In retrospect, he said that President Copeland "tolerated me, I guess. . . . I hope he felt that it was valuable for Wooster's reputation to have a vice president out around the world doing things." It wasn't until 1999, by which time he had been president of the College four years, that his serious badminton involvement ended, primarily because, as Hales remembered, "Stan Gault said to me, we're concerned about your being gone too much."

The road to Wooster for Hales had begun many years earlier. As an associate dean at Pomona, he served under Bob Voelkel, Wooster class of 1954, Pomona's dean (chief academic officer) at the same time that Fred Cropp, Voelkel's classmate and close friend, held the same responsibilities as vice president for academic affairs at Wooster. Separated by more than two thousand miles, Pomona and Wooster were enough alike, Hales said, that Voelkel and Cropp "were in constant contact, trading ideas. I'd have meetings with Bob, and he'd say, 'At Wooster they're doing this.'" (Voelkel died of a heart attack in the fall of 1987 at the age of fifty-five; Pomona named its varsity basketball gymnasium for him.) Thus, when a recruiter called in 1989 to say that Wooster was searching for an academic vice president, Hales was more than interested.

Among his first assignments after he arrived in the fall of 1990 was a paper outlining prospects for adding an Asian language; Japanese and Arabic were among those considered before Chinese became the choice. Dealing with the faculty was clearly the vice president's principal task, no element more important than chairing the Teaching Staff and Tenure Committee, with its responsibility for recruiting and hiring new faculty and making promotion and tenure decisions. Hales was completing his fourth year as vice president by the time the search for Copeland's successor had begun, and although he had considered the possibility of a college presidency, he thought it more likely that the opportunity would come from somewhere other than Wooster. Then came the failed search, and by the second go-round he declared himself open to the Wooster job.

Once the interim year was completed and his appointment made effective for the 1996–97 academic year, Hales understood that he faced two obstacles beyond his control: he was not a woman, as some faculty members (including some men) had hoped for, and he was not an out-sider, or fresh face, as most had wanted. "I realized that there was at least some fraction of the faculty that had real doubts and were upset about this. I knew that I had, from that point on, to do a strong job of calming things down and reassuring people." So he plunged into his new role, as anyone who knew him would have expected. "You had to start by knowing everybody. If you didn't know everybody, you'd immediately start losing people's confidence in your oversight of the institution. . . . If anyone in the community felt that they weren't known by or appreciated by the president, then you've lost them." At the time Wooster enrolled about eighteen hundred students, and it can be estimated safely that Hales knew hundreds of them, probably most of them, by face and name. The faculty numbered about 130, and the full-time support staff nearly 400 more, and Hales counted on knowing them all. "I have to confess I didn't know all the part-timers," he confessed. Badminton helped; he would go to the gym late at night or early in the morning, so he knew all the custodians. "It's just part of my belief in the nature of the institution. It was not the kind of thing that got you points in public ways, but it was an investment in the strength of the community."

Another critical early task was to find his own successor as the chief academic officer. Given that Hales was an insider—and conscious of the faculty disappointment that an outsider had not become president—this meant off-campus recruiting. "The chorus of people worried about . . . too much of an internal thing would have been too much to overcome." That meant bypassing his good friend and regular tennis partner Hayden Schilling, historian, faculty leader on several levels, who had served as admissions director and stepped forward as academic vice president for a second time during the search that had led to Hales. "It was hard because I respected Hayden so much, and he'd done such good things as an act-ing vice president," Hales said. But he constituted a search committee for the job, which led to the appointment of the sociologist Barbara Hetrick, who had been at Hood College in Maryland, the first woman to serve as chief academic officer at Wooster.

The start of Hales's presidency included an ending as well—the wrap-up of Wooster's Campaign for the '90s, which had been led by Copeland, Sally Patton, and Stan Gault. Before long, however, it was apparent that a new campaign should be started. Again Patton would direct operations,

President Drushal addressing, and calming, students in Lowry Center at a tense rally after the killings at Kent State (1970)

Students, black and white, on football field at Homecoming, protesting perceived racism (1972)

Coach Boles's "four horsemen," from left, Johnny Swigart, Mose Hole, Carl Munson, and Art Murray; below: Maria "Doc" Sexton, leader of women's athletics at Wooster and nationally (1989)

Above: Basketball coach Al Van Wie celebrating a conference championship (1971); right: Steve Moore, who has compiled the best winning record of any college basketball coach in the twenty-first century

Joanne Frye (left) and Carolyn Durham, at a turning point for feminism at Wooster (1982)

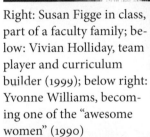

Right: Susan Figge in class, part of a faculty family; below: Vivian Holliday, team player and curriculum builder (1999); below right: Yvonne Williams, becoming one of the "awesome women" (1990)

Left: Historian Hayden Schilling in class—his was a Renaissance career; above: Don Harward, who brought new life to the curriculum (1985)

Left, above: Geologist Mark Wilson, scholar and teacher (1993); left, below: Fred Cropp, academic leader, whitewater leader; above: David Gedalecia, a new identity on the faculty (2000)

Buck Smith, to the financial rescue

Sally Patton knew more Wooster alumni than anyone else, ever (1985)

Hans Jenny: imaginative budgets, unusual life (1982)

Bill Snoddy, honest broker (1967)

Above: First Lady Lolly Copeland and President Henry Copeland; right: Flo and Stan Gault with model of the Flo K. Gault Library (1995)

Stan Hales, happily with students

Board leaders Marge Carlson and Jim Wilson (2000)

Left: The cold comfort of filling the Arch (1984); below: Kilt-clad Scot band heading over the hill to the gridiron

Grant and Peg Cornwell, the new team (2007)

Above: Scot Center: Every student, every day (2012); below: Presidents Copeland, Cornwell, Hales at the Final Four (2011)

Board chairman Dave Gunning

and now trustee Jim Clarke would be chairman, with Gault as "honorary chairman." By this time, Patton was a tireless veteran, vice president for development for more than two decades, respected speaker and consultant to colleges across the nation, tested by two successful campaigns. Clarke, a leading trustee for more than thirty years, had been an assistant secretary for management in the U.S. Department of the Interior, had helped facilitate the worldwide merger of Price Waterhouse with Coopers & Lybrand, and retired as international executive partner of the resulting global accounting and consulting firm PricewaterhouseCoopers.

As years go by, both dollars and needs become inflated, and as the steering committee laid out twenty-first century needs, the 1960s' $20 million Centennial Campaign seemed almost quaint. The committee identified six capital projects, a major burst of endowment income, and short-term operations needs during the seven-year campaign period. (See chapters 8 and 17 for fuller details on these and other building projects.) Independent Minds: The Campaign for Wooster, produced a shade under $148 million, or more than 120 percent of its $122 million goal. Hales made a number of trips during those years and particularly remembers his "farewell tour" to visit alumni in 2006–7. "It was a dream come true, to be able to transform a campus in every possible way and to be able to show slides on those trips and to share that enthusiasm." He was "the consummate team player, just absolutely a team player," said Patton, adding that he "thought a college campus was the most exciting place in the world." The chairman of the Board of Trustees during the campaign, Jim Wilson, praised Hales's energy. "Stan was great with alumni," Wilson said, adding that the campaign "transformed the campus and raised a lot of money for endowment. It happened on his watch."

Wilson's ascendance to chairman, following Gault's retirement to emeritus status in 2000—Vice Chair Marge Carlson said later, "Jim Wilson is the only person who ever succeeded Stan Gault successfully"—was another transition for Hales to cope with. Wilson recalled that he had almost lost touch with the College until invited to serve on a visiting committee to the economics department, in which he had been a major, then joined the Board of Trustees in 1980, which he would serve as chairman of both the investment and finance committees. He was chief financial officer of three Fortune 500 companies, becoming chief executive of Thiokol before retiring after the company was sold to Alcoa in 2000. Wilson remembered his first years as chairman as particularly challenging. "We had a relatively new president, a relatively new vice president of finance [Bob Walton, who had come in 1999], and a brand-new vice president of academic affairs [Iain Crawford, 2003, following an interim year with Tom Falkner] . . . and then we got into the campaign. . . . I did ask Stan [Gault] regularly for counsel and advice."

Like Pocock and Gault before him, Wilson regularly visited campus, not especially easy, given that Wilson lived in Park City, Utah (and had given up a company plane upon his retirement). He chatted with other administrators and faculty and offered the president his CEO management experience. Coming from different perspectives, they discussed a particular phase of Hales's leadership: attention to detail. Wilson saw it sometimes as micromanaging, spending too much time on details that could be left to others, which allowed matters to pile up. Hales saw it as a legacy of his mathematical training: "It's just a statement on myself as a person. A mathematician, raised to aim for perfection in detail, and not to discount things. . . . So I probably had the tendency not to want to make a decision on some things until I felt I truly understood all the details. . . . But it's probably a fair criticism that there were some decisions that took longer than they should have."

Among the leading examples both associates and Hales himself cited was a delay in personnel decisions, which resulted in part from his personal outlook. "Stan is the eternal optimist, the glass is always half-full," said Wilson, citing an example. "One day I said, 'Stan, you've got to make the change'"; if not, the Board of Trustees might force a change. "Once he realized and decided, 'Yes, I've got to do this,' he handled it very well." In a particular case, Hales conceded a mistake because the person concerned was performing so well. This was Bettye Jo Mastrine, who was his executive assistant as she had been for Henry Copeland before him. Mastrine, who in three decades had worked her way from a clerical secretary to the chief staff assistant in the president's office, was not only effective but also beloved at the College. "In retrospect I would have been very wise to take on an assistant in addition to Bettye Jo," Hales said. "Most presidents I know had at least one if not two more persons. . . . I didn't have anyone like that." Hales's successor, Grant Cornwell, relied on Mastrine's institutional memory, but he brought a chief of staff to the office, spreading the burden. In January 2012, on a gala evening in which the College community was celebrating the opening of the Scot Center, Mastrine did not appear. When she was missed, friends called her son, Erich Riebe, a Hall of Fame basketball star at the College who lived nearby. He found her in her Apple Creek home, crocheting hook in hand, having passed away quietly at the age of sixty-two. The community mourned her in a McGaw Chapel service.

No one doubted Hales's likability, and everyone knew the students loved him, but over the years he was receiving mixed responses from faculty and trustees. Part of the leadership difficulty, as Wilson saw it, could be traced to the fallout from the previous search, when the trustees thought they had found a star yet ultimately had to fall back on a second choice. "I don't think Stan really felt he had a mandate to be president of the College . . . from the board or from the faculty, that it was his college to run with," the chairman opined. This made him, as one former administrator put it, "reluctant to change things, or to push in new directions. He was maintaining, carefully maintaining the structure and the traditions and the past practices of the College." Hales believes that the confidence the Board of Trustees had displayed in appointing him had indeed given him a mandate, which was added to by the confidence that the successful Copeland had shown in choosing him as vice president. "I think part of the mandate came from what had happened in my interim year," Hales said. "I'd tried to work very hard . . . to bring everybody aboard and to reassure them, too. I was trying to use the momentum that I had created in that year."

In the course of "maintaining the structure and traditions" of the College, a number of things did change unmistakably under Hales. One might turn back to Louis Holden's presidency and the rebirth after the Old Main fire to find so much change in the look of the College. The Severance Chemistry and Kauke renovations, of course, and a new academic building, new dorms, a health center, and an admissions center—and something else: a campus mall. Hales recalled scrambling up scaffolding to the third floor of the chemistry building along with Art Lidsky—the planning consultant whose care and imagination helped revitalize the campus—and marveling at the view. "You could see Kauke, you could see University Avenue, and then down College Avenue. We looked at each other, and Art Lidsky kind of said, 'You know, it sure would be nice if we could close that off and . . . make it feel like it was all one college down to [Pine].' I'd had the sense that it was unfortunate that the College seemed to stop at University and everything below . . . seemed like almost an appendage. It was that discussion that led to what we now know as a mall."

Academically, Hales walked a careful line between teaching and research. He believed that teaching needed to be the primary purpose of a small liberal arts college. Yet, he encouraged research by increasing faculty travel and research funds. This ultimately benefited classroom and laboratory instruction and so did support of academic work outside the classroom—such as a forensics program directed by political scientist Mark Weaver, which produced national debate champions. Given Hales's penchant for seeing the best in people, he intervened in the case of a bright young faculty member, praised as a teacher, who had been denied tenure in a close vote within the Teaching Staff and Tenure Committee because she had not published enough. The president, responsible for the final decision, thought she was worthy and confronted her in her office. It turned out she had several articles prepared but found tiny faults in her own work that gave her excuses not to submit them for publication; she suffered from an academic syndrome sometimes known as "publication phobia." He demanded that she send her work off to journals, and within a couple of months two had been accepted for publication. She received tenure.

One of any president's roles is to represent the college in affiliated groups, and Hales carried Wooster's flag high in regional and national higher education organizations. He served as president of the Five Colleges of Ohio Consortium and chairman of the Executive Committee of the Association of Independent Colleges and Universities of Ohio; he chaired the Executive Committee of the Great Lakes College Association and the board of the Association of Presbyterian Colleges and Universities; and he chaired the Executive Committee of the Annapolis Group, the nation's most prestigious association of liberal arts colleges. Such activity, board chairman Wilson said, "contributed a lot toward the growing recognition of Wooster."

Over and over, though, Hales and others at the College came back to his relationship with people, and particularly students, in and outside of the classroom. "Cocurricular, the fact that I enjoyed that and worked at it, it's part of the bigger picture. I thrived in an environment where I had a foot in every single activity of the institution. . . . I was an athlete, so I identified pretty well with all of the coaches." No sport went unnoticed. Some of Wooster's students from India and Pakistan had organized a cricket team, playing informally against nearby schools, but the president wanted something more. So he persuaded a trustee, Bob Wilder, who was also associated with the prestigious Haverford College, to offer what became the Wilder Cup, the cricket trophy passed between the two schools.

What follows is a little tale illustrative of Hales's relationship to students (and badminton) and of Wooster's effect on its alumni. The message was written to the author by Julia F. Jones, class of 1997, on May 9, 2011:

> I played badminton all through high school. . . . Of course I mentioned this in my Wooster application. . . . Well, imagine my surprise when the Vice President for Academic Affairs, Dr. Stan Hales, personally called me on the phone! . . . That personal touch, and the assurance of continued badminton! certainly tipped the scales in Wooster's favor in my mind. During my time at Wooster, whenever I ran into Dr. Hales he always remembered my name and was genuinely interested in how I was doing. And we did even play badminton together on a couple of occasions. . . . Currently I'm working for Church World Service, doing community organizing and educational work in Illinois toward ending hunger, locally and globally. The sense that I, and each student, was important in the eyes of each faculty member has impacted me greatly as I strive to treat everyone with respect and as I work to make sure that even the most basic needs of all people are met.

Susan Figge, professor of German, had been appointed by Henry Copeland as dean of the faculty while Hales was vice president and continued into his term as president, which gave her a special perspective on those years. "The faculty saw him as not only an administrator but a guy out there having fun. And he did have fun. Stan had boundless energy. He created an alumni body for us that is going to love Wooster until they die."

CHAPTER 19

Alpha and Omega

The capstone of the academic program at The College of Wooster, as everyone who knows anything about the College knows, is Independent Study. For more than six decades, it has offered students an intellectual challenge, but more, it has demanded discipline and resilience. If I.S. is the Omega of Wooster student scholarship, the Alpha is a program for first-year students that has gone through a number of iterations, a number of identifications—and is almost as old as I.S.

An important difference between the monumental Independent Study and its freshman bookend is that while I.S. has become a national hallmark for Wooster, the freshman program is similar to that in scores of other colleges, an attempt to pry teens away from rote learning and introduce them to an educational experience that most secondary schools don't offer. In effect the Wooster program started as a replacement for the standard freshman composition courses, good old English 101 and English 102, the subjects of many a student complaint. A 1955 Student Senate survey discovered "an astounding condemnation of Freshman English." That led the College to examine programs elsewhere, the principal model being Lawrence University in Wisconsin, where such a course began just after World War II; in 1956, a new course came to Wooster, called "Introduction to Liberal Studies."

Over the years, the faculty labored to find a program that it was comfortable with, perhaps exemplified by the names by which it has been called. For its first fifteen years, it remained "Introduction to Liberal Studies." From 1970–71 until 1975–76, it was "Freshman Colloquium"; from 1976–77 until 1982–83, "Freshman Studies"; 1983–84, "Freshman Seminar"; 1984–85 and 1985–86, "Liberal Studies and Freshman Seminar"; 1986–87 and 1987–88, the "Wooster Seminar." Beginning with the 1988–89 academic year, the word "freshman" disappeared from the Wooster lexicon, replaced by "first year"; so through 1994–95, it was the "First-Year Seminar." Then in 1995–96 emerged the "First-Year Seminar in Critical Inquiry," the title through 2011–12. Eight names over fifty-six years. As with freshman English, one critical intent of the seminar is to require new students to write, to write a lot. Some elements, though, are different: the seminars demand class discussion, and, unlike English 101 and 102, they are not taught exclusively by faculty of the English department. Because the seminars are led by faculty of different disciplines, with outside speakers added to the mix, students are exposed to a wide range of knowledge and ideas.

The great CBS news producer and communications scholar Fred Friendly directed a long-running television series, *The Fred Friendly Seminars,* in which he proposed a challenging issue to a panel of authorities and, like a tough appellate judge, demanded responses that made their hard-held views difficult to defend. In short, he liked to say, he would create "an agony quotient so high that you can escape only by thinking." Ideally, by whatever name it has been called, that is what Wooster's program has always intended to do: force first-year students to think.

Although some thought Lowry was lukewarm about the replacement of freshman English with the new course, Lowell Coolidge of the English department rallied the faculty for Introduction to Liberal Studies: "More often than not, the entering student has only the vaguest notion of what a liberal education is about," said Coolidge. "He needs to be intellectually aroused, to be made aware of the great questions which are the common concern of the various academic disciplines. Once he is aware of these questions, techniques for dealing with them become meaningful. . . . The first object of the course, therefore, is to bring the freshman into contact with ideas, to introduce him to what President Lowry has called 'the humane themes.'" In its initial incarnation, Liberal Studies was something of a "Great Books" course. The first semester reading list included Thoreau's *Walden,* Sophocles's *Antigone,* Plato's *The Republic,* and *The Book of Job;* the second semester, Benedict's *Patterns of Culture,* Mill's *On Liberty,* Heilbroner's *The Worldly Philosophers,* Dostoyevsky's *The Brothers Karamazov,* and Arnold's *Selected Poems.*

The classes, fifteen or sixteen students, met twice a week with their professor for informal discussion of the reading, and a third session brought in a guest speaker to lecture on topics related to the reading. In the first semester, short essays were required; these were followed by a "fully documented reference paper" in the second. "The total amount of writing is probably somewhat less than in the typical composition course," Coolidge admitted, "but it is far more purposeful. Trivial topics are automatically excluded." It is a virtue of the course, Coolidge said, to have faculty from the departments of economics, history, Latin, mathematics, music, political science, religion, and English. "That the professor of economics or of mathematics should be associated with instruction in rhetoric is no anomaly. Indeed it is of very considerable psychological advantage. Too often in the past," he wryly added, "students have assumed a concern for good writing to be a departmental idiosyncrasy safely ignored outside the English classroom."

In an eighth-year evaluation, Ray McCall of the English department, then the program coordinator, wrote, "I still find it easier to say what it is not than to say what it is. It is not a course in philosophy; it is not a Great Books course [although many of the books were the same as in the earlier years]; it is not an indoctrination course." Rather, he said, "Liberal Studies is dedicated to the proposition that intellectual curiosity, with which most freshmen are so abundantly equipped, is a good thing and ought to be encouraged and intensified. Through a program of readings, class discussions, lectures, and writing assignments it tries to demonstrate the interrelatedness of the various branches of learning and to sharpen the student's perspective on certain basic questions that must be posed in any genuine college education." McCall observed that the course might have to be toughened, since the faculty discovered that a growing number of freshmen had taken advanced placement courses in high school and had read books like *The Republic* and *Walden*. And if the students were supposed to think big thoughts, they had developed a sense of humor about it. A cartoon in the *Voice* by Bill Shear showed a freshman preparing an essay, with the caption: "For my first Liberal Studies paper I will write on Man and his place in the cosmos. Of course I realize this is ambitious. But I think I can expand it to 500 words."

Coincident with the College's move to an academic quarter system in 1979, "Liberal Studies" became "Freshman Colloquium" and was reduced to a single quarter from a full academic year. For teachers, the course became more flexible, allowing them to structure the courses toward their own expertise. Possibly for this reason—after all, preparation was easier, since little extra intellectual study was needed—the faculty turnout was strong, thirty-seven professors from seventeen academic departments, including President Drushal and Vice President Hans Jenny. These faculty members also became academic advisors for their dozen or so students, until, as sophomores, they chose their majors. After a lengthy and sometimes heated debate, the faculty voted to grade the course on an S/U (Satisfactory/ Unsatisfactory) basis. The winning argument was that letter grades were hard to decide upon in such a personal course where "quality of mind" counted more than "actual mastery of the content"; the counterargument was that students wouldn't work as hard if all they needed was an S when other courses measured them A to D. Altogether, the somewhat looser course seemed a sign of looser academic times.

Despite the many changes in names, the course remained fundamentally similar to what it had been in the '70s—class discussion, rosters of just fourteen or fifteen students; intensive writing demands; and, for much of the time, faculty members from different departments choosing their own basic topics as well as serving as advisors to the students during their first year or two. When the College returned to semesters in 1983–84, the course became one semester long, never again the full year. In 1985, under the auspices of Don Harward, the vice president for academic affairs, and Glenn Bucher, dean of the faculty, an annual common theme was instituted—for example, "Individual and Community"—and faculty members could configure their courses within that theme and their own discipline. In 1986, a Wooster Forum was inaugurated, at which guest speakers, many of them nationally known, would address some element of the theme, leading to discussion in the small classes. In 1990, under the new dean of the faculty, Yvonne Williams, the program took on a three-year theme, revolving around race, ethnicity, and gender, which meant that instructors did not have to change their course every year. In 1994 came a return to a one-year theme.

It has not been a smooth road. For decades, the faculty appeared to approve of a first-year program in the abstract, but, as the cliché goes, the devil is in the details. Some departments cooperated much more fully than others, holdouts occasionally claiming that it was the English department's responsibility, not theirs, to teach writing. At various times, faculty members have said, they declined to teach the first-year course because it took time away from their departmental courses, it interfered with their research, they needed to prepare for and spend more time advising their I.S. students, their department was short-handed because of faculty leaves—an endless array of reasons. As one veteran professor observed, "The faculty always found a topic everyone can agree to hate." At the same time, many faculty members have been regular and enthusiastic participants, believing that a writing-intensive, discussion-intensive course is just what freshmen needed—that it was, in fact, a stepping stone toward the Independent Study project that would soon be a major part of their academic lives. As historian Madonna Hettinger put it, "With the very first paper, I tell them this is page one of their I.S."

A turning point came in the mid-1990s when more than half the faculty signed a petition to abolish first-year seminar entirely. Susan Figge, professor of German, who had only recently become dean of the faculty, appointed a faculty commission to propose new rules, and in spring 1994 it set forth goals that were approved by the faculty and have been largely in effect ever since. The first-year seminars should strengthen students' abilities "to read a variety of texts . . . with understanding and critical judgment; write clearly and use writing as a tool for the exploration and expression of ideas and arguments; synthesize in writing and in discussion material from several sources . . . ; perceive, analyze, and value the perspectives of other thinkers . . . ; move, in writing and discussion, from the expression of an opinion to the formulation and grounding of an argument; understand the validity and uses of different kinds of evidence; formulate meaningful questions . . . within the topic area."

The 2011–12 catalog explained the required "First-Year Seminar in Critical Inquiry," given annually in the fall semester: "First-Year Seminar provides a unique intellectual opportunity for faculty and first-year students to participate in a small, discussion-oriented, multidisciplinary course. The course introduces students to critical thinking and other academic skills that will be needed in subsequent courses, including Junior and Senior Independent Study. Students are expected to develop their abilities in writing, interpreting complex texts, constructing an argument, supporting the argument with evidence, and defending the argument orally. The course also requires students to appreciate and critique multiple perspectives, including their own."

How long this delineation will survive is anyone's guess. On the other side of a Wooster education, I.S. appears to have survived stupendously well. For one thing, the faculty has never even remotely challenged its very existence. If anything, the faculty—the College itself—is prouder of I.S. in the twenty-first century than it was during its uncertain days immediately following World War II. At his inauguration in 2008, Grant Cornwell, a newcomer capping his first year as president, made that clear: "Our unique educational program that culminates in the senior Independent Study is what we do that makes us who we are. Our excellence is to be understood in those terms. Our integrity is measured in it."

If I.S. has a problem, it is external: too many people outside the College, most seriously prospective students and their parents, appear not to understand it. Admissions officers have discovered over the years that to some outsiders "independent" connotes students somehow being required to work on their own, without assistance. Lowry was aware of this danger from the start. He said, "This word 'independent' causes the plan to be misunderstood in some quarters. The word is not a synonym for loneliness." Although the College tried many explanatory remedies, it suffered to some extent, in modern parlance, from a failure of marketing. Wooster did hit upon a major improvement when, coming out of the turn-of-the-twenty-first-century financial campaign, it adopted the theme "Independent Minds, Working Together." That theme has been continued, with an additional fillip: "America's Premier College for Mentored Undergraduate Research"—"Premier" and "Mentored" emphasized in the typography.

Inevitably, though, this landmark intellectual program has definitely changed—for the better, everyone would agree, not merely I.S. but also the faculty leave program. By twenty-first-century standards, some of the early professorial efforts indeed would seem modest. But as historian Clayton Ellsworth said in 1948, "If the research is well done, it brings prestige to the professor and to his college, and ultimately may be of value to society." And in six-plus decades of research leaves, Wooster's faculty members have reached far beyond their original efforts. They have produced dozens of books, scores of compositions, hundreds of peer-reviewed journal articles. They have taken leadership roles in professional associations. The very idea of an entire, untrammeled academic year for serious research every five years or so, combined with the opportunity to teach bright students, has made Wooster an attractive goal for teacher-scholars. And, as Lowry hoped, the intellectual challenges to the faculty, and its broadened horizons, have come home to Wooster classrooms and laboratories, redounding to the benefit of its students. (See chapter 2 for more on Clayton Ellsworth's description of the academic leave program.)

Like a number of early faculty works, some of the first student I.S. efforts could be looked back upon as not far from lengthy term papers; everyone was feeling his way. But the confidence of both faculty mentors and their students has increased phenomenally, leading to astonishing I.S. results worthy of many a graduate-school thesis. Indeed, considerable numbers of Wooster seniors assist their professors at the level of a graduate research assistant. To highlight the seniors' work, Cornwell postponed his inauguration from the fall, when such events are common, to the spring, connecting the ceremony to an I.S. symposium. So successful was that symposium that it became an annual event—seniors conducting exhibitions, demonstrations, and lectures for audiences from the campus and beyond—classes cancelled so that freshman, sophomores, and juniors could observe what the seniors have accomplished and what was in store for them.

I.S. in the twenty-first century knows no boundaries, either literal or figurative. Thanks to the Henry Copeland Fund for Independent Study, students can travel the nation or the world in their research. And as for boundless imagination, it should suffice to elucidate a tiny sampling of the work performed by seniors—some daring, some dangerous, some charming—in the modern era of Independent Study.

2007–8:

> "Post-Colonial Identity on the Isle of Flowers," Jaimy Stoll, anthropology major and Africana Studies minor—studying race theory on the island of Martinique, the influence of Negritude, and the development of the Creole language.
>
> "Empowering the Uninsured," Nick Weida, self-designed major in economic history—examining the history of health insurance and resistance to it in Tanzania.
>
> "Becoming Paijo," Ryan Barnett, geology—including service on a government team to stop poaching of rhinoceros and elephants in Sumatra, in the course of which he contracted malaria and was stabbed by outlaws.

2008–9:

"The Language of Fat; *La Langue de la Graisse*," Lindsay Galan, double major in French and women's studies—eating disorders as a feminist issue, comparison of French and American attitudes toward women's eating disorders, and asking if it's true that French women don't get fat.

"You . . . Only Better," Sarah Green-Golan, anthropology—examining the culture of cosmetic surgery.

2009–10:

"Sadly, He Isn't Barry Gibb: A Study of Modern Depictions of Jesus . Christ," Chris Weston, religious studies—nontraditional looks at Jesus Christ, including presentation on the satirical television show *South Park.*

"The Two-Higgs Doublet Model and Sonification: Using Sound to Understand the Origin of Mass," Mike Winters, double major in physics and music—using music to better understand the universe.

2010–11:

"Harry Potter and the Prisoner of Gender," Lauren Camacci, communications studies—exploring Harry's relationship with other males.

"What Hip-Hop Teaches Us about Adolescence," Ana-Nicole Baggiano, anthropology—a new way of life, music, clothes, and "a religion of the street."

"The Decline of African-American Players in Major League Baseball," Brandon Jacobs, double major in sociology and communications studies—discovering a series of interrelated and cumulative conditions that lead far away from Hank Aaron and Willie Mays.

"Gourmet Pioneers," Amanda Gottesman, anthropology—the role food writers play in American society.

In his academic manifesto published in December 1945, Howard Lowry wrote: "The new program is democratic and aristocratic at once—aristocratic in that it challenges a student to come to his own best; democratic in that it offers the opportunity and challenge to everyone." It appears to have worked.

CHAPTER 20

Teaching and Research, Well Remembered

Since the moment Howard Lowry recommended, and the faculty approved, Independent Study in the 1940s, a fundamental principle—it can be called a grand bargain—has shaped the role of the faculty: its members must combine attention to and skills in teaching and mentoring students, and they must pursue with energy and ambition scholarly research. This principle has applied, from the College's perspective, to how faculty members have been selected and how they have been promoted. It has also applied to the type of teacher/scholars who have chosen to come to Wooster and have chosen to remain. The principle was valid in Lowry's era, and it continues to be true in the twenty-first century.

Admittedly, the bargain has not been perfectly maintained. No one would contend that every man or woman who stood at the front of a Wooster classroom or laboratory was a flawless, skilled teacher. No one would contend that every woman or man laboring in an office, a library, a laboratory, at Wooster or somewhere else, was adding measurably to the world's storehouse of knowledge or offering fresh insight into accepted knowledge. But a significant number of faculty members have achieved an appropriate balance, to the benefit of both their students and their disciplines. Reports of scholarly associations over the decades note significant contributions from Wooster faculty. And it hardly needs saying that many of the warmest memories of the College carried lifelong by alumni result from their relationships with professors.

Achieving this balance has been, in fact, a continuing source of tension within the faculty. Some professors believe some of their colleagues are not serious enough about scholarship, that they either do as little as possible, or that they undertake relatively simple projects which enlighten no one. And the professors in question may respond by pointing to their teaching abilities as measured in student support or respond that some colleagues pay more attention to research than to students—the latter a complaint more legitimately offered by victimized students at many a large and famous research university.

It is a fool's errand to identify a handful among faculty members who have offered such a bountiful feast of information and insight to generations of Wooster students. A few readers will ask rhetorically: How could you include him or her? A great many more will exhibit dudgeon at the inexplicable absence of their favorite(s). Over several chapters of this story, a number of worthy faculty members have been named. Many are women—the extraordinary group who controlled several departments into the 1950s and '60s, the hardy band who held the fort into the '70s, and their strong-willed successors who have successfully demanded equality and influence in later years. Some are African American; their contributions, occasionally against peer resistance, are identified in chapter 7. Most notable, of course, is the chemist Ted Williams, who must be named again here—not simply as a teacher and scholar but as an advisor to everyone from freshmen and custodians to deans and presidents—indisputably among a tiny group of the most influential figures of the last half-century. Among a number who could be named in the former religion department—an especially sensitive area, given the College's history—are those scholars who led its evolution to the Department of Religious Studies, in particular the historian of religion Gordon Tait and the archaeologist Bob Smith. In recent years, its more cosmopolitan faculty has included Ishwar Harris, who taught Eastern religions, and a rabbi, Joan Friedman, who shared an appointment with the history department.

One way to observe momentous change over the years is to study the application forms required of prospective Wooster faculty. On forms presumably authorized by the Board of Trustees and administration, they were asked until 1948 if they used tobacco and until 1964 if they used liquor or alcohol. Regarding religion: they had to state what church they belonged to, until 1954; what church activities they participated in, until 1964; whether they belonged to any church, until 1978. Ted Williams might have been overly cautious when he admitted using alcohol because every chemist did; it is indisputable that, however they answered the question, some on the faculty before 1964 did use liquor. Others said they ignored certain questions and still got a job. It would appear that the administration made ad hoc decisions depending on need and circumstances.

Illustrative both of the value in paying homage to particular instructors and the touchy path it offers is this message from Gene Bay, one of the nation's leading Presbyterian ministers (and an important advisor in the preparation of this book): "I think of faculty such as Kieffer, Fobes, Spencer, Wolcott, Dunham, Kaslo Osgood, Craig . . . and others more recently. I recognize that some egos of current faculty may be bruised if they are not mentioned . . . I would include something about how the College has managed to attract and retain superior faculty despite modest salaries."

A starting point is that whenever the subject of great teaching at Wooster has arisen, almost always the first name mentioned was Melcher Fobes. A New Englander with a Harvard PhD, Fobes joined the faculty in 1940 and served until 1980, presiding over the Department of Mathematics in Taylor Hall for most of those years—and teaching navigation to navy V-5 cadets during World War II. Beyond the classroom, professors and administrators remembered receiving short Fobes notes of support at difficult moments. Jim Wilson, who became chairman of the Board of Trustees, recalled Fobes advising him into a difficult science course, with which he struggled but which Fobes thought good for him. Hayden Schilling, professor of history and high-level administrator, remembered that as he was considering leaving the South for a small midwestern town he knew nothing about, Fobes, who had been one of Schilling's interviewers, took it upon himself to drive the young man around the city, touting its virtues and making him comfortable.

The Fobes tales are legion. The art historian Arn Lewis recalled a Teaching Staff and Tenure Committee discussion about how to arrange academic contracts for a specific married couple: "Melcher suggested two half-time contracts, saying 'You never know what's going to happen to this relationship.' I said, 'Melcher, this couple is really in love.' Then they divorced two years later. I didn't always agree with Melcher, but there was an integrity to him. He was consistent, he was intelligent, and he could speak without losing control." Then there is the story from Sally Patton, vice president for development, who was entertaining faculty at her home. At one point in the evening, Fobes confided that when he was troubled by an issue he liked to seek counsel from the late president Lowry. The prominent historian

Jim Hodges rushed to question him: "Well, Melcher, what do you say to Howard?" To which Fobes softly replied, "Actually, Jim, Howard speaks to me."

Among other names from Gene Bay's message, one would consider at once Bill Kieffer, a Wooster graduate who taught briefly at the College before leaving for the research university Western Reserve, then was quickly retrieved by the new president Lowry. A lanky man who could be a formidable presence as he leaned over a budding chemist in a laboratory, Kieffer awed and charmed both students and faculty on and off campus. In an era when alcohol consumption was officially forbidden to students and discouraged for faculty, Kieffer's quiet Friday afternoon faculty cocktail parties were a favored respite for a select few. (Years ago, the only place to buy bottles of alcoholic drinks in Ohio was in a state liquor store. The English professor Larry Stewart reported that as a newcomer he was advised by the professor of music Karl Trump that one should not be seen in the state store until he had gained tenure.) Kieffer was frequently invited to teach at research universities—Stanford, Berkeley, and MIT, among them—and he also became editor of the *Journal of Chemical Education,* which meant that every article for this widely read journal had to pass through The College of Wooster. Upon his retirement from the College in 1980—the same time as Fobes, a brutal double loss that led some to fear for the future of faculty quality—Kieffer taught at the Naval Academy and elsewhere before settling into full retirement in California's Oakland hills.

Kieffer was only one of the stalwarts in Wooster's renowned chemistry department, which has regularly ranked at or near the top among independent colleges in the number of graduates who earn PhDs. Roy Grady, who taught from 1918 to 1959 was the first of three Wooster chemists to receive the Catalyst Award from the Chemical Manufacturers Association for excellence in teaching; Kieffer was the second, and Williams the third. The group would include John Chittum, chairman for many years, a conservative Methodist who determined that he would recruit a black professor to the department and the College and found Ted Williams. It could occupy its own chapter, or book, to recite the many accomplishments of Wooster's chemists, but anyone associated with the College would recall such memorable names as Roy Haynes and Dave Powell, who among other things developed a "kiddie chemistry" program for junior high and high school pupils; John Reinheimer, a pioneer in introducing undergraduates to serious research; Monte Borders, a biochemist; Virginia Pett, a computer science authority; Dick Bromund, an oceanography specialist; and Paul Gaus, who not only brought computerized literature searching to the department but also spent off-hours and retirement days writing Agatha Christie–like murder mysteries set in the Amish country of Holmes County in which the shrewd crime-solving hero was a professor at a fictional liberal arts college in Millersburg.

Then came a new generation of chemists such as Judy Amburgey-Peters, Paul Bonvallet, and Paul Edmiston, who invented a product called Osorb, an organosilica—or swellable glass—material that has been nano-engineered to capture contaminants like oil, pesticides, and pharmaceutical products while excluding water. Thus, it can treat water after oil spills, for example, and it is cost-efficient: because of its spongelike quality, it can be squeezed out and reused. Like his colleagues, Edmiston has supervised many students in research, and some of them have conducted directed experiments with the materials. In 2009 a company named ABSMaterials, Inc., was founded to promote the commercialization of Osorb; if it is a success, Wooster could benefit financially.

In considering his students' research assistance, Edmiston said:

> It's a tribute to Wooster, because we do have this caliber of student here. It is not unusual to have a student that is working in the lab in their younger years and going on to great things. I have first-year students working in my lab right now. I just give them the keys to the lab and say, "Go work. Here's what you're going to do." . . . It's the confidence that does it. They're already intelligent. They were born with it. They cultivated it in their high school years. . . . They just need an opportunity to use it. Ted Williams's advice to me was always, "Just don't mess 'em up."

If men like Kieffer were revered as chemists, the equivalents in the also renowned history department would be Aileen Dunham (whose influential career is discussed chapter 6) and Bob Walcott. They shared their scholarship in the classroom; what most of them also had in common were political views that they did not foist upon their students but made no effort to hide elsewhere. Dunham, the longtime department head, was an openly fierce critic of Wisconsin senator Joseph McCarthy before Edward R. Murrow was. Walcott defended presidential candidate Adlai Stevenson in public debate with Howard Lowry and later withheld the fraction of his income tax that he thought helped fund the Vietnam War; his colleagues thought enough of him to establish a Robert Walcott Reading Room (it disappeared during the most recent Kauke Hall refurbishing, as, similarly, did the English department's Lowell Coolidge Room).

Hayden Schilling was something of a Renaissance man—he did things he wanted to do and performed services the College needed. When Schilling joined the faculty in 1964, Dunham pointedly assured him, he recalled with a smile, that it was a one-year contract for that year and the following year as well, indefinitely; he was still teaching in 2012, the Robert Critchfield Professor of English History. That's part of it. Having been a tennis star as a young man, Schilling satisfied a long-held desire to become Wooster's tennis coach in 1980. When, in 1984, the new vice president for academic affairs, Don Harward, wanted to rebuild the admissions office, he identified Schilling and doggedly pursued him to take the dean of admissions position—which Schilling finally agreed to do on the single condition that he would remain tennis coach. After eight years, Schilling went back to the classroom, but when his successor failed, he returned to admissions for another six years. Twice, he served as acting vice president for academic affairs while the College conducted searches for outsiders to fill the place. He was one of the Wooster faculty who volunteered to teach at little Miles College in the 1960s. In the '80s he organized a program that for almost thirty years has introduced disadvantaged inner-city Youngstown teenagers to the College. They come for two weeks every summer through their four years of high school, and their progress is monitored during the academic year; nearly all of them attend college, many at Wooster. In 2006, the Carnegie Foundation for the Advancement of Teaching selected Schilling as Professor of the Year for Baccalaureate Colleges in the United States, the only faculty member in Wooster's history to achieve that recognition. This might have been the capstone of his career, though he kept on teaching—a course he long taught, "Hitler and the Nazi State," sometimes had a waiting list of over a hundred—and coaching tennis.

Although the history department's liberal bent showed in many ways—Dan Calhoun's public statements and writing that occasionally unsettled the Wooster community, Jim Turner's leadership in developing the College's women's studies program—its most distinguishing trait was an intense intellectual camaraderie, frequently expressed in witty barbs. Everyone

learned to take it and give it. After the strong reigns of Dunham and Clayton Ellsworth, the official leadership was tossed around like the prover-
bial hot potato. With such notable carryover from the 1950s as Helen Kaslo
Osgood and Floyd Watts, the powerhouse 1960s additions to the department
included Jim Hodges, an Alabamian with a national reputation for his work
in southern and educational history; John Gates, resident curmudgeon and
military historian—he offered the first courses on Vietnam with military
and social context at a time when students thirsted to learn about that
faraway place—John Hondros, who helped introduce students to southern
Europe and World War II; as well as Henry Copeland, a French historian.
Through the decades the department reloaded: David Gedalecia brought
a new face to Asian scholarship in 1971; Madonna Hettinger arrived in 1989
to bulwark medieval history after that subfield had suffered less successful
efforts by her predecessors; Alphine Jefferson also joined the faculty in
1989, with responsibilities in both history and black studies; followed by
Peter Pozefsky in 1994, Greg Shaya in 2001.

And language. The Department of English, home of such longtime and
deservedly praised teacher-scholars as Lowell Coolidge and Ray McCall,
and George Bradford, who fought in the trenches during World War I
before bringing his gentle touch to poetry and literature. Then came
Paul Christenson; Joanne Frye; and Larry Stewart, who for much of his
four-decade career was a leading figure on the decisive Teaching Staff
and Tenure Committee and taught the always oversubscribed "Children
as Readers" class, which students lovingly called "kiddie lit." And there
were Henry Herring; Dave Moldstad; and Peter Havholm, who not only
energized students in the classroom but also served the College for many
years as editor of the alumni magazine, during which he authored a series
of striking mini-histories of a number of academic departments. Then,
more recently came women such as Deb Shostak, who followed Stewart
as the Mildred Foss Thompson Professor; Jenna Hayward; Nancy Grace;
and Terry Prendergast.

Wooster's foreign language departments have long been a point of pride.
French, once led by John Olthouse, Pauline Ihrig, and Fran Guille, has more
recently been captained by Carolyn Durham, the Inez K. Gaylord Professor
of French Language and Literature, and Harry Gamble. In Spanish, the
beloved Myron Peyton was followed by scholars like John Gabriele, the
inaugural choice to hold the Raymond and Carolyn Dix Professorship.

In German, everyone remembered one of the First Couples in College history—Willy and Clare Adel Schreiber. The longtime chairman of the German department, he never lost his native accent; as an outsider he won the trust of Wayne and Holmes County Amish to become a chronicler of their lives (and an authority on the German beginnings of the Christmas tree); and in 1960 led a contingent of eager Wooster students for a summer in Vienna, an excursion so successful that it continued annually for a quarter century. She had been a journalism major at the University of Illinois and was a frequent reporter of College affairs for both the alumni magazine and the *Daily Record,* but she became something of an aunt to generations of faculty children and children of many other educated families in Wooster as the longtime director of the Nursery School. She worked for more progressive causes in the city than one could count, almost every single day until the day she died in early 2011, a month short of her ninety-seventh birthday. Remarkably, the German department benefited from a second of the most admired couples Wooster knew. Susan and Dick Figge met in graduate school in California and came to the College in 1974. Dick was hired first, then they shared a position, then Susan joined the faculty full time, he becoming the Gingrich Professor, she dean of the faculty. In retirement, he continued to perform as an actor in theaters all over northeastern Ohio and to delight readers with his movie criticisms on a Wooster Web site. She delivered the eulogy for Clare Adel Schreiber.

The other departments contained notables, as well. Economics was once base to men like Alvin Toatlebe and Kingman Eberhart; and Hans Jenny before he moved to administration; then Gene Pollock; Bill Baird; Dick Reimer; Barbara and Jim Burnell; and John Sell, yet another scholar who served the College in many ways, not least as an interim vice president for finance and business. Vivian Holliday was a classicist—who could have predicted her rise from a rural South Carolina background?—and classic team player who team-taught in a variety of departments and served eight years as dean of the faculty, working with Copeland to rebuild the curriculum. Sheila Garg was a physicist and a dean of the faculty who served a year as acting provost. The biologist Don Wise, among other academic contributions led a college-wide self-study as required for renewed accreditation, and one of his key successors, Dean Fraga. Josephine Wright, multi-accomplished, was both the Josephine Lincoln Morris Professor of Black Studies and professor of music; her colleague Boubacar N'Diaye held a joint appointment in black studies and political science; and of course, one must mention Yvonne Williams, a political scientist who created the black studies program. Among Williams's and N'Diaye's political science colleagues were Gordon Shull, the soft-spoken scholar and mentor to many, and Mark Weaver, coach of Wooster's perennially and extraordinarily successful debate teams.

Gordon Collins, whose father had been president of a Presbyterian college, was for decades the mainstay of the psychology department, an athlete himself who volunteered to help coach track and field; followed in the department by leaders like Susan Clayton and Amy Jo Stavnezer, whose work extended across disciplines into burgeoning fields like neuroscience. For more than four decades in the rapidly changing field of sociology (which now shares a department designation with anthropology), Atlee Stroup taught nearly every student who took a course in that department; for two of those decades Chuck Hurst joined Stroup to give the department new prominence. Hurst was joined by Heather Fitz-Gibbon, who became the first dean for faculty development, and Anne Nurse, whose incisive studies of the relationship between incarcerated young people and their families earned national respect; she introduced a course named "Criminology and Deviance"—students called it "the prison class"—in which half the class were Wooster students and half were inmates at the juvenile correctional institution in Massillon. The Department of Communication, led for more than a decade by Denise Bostdorff, is relatively new, yet it traces its origins to the ancient Greeks who studied public speaking and in modern guise teaches students "how to be more effective communicators and how to be critical analysts of communication, thereby preparing them for life as enlightened citizens and professionals in a variety of career paths such as business, education, law, politics, media, and the ministry."

In Scovel Hall lived a seemingly mismatched pair of disciplines: philosophy and geology. Another College legend was Vergilius Ture Anselm Ferm, prolific writer, careful thinker, and tireless teacher, who retired in 1964 as Compton Professor of Philosophy after thirty-seven years on the faculty; he was occasionally the only member of the department at a time when an introductory course in philosophy was required. His successor as Compton Professor was Auburey Castell, whom Lowry seduced away from the University of Oregon in 1963. During his decade at Wooster, Castell mentored Ron Hustwit, an outspoken leader and thinker who joined the department in 1967 and carried it prominently into the twenty-first century, becoming one of the most sought-after I.S. advisors on the faculty; in 1990 Hank Kreuzman arrived to the department, then took leave in 2009 to become part of an administrative reorganization as the College's first dean for curriculum and academic engagement.

Speaking of legends, there came Karl Ver Steeg, who joined the faculty the year Lowry graduated in 1923 and taught geology until his death in the fall of 1952. One of his students, Charley Moke, returned with his PhD in 1936 and taught until 1972, becoming one of the leading citizen volunteers in Wooster. In 1964, alumnus Fred Cropp arrived from Illinois to become a dean and teach what had been his major, geology. Although Cropp went on to become vice president for academic affairs, many alumni likely remember him for the whitewater rafting trips he led for two decades down the Colorado River through the Grand Canyon, voyages that exhilarated hundreds of Wooster alumni, some of whom made more than a dozen jaunts. Excellence in geology was carried into the new century by Mark Wilson, a teacher-scholar respected by his students and peers in the Kieffer-Fobes mode, which is saying a good deal. Each spring, Wilson offers an introductory course (cross-referenced with archaeology) in the largest classroom of Scovel, at 8:00 A.M., hardly a potent time to attract students, but they fight to enroll, as do auditors who beg for any available extra seat. Quaintly called "History of Life," it covers the "origin and evolution of life, with emphasis on biologic innovations and crises in the context of Earth history" and may be the most popular course on campus.

Among the extraordinary departmental tales are those of the fine arts faculties, art and music. The art department bounced through several venues before landing new quarters and a museum in the remodeled Severance Gym, which became the Ebert Art Center, all the while maintaining a particularly close relationship with students. George Olson, who joined the faculty in 1963, was a strengthening force during those transient days. Art also included an academic couple, Walter Zurko as a longtime professor and Kitty Zurko as director and curator of the art museum. The College got lucky in 1968 with the arrival of Thalia Gouma-Peterson. Married to an Oberlin faculty member, she was used at that college as a part-time utility player; tired of that, she accepted a full-time position at Wooster, where she served for thirty-two years as both an artistic and feminist leader. The person best remembered by many students is the art historian Arn Lewis, who came to the College in 1964 and in a stellar thirty-two year career became something more than a teacher: a campus wise man, a leader in Wooster's civil rights and diversity efforts, a calming influence in times of unrest, a confidant to students and presidents.

Like those in the art department, the dedicated teacher-performers in the music faculty suffered through years of agonizingly inadequate facilities—which, however insufficient, could not spoil their record of success. For a long time, the College had tried and failed to find a principal contributor for a worthy building, until Richard Gore, the renowned organist and professor of music, connected Wooster with a New York friend, William Scheide, which led to Scheide Hall in 1995. Actually, Gore's academic roles—his teaching skills, compositions, and bravura organ performances—almost paled in relation to the number of anecdotes he inspired, possibly more than any other single faculty member. Everyone at Wooster knew about his phenomenal memory for all things musical, but the whole country found out when he was offered up as a sacrificial contestant on the hugely popular television show, *The $64,000 Challenge*. His opponent was a St. Louis civil service clerk named Teddy Nadler, who had charmed the TV audience as he systematically knocked off opponents. But Gore answered correctly at the $16,000 level, and Nadler failed, to the disappointment of the show's producers, among others. (They kept bringing Nadler back against new opponents and gave him a rematch against Gore; he never lost again.) At the College organ, if Gore decided a chapel speaker had exceeded the proper time, he might rattle the screen that hid himself from the audience or hit the foot pedal hard; once, when a visiting preacher gave an overlong temperance sermon, as postlude, Gore played "Little Brown Jug." Then there was the evening he attended a party at the home of Carol and Ray Dix, along with a number of leading citizens of the College and city. Midway through he got bored, so he lay down on a sofa in the living room and took a nap.

The music ranks were filled with names that reverberate with alumni. Two noted couples began at Wooster in the second decade of the twentieth century on what was called the "conservatory staff." Dan Parmelee, who founded the Wooster Symphony, and Clarice Parmelee were both professors of music until they jointly retired in 1960. Neil Rowe retired in 1945 and Gertrude Rowe in 1953; their daughter Genevieve, class of 1930, sang worldwide on operatic stages. Eve Roine Richmond led the Girls'

Chorus into the 1960s, and Karl Trump led the Men's Glee Club into the 1970s (those were the official names), both groups performing regularly in Wooster and on tour for alumni and church audiences nationwide. Alan Collins taught instrumental music and played clarinet in several northern Ohio symphony orchestras; Brian Dykstra's jazz and ragtime piano renderings delighted scores of audiences; Jack Russell not only worthily succeeded Gore as an organist but is warmly remembered as director of the Wooster Chorus, women and men combined, for thirty-four years. Then there is the Scot band—the kilt-clad marchers and the well-honed instrumentalists in the symphonic band—built and directed for many years by Stu Ling and directed to new heights by Nancy Ditmer.

Wooster's theater and dance department has benefited since 1976 from the roomy surroundings of Freedlander Theatre, but much of its fascinating history played out in the cramped setting of Scott Auditorium in Taylor Hall—or, in something of a side note, in Memorial Chapel. It was in the Chapel, each December for fifty years, that Delbert Lean, who had come to the College in 1908 as a "professor of oratory," would stride on to the rostrum in black tie and pronounce, "Marley was dead, to begin with." Lean's recitation of Dickens's *A Christmas Carol* was a highlight of the season not only for the campus but also for the city of Wooster, and it played to overflow crowds each and every year, through his final performance in 1959. Lean's successor as chairman of the department was Bill Craig, whose insatiable love of the theater and solid connections in New York brought stars to Wooster—among them, Wooster alumna Ruth McDevitt (class of 1917) reprising her star turn in *The Solid Gold Cadillac*, and Charles Laughton as a visiting lecturer. (Craig also recruited graduate school friend Garber Drushal to the speech department.) Lowry attracted his friend Thornton Wilder to Wooster, and Craig directed him as the stage manager in *Our Town*. In Craig's always oversubscribed "Theater Appreciation" course, he would maintain the minority position that Katharine Cornell, not Helen Hayes, was the "first lady of the American theater." Each year Scott Auditorium would be packed for an old chestnut of a faculty play, *Abbie's Irish Rose*, for example, which usually featured Howard Lowry delivering a single semiliterate line. Remarkably, through the 1950s and 1960s, Wooster would mount a production of a Broadway hit nearly the moment it was licensed for amateur companies, directed either by Craig or by his longtime colleague and successor as chairman, the witty Win Logan, whose popular faculty service ran from 1948 until 1982 except for his recall to military service during the Korean War.

So, these are some of the names that have come through in research, from the memories of a number of either older or younger alumni, or from comments by current or recently retired faculty and trustees. The list is by no means random; yet it is not intended to be comprehensive. Attempting to be all-inclusive can create anguish for an author faced with choices among the roster of outstanding teacher-scholars who have graced The College of Wooster faculty.

CHAPTER 21

The Future Is Now

There is a tale that in 1972 Richard Nixon, upon meeting Zhou Enlai, the scholarly Chinese premier, attempted a friendly conversation opening by asking Zhou what he thought of the French Revolution. Zhou, who had studied in France in the 1920s, is said to have responded, "Too early to say." Whether true or not, the story illustrates the long-range perspective that some historians bring to their work. It is difficult to bring historical perspective to a presidency so recently begun, as was Grant Cornwell's at The College of Wooster. That said, it can be stated confidently that the Cornwell presidency is off to a very good start.

The Stan Hales years had ended with a record-setting financial campaign and a spectacular building boom, which, Jim Wilson, chairman of the Board of Trustees, observed, laid firm groundwork for his successor. As the trustees began to consider the succession, no on-campus candidate was in sight, and after the abortive search of a decade earlier, it seemed obvious that the whole College was aching for a fresh face. Wilson had been a member of both search committees in the mid-1990s and like everyone else was disconcerted about how the first one ended. Aware that Hales would retire at the age of sixty-five in 2007, and determined to follow a better-organized path, Wilson began preparing for the new search two years in advance. He started with workshops at the Association of Governing Boards, where he had been elected to the Council of Board Chairs. He was appalled to discover that the College had kept no record of previous searches: "They didn't exist. They'd all been destroyed. No notes, nothing." So he pieced together the process by interviewing Jack Dowd, who had chaired the two most recent searches; Deb Hilty, who as secretary of the College had organized them; Mark Wilson, the faculty chair of the Woods search; and the retired president Henry Copeland.

Then he and Marge Carlson, vice chair of the board, persuaded Sol Oliver, a trustee and federal judge, to lead the search committee. In addition to Wilson and Oliver, the trustees were Jim Clarke, Steve Gault, Dave Gunning, Diane Hamburger, Jennifer Havercamp, Deb Schwinn, and Reggie Williams. The members elected by the faculty were Judy Amburgey-Peters, chemistry; Shirley Huston-Findley, theater; Hayden Schilling, history, and Greg Shaya, history, the last not then tenured, because the faculty wanted at least one younger, non-tenured member (Shaya was later tenured and became department chair). The committee included one staff member, Mike Thompson, director of institutional research, and one student, Elizabeth Wojtowicz, a senior biology major. Wilson and Oliver then interviewed prospective consultants and chose Tobie van der Vorm of Academic Search Consultants. Two things favored her: she had done a number of searches for liberal arts colleges, and she was a career professional consultant, not a retired college president. Wilson said the committee was pleased with her skill and hard work.

From among the scores of original possibilities van der Vorm gathered, several of whom were interviewed, the committee invited three to campus. One of them was Cornwell, whose interest in the job came as something of a surprise. He had been a lifer at St. Lawrence University in Canton, New York, twenty-five miles from the Canadian border. His father and brothers had attended St. Lawrence, and he entered there as a pre-med student—"because my mother told me I wanted to be a doctor." Not entranced by his biology courses, he began sampling—Buddhist religious traditions, art history, international politics—before becoming entranced by philosophy, "and that's where I sank my teeth in deep." After graduating as a double major in biology and philosophy, Cornwell completed his PhD in the philosophy of biology at the University of Chicago—"How do we assess claims in biology? How has knowledge in biology evolved over time?" He immediately joined the faculty at his alma mater, rose to the top academic position, and was widely considered the president-in-waiting at St. Lawrence, who would take the reins when Dan Sullivan, one of his mentors, retired.

Cornwell's ties to St. Lawrence were strong indeed. In a college ritual, at dusk on the first day of orientation, when the freshman class forms a circle around the quad, lights candles, sings the alma mater, hears greetings from the president—and the five hundred or so freshmen hold hands with the persons beside them—Cornwell held hands with Peg Kelsey. They became friends, then dated for most of their four years in college. There were ups and downs. Grant went off to Germany upon graduation, still not certain whether he would pursue an MD or PhD; Peg, an economics major, went to Wall Street. They spent romantic days in Paris. Then, a year after graduation, they married, and he entered the University of Chicago, she having arranged a transfer with Chemical Bank to the city. About fifteen years later, when he had become a tenured associate professor at St. Lawrence, Peg reminded Grant that he now made as much money as she had as a young banker.

At St. Lawrence, Cornwell moved into administration early, as a dean of first-year students. The family spent a formative sabbatical year in St. Kitts—their two elementary-school-age boys the only white children in a West Indian parochial school—while Grant researched the related history of sugar and slavery on the island. Not long after their return, Grant, having won all the university's teaching awards and having years of administrative experience, was appointed vice president of the university and dean of academic affairs. In a couple of years, search firms began inquiring about his availability, but by then Dan Sullivan was making retirement noises, and a campus consensus was building about his successor. "Peg and I figured ourselves to be lifers; we were committed to the college whole cloth; we had a wonderful family summer home in the Adirondacks. Our roots are deep there—deep, deep roots."

The call about Wooster was the first one Cornwell talked to Sullivan about. The president had a midwestern background and recalled giving his first academic paper there: "A very good place, a place with high integrity," Sullivan said, as Cornwell remembered. "I don't want you to leave St. Lawrence, but you should take this seriously." Cornwell began talking with Sol Oliver, and "it looked better every step of the way." By the time Cornwell had spoken with other Wooster trustees, "it really felt like a calling." He even spoke with Susanne Woods, with whom he had worked when they were both deans in the Northeast. Cornwell thought his visit to Wooster went well, meetings—"dynamic" meetings—in small groups, larger groups, one-on-one, although he sensed that another candidate, whom he knew and respected, had considerable faculty support.

Then, as required of all candidates, Cornwell gave a formal presentation in Freedlander Theatre—disaster. He is six feet, six inches tall, and the microphone on the lectern was set for an average height. He struggled with his glasses, putting them on, taking them off. "I couldn't really see my text. I fumbled it up quite a bit. I also read the venue wrong. It was basically sort of a formal text . . . my philosophy of what liberal education [should be], and the way I saw the landscape. Not much wrong with the content, [just not] the venue to read a formal text. It fell flat." One member of the search committee remembered, "His talk was uninspired and uninspiring, and his answers to questions didn't show a lot of energy or imagination." In retrospect, that same person said, "I'm happy how the search turned out. And I think that Grant has shown he can be very strong in public meetings from convocation to commencement and beyond." If the presentation dismayed many in the audience, some of the listeners, who had met Cornwell privately, knew better—and the trustees' confidence was not shaken. "These public appearances by prospective candidates are sort of like the bathing suit competition for Miss America," Wilson joked. "But at the end of the day, the committee had the benefit of all the referencing that was done, and the benefit of having spent a lot more time with the candidates, and observed them in different settings, which I think was key." Although some faculty members on the committee expressed a touch of disagreement, the trustees felt strongly and invited Cornwell to the Wooster presidency.

On one thing, though, search committee members had grilled Cornwell hard: What was the chance that he was really just waiting for the St. Lawrence presidency to open up? (It soon thereafter opened and was soon filled.) Cornwell convinced them of his sincerity and even years later reflected on the difficulty inherent in his and Peg's decision.

It's probably the single most profound decision that we've made that has shaped the course of our lives, the decision to leave St. Lawrence and come to Wooster. It's the best thing we've done. St. Lawrence was cozy for us; we were St. Lawrence. But . . . coming to a new place and being challenged in a new way, and having to learn and love a whole new institution . . . that has helped us grow and feel like we've made contributions that we never would have made at St. Lawrence. . . . We have not for a single moment looked back.

Just in case there remained mutual misgivings, Wilson had one more request. It came on Cornwell's first visit to campus after his appointment, when he was meeting with senior staff, department chairs, various other groups. "In his subtle way," Cornwell remembered,

> he said, "I want you to have dinner with a small group of faculty leaders." I said, "Great idea." He had three in mind. They were Carolyn Durham [professor of French and women's studies], Mark Wilson [professor of geology], and Hank Kreuzman [associate professor of philosophy]. It became clear to me very quickly that those three, maybe they didn't oppose my presidency, but they must have at some point voiced their clear opinion that Wooster should have chosen [the other leading candidate]. At that dinner they were each sort of saying, "Okay, you're here now, what are you really made of, who have we really got." I remember that dinner to this day, and I count the three of them among my closest colleagues. I have the highest esteem for those three people. It was one of my rites of passage. I think it went well.

Cornwell is nothing if not confident. And nothing if not decisive. As the trustees had expected, and wanted, he spent little time before modifying some elements of the College and adding new ones. In the senior administration—the president's cabinet—only two people remained in 2012, five years after Cornwell's arrival. They were Kurt Holmes, dean of students, and John Hopkins, associate vice president for college relations and marketing; "marketing" was added to Hopkins's title, and he moved from the development to the enrollment and marketing division. All the vice presidents were new. Bob Walton, the vice president for finance and business, who had already announced his resignation in 2007 to become chief executive of the Claremont College Consortium in California, volunteered financial advice before departing; Cornwell turned to John Sell, professor of business economics, who shepherded the office smoothly during a two-year search that brought Laurie Stickelmeier from St. Mary's College of Indiana. Sally Patton, who had served thirty-two years as vice president for development, directed three over-the-top campaigns and made countless alumni visits, retired in 2011, succeeded by Laurie Houck, who came from Whitman College in Washington.

Cornwell took it upon himself to recruit the person he coveted for vice president for enrollment and marketing, even to the point of clandestine meetings in places like Youngstown, in between Wooster and Meadville, Pennsylvania, where Scott Friedhoff was compiling an enviable record at Allegheny College; it took more than a year to persuade Friedhoff he should move. For chief academic officer, Cornwell elevated the title and responsibilities to "provost" and appointed Carolyn Newton, who had held that position at Berea College in Kentucky. He also made two additions to the cabinet. Ellen Falduto, held one, chief information and planning officer, a signifier of the College's adjustment to the advancing technological world. And the president got his chief of staff in Angela Johnston, who took over the roles of secretary of the Board of Trustees and secretary of the College as well. Sally Whitman, who had served as executive assistant Bettye Jo Mastrine's deputy, was promoted to executive assistant for presidential events.

One of the factors that attracted the trustees to Cornwell was his proven commitment to ethnic diversity, in the United States and around the world. Even before he had officially taken charge, July 1, 2007, he assembled a Diversity Task Force from faculty and staff with a specific instruction: How should we organize to advance the process of diversity? (President Hales had created a similar task force, one result of which is the Posse program, described in chapter 7). The task force worked with the new president over several months, researching material, using consultants, visiting other campuses. During the same period, Cornwell met with the Black Alumni Council; spoke with Josephine Wright, the longtime professor of music and black studies; reached out to Yvonne Williams, the retired former dean and organizer of black studies; and absorbed the legacy of the iconic Ted Williams. "I wanted to understand some of the history and set of concerns," Cornwell said. "It was all part of my orientation to Wooster, one of the things I was going to dig deep on." Ultimately this process coordinated into a single structure—the Center for Diversity and Global Engagement—such programs as the Office of International Student Affairs, the Office of Multicultural Student Affairs, and Off-Campus Study, which are housed in Babcock Hall. Subsequently, Linda Morgan-Clement, the campus chaplain, brought her many and varied interfaith programs to the Center. By 2012, nearly one-quarter of all students at the College were minority or multiethnic Americans or international students, numbers never before known, never imagined a few decades earlier.

As the first outsider to take the Wooster presidency in eighty-eight years, Cornwell had a great deal to learn about the College. Before arriving, he had read data and books and talked at length to Wilson and Oliver, then other trustees. During his first few months, he also engaged in what politicians like to call a "listening tour," visiting tenured and tenure-track faculty members in their offices. St. Lawrence was his baseline, but he was now in a different place. "Everything St. Lawrence did seemed natural and normal to [Peg and me]. We came to Wooster and nothing seemed natural and normal, so everything was new. We would say, 'Why do we do it this way?' For many things, there were good answers. For other things, we were told, 'We don't do that.' 'Well,' [I thought,] maybe we need to do that.'"

Cornwell was startled particularly as he read through the Statute of Instruction, which lays out faculty (and administrative) responsibilities and is more elaborate at Wooster than at most colleges. "I got out a yellow highlighter, and it looked like a coloring book," he remembered. "It read to me like a constitution written by a monarch." The Statute gave the president what he considered inappropriate powers, ex officio on every governance committee, chair of faculty meetings, participant in teaching staff and tenure meetings, when that committee's recommendations would eventually come to him. One of his first steps was to remove himself as chairman of faculty meetings, a role the revised Statute gave to an elected member of the faculty. "It was a document that placed the president in a position of power that I thought unhealthy for the system and as a model of shared governance."

Cornwell was particularly keen about removing himself from curriculum decisions. The role of "the faculty designing and implementing curriculum is absolutely sacrosanct. What I was trying to say to the faculty is, the sphere of curriculum and pedagogy of this institution is yours to steward. That means you have responsibility for it. As president (and, as a tenured professor of philosophy), I can have opinions about curriculum, but . . . I don't set curriculum by my mandate." He also tried to persuade the faculty—more than once—that it should create a smaller governing body, a faculty senate, as many larger institutions have, and he was regularly rebuffed. So, seeking a smaller forum, he invented Cross-Talk, which consists of the president, the provost, the convenor of faculty meetings, and chairs of elected faculty committees. It allows for helpful conversation, although it had no official standing and could not set policy.

Cornwell also established a number of other procedures and groupings. First Fridays was an informal gathering at the president's home once a month so that faculty members from across the disciplines could chat with colleagues they seldom saw. The Hales Group—funds from an endowment created by the trustees to honor retired President Hales—became an interdisciplinary study group to keep faculty current with issues of globalization. A dozen or two faculty members may participate each year, and small groups suggest global issues to study, from which the president selects one, and the entire group meets monthly in his home to exchange ideas.

During the summer, members of the Hales Group travel abroad to sites they have been studying, with the proviso that each member return to create a new course or revise an older one that includes material garnered from their study and on-site travel. Over the early years, faculty traveled to such destinations as Cuba, Ghana, India, Israel, Jordan, China, Denmark, and Iceland, exploring themes such as regional conflict and cooperation or how tourism as a global industry affected local culture.

A more recent effort has been the Horizon Group, senior administrators and faculty, again meeting in the president's home, to consider how the College should view long-term prospects for higher education in general and Wooster in particular, amidst changing demographics, technology, globalization—in short, how Wooster should prepare itself for what is "over the horizon," ten or fifteen years down the road; an outside evaluation team called it "a weather vane for the institution."

The new president and the Board of Trustees, conscious of a slumping faculty salary scale measured against the Great Lakes College Association peer group, worked over the early years to raise salaries at all levels; by 2012 it had reached the GLCA mean for non-tenured assistant professors, but it had also moved nearly to the mean for associate professors and professors. Cornwell used a Mellon Foundation grant to add eight tenure-track positions in humanities and social-science departments, bolstering the departments for when faculty members take research leave. His theory is that I.S. mentoring is such a special skill that temporary "leave replacements" are often not adequate and that Wooster's tenured and tenure-track faculty in bulked-up departments should be able to pick up the slack. The newcomers are also hired with a special edge toward diversity.

Given how the Hales years revitalized the campus footprint, the College looked not all that much different five years into the Cornwell period—with one significant exception. That was the Scot Center, the most expensive project the College had ever undertaken, fulfillment of the long-deferred dream for an athletic field house and a recreation and fitness center for "every student, every day." (See chapter 9 for details of the planning and construction of the Scot Center.) Several campus structures looked different inside—for example, Babcock, the onetime senior women's dorm became headquarters of the Center for Diversity and Global Engagement. More consequential interior changes, though, came in the libraries, both the 1962 Andrews Library and the adjoining 1995 Flo K. Gault Library for Independent Study.

First came CoRE, for Collaborative Research Environment, in which much of the first floor of Andrews was converted to a space for students and faculty to "brainstorm ideas, develop collaborative projects using digital or traditional media, sketch out a new concept, or practice a presentation." In private rooms, they can work individually or in teams. Research librarians and Writing Center counselors are available to assist. So are flat-screen monitors and a digital "media bar." At the center of CoRE is a glassed-in Cube, where flexible seating for more than a hundred allows for discussions and presentations. In the ground floor of the adjoining Gault Library are offices and research material that are known collectively as APEX for Advising, Planning, Experiential Learning. Its purpose, simply enough, is to make connections between the classrooms and labs of a liberal arts college and the lives of its prospective graduates in what students call "the real world." One element is the Learning Center, an academic support service staffed by professional consultants to help students maximize their time management and study skills; it is also a special resource for students with disabilities. Others are the Experiential Learning Office, which encourages volunteerism and assists students in finding off-campus internships, and the Center for Entrepreneurship, designed to help students "translate their creativity into a sustainable venture." As students near graduation, they can turn to Career Services, where they can examine and prepare for opportunities in both the world of work and graduate or professional school.

After APEX became a one-stop advice center, the number of students using its various elements doubled.

Just as a corporate chief executive officer must deal with a board of directors, a college president must be comfortable with his board of trustees, especially with the chairman, and almost every president in Wooster's history has faced a change at the top. Having led the board through two major accomplishments—the largest financial campaign in Wooster's history and selection of a new president—Jim Wilson decided he had spent enough time in the taxing job (to say nothing of frequent trips from Park City, Utah) to give up the position a year after Cornwell came to Wooster. But Wilson said Henry Copeland persuaded him to "have two years overlap. I respected that advice. And it worked well." It was assumed that each board chairman would be a graduate of the College, and with the exception of Arthur Compton, every one in recent history was also a businessman. So it was a significant break when Dave Gunning became chairman of the board in 2009. Gunning had gone to college at Cornell, then to Harvard Law School; as a lawyer, he had spent much of his career working in or with businesses. He had first joined the board as a parent trustee in 1989 and after a two-year break returned in 1994. He said he had never thought about becoming chairman and was surprised when Cornwell raised the possibility at a luncheon—a few senior members of the board had obviously considered this prospect. Gunning understood that some trustees were, "quite legitimately, taken aback," but no one questioned the validity of the selection. The disadvantage, Gunning said, was "you can't process the kind of emotional connection that can only come from having gone through that [Wooster student] experience." But given his long "intense and committed" ties to the College, plus the "echo experience" of having been a Wooster parent, he said, "it's been a wonderful experience." For that he credited mostly Cornwell's strong leadership and the board members "who share this absolutely uniform commitment to Wooster."

The pace of change in the new presidency unsettled some faculty members, who believed that it occasionally came almost by administrative fiat, without the transparency the president promised. Sometimes the irksome problems dealt with nonacademic matters. For example, the Taeusch Lounge in Lowry Center, the de facto faculty lounge where professors could gather for morning coffee or lunch, read newspapers and magazines, or simply touch base with colleagues from other departments, was quietly renamed the Tartan Room, and its uses became campuswide; faculty continued to speak hopefully about finding a new place on campus to share each other's company informally. Cornwell dismissed the issue of transparency, insisting that many missed out on changes while on leave or simply because they weren't paying attention. "I just have so much confidence in Wooster's bones," he said about the new order. "I think we could move further faster, take on greater risks, to our great benefit."

In one area, though, the requirement of change is beyond the control of either a president or a faculty: technology. Most students who entered the College in the autumn of 2011 were born in 1993 and would find life without advanced technology unimaginable and Wooster's early efforts, some of them even pioneering, to be amusing. In 1961, because the College's manual accounting systems had fallen behind the times in providing timely budget information, the Board of Trustees approved leasing an IBM punch-card system; Bill Snoddy, then a relatively inexperienced employee in the treasurer's office, was sent off to train to use the equipment. In 1964 the College acquired its first IBM computer, and Snoddy was now trained in Fortran and Symbolic Language to write the programs for budget applications. Four years later, to speed the accounting process, the vice president Hans Jenny cut a deal with Battelle Memorial Institute in Columbus to install a high-speed telephone line between Battelle's mainframe computer and a terminal in Wooster. It worked well, despite unexpected problems. in the spring, farmers plowing the fields of north central Ohio occasionally snapped the wires; microwave towers soon replaced the wires.

In 1968, Carl Zimmerman, a onetime Wooster physics major with a graduate degree in mathematics who served as a systems analyst for the navy and then at the Ford Motor Company, became the College's first director of academic computing services, working in lower Galpin Hall. Much of his early work resulted from specific requests—a program to solve quadratic equations for a mathematics textbook, for instance—but soon students, well before faculty, were demanding computer courses, so Zimmerman received an academic appointment as well. From the late 1970s into the early '80s, Wooster developed a national reputation for its use of technology in teaching. John Ramsey, Jim Hartman, and Chuck Hampton in the Department of Mathematics, and Larry Stewart and Peter Havholm in English were using the Rubbermaid Computer Lab in Taylor Hall for occasional classes; Stewart and Havholm even encouraged students to develop software that could be used to create original stories.

By the mid-1990s, fiber optics had been installed underground, knitting the campus together for telephones, television, and data. But less attention was paid to instructional technology until the turn of the century. Then the biology department began experimenting with the creation of flash modules to help instruct students in lab methods, and the mathematics department as well as the new computer science department explored course management software and blog software. In 2005 the College created an instructional technology department, which worked on everything from curriculum assistance to filming guest speakers. As a sign of IT's growing consequence, its director, Ellen Falduto, became a member of the president's cabinet. As instructional technology's role continued to grow, a new division, called digital infrastructure, headed by the veteran staffer Vince DiScipio, took over maintenance and events responsibilities. That allowed IT to concentrate on helping faculty incorporate technology into the classroom—implementing a course management system, introducing podcasting and a blogging service, maintaining a media lab, and assisting faculty ad hoc with tech projects.

Some matters that have occupied the attention of the Board of Trustees for years remained unsettled. What is the value of the L. C. Boles Memorial Golf Course? Wooster's championship-level varsity golf team years ago abandoned the nine-hole course for the more challenging eighteen-hole Wooster Country Club course, and the campus facility was losing enough money that the Board of Trustees considered closing it. More careful collection of fees and a reorganization of groundskeeping reduced the losses to a manageable figure. Still, the 250-acre course on the eastern border of the campus has remained a tempting site for expansion in a number of different ways. And what of the Ohio Light Opera Company? The Light Opera, whose professional performers are recruited through competitive auditions around the country, has for three decades played a schedule of operettas, primarily Gilbert and Sullivan, and Broadway musicals in Freedlander Theatre from mid-June through mid-August. The OLO has brought the College praise from theatergoers and critics nationwide, putting Wooster on the map in a way it could not be otherwise. Yet it has been a slight money-loser more often than not, marked against the

College budget. Although tightened practices reduced deficits, the College continued to subsidize OLO with various in-kind assistances, and the board had yet to decide how to reach a balance.

Five years into his presidency, Cornwell and the Board of Trustees were confident. Wooster's academic program continued to draw praise from peers around the country. Student applications set records almost every year, both in numbers and quality. In 2012, Wooster submitted to the rigorous ten-year accreditation review required by the Higher Learning Commission of the North Central Association of Colleges and Schools, and the report the experienced and no-nonsense visiting team submitted was glowing: "The Board, administration, faculty, staff, and students of the College of Wooster are to be complimented for their focus on mission and willingness to allocate resources sufficient to support and enhance it. . . . The administration is trusted by the campus community, works collaboratively, and is even sacrificial in its allocation of resources. . . . The faculty is truly committed to the mission and engaged in the decision making of the institution. Even students feel empowered and informed." It also observed: "The campus facilities and grounds are beautiful and a true asset to the institution."

It should come as no surprise, however, that on the eve of its Sesquicentennial in 2016, the College continued to set ambitious goals. One significant need would be to build up the endowment; as of July 1, 2012, it was about $232 million, a recovery from Great Recession years, yet millions lower than at the close of the last financial campaign. The school would certainly require a new science facility, a project comparable in planning and cost to the Kauke remodeling. Over the years Wooster has educated an astonishing number of successful chemists, geologists, physicists, and biologists. The chemistry and geology buildings received updated treatment during the Copeland and Hales years, but Mateer Hall, built for the biology department in the 1920s, was not only hopelessly out of date but also an admissions embarrassment. A considerable number of the most promising prospective students (and their parents) express strong interest in emerging fields of science, but most of them have little or no sense of Wooster's exemplary record, and the out-of-date facilities unnerve them. "Biology" itself has become essentially a misnomer; "life science" is the larger, more accurate generic term. A life science structure could bring biology, biochemistry, and molecular biology together with newer departments, such as environmental studies and neuroscience, an interdisciplinary field that incorporates biology, genetics, nanotechnology, psychology, chemistry, philosophy, and computer science in the study of the nervous system.

Those things are part of a proud college's dreams, the denouement of which no simple book of history can dream of judging. Who would have dreamed in 1944 of the historic changes that would be wrought at The College of Wooster as it grew into the world of the twenty-first century. Over sixty-eight years it became, inevitably, a much different place from the modest midwestern institution that an untried new president awakened intellectually. He might be surprised at all the change, even chagrined by some of it. But it is fair to guess that Howard Lowry would be pleased.

Notes

This book, as scholars will instantly observe, is not styled academically. It was planned, as a fellow trustee suggested, to be "a story." The research sources cited do not follow the text line by line, as a pure academic volume might. I thought it pointless, bordering on affectation, to follow this procedure, one "ibid." after another when so much of the material cited is obvious and/or repeated. All the printed research—volumes such as the alumni magazine, yearbooks, student newspaper—are available in Special Collections, ably presided over by Denise Monbarren, and the city newspaper in the library proper. Material shared from private files by faculty or other friends of the College will be added to Special Collections. Transcripts of all interviews will go to Special Collections. Thus, anyone who is seriously interested in pursuing details of the research should have access to it—and those who find that unnecessary will not have to bother.

Because the alumni magazine at the College was given different names during this period, it is referred to throughout these notes as "alumni magazine." (Since the magazine began in 1886 as *The Post-Graduate*, it has been published as *Wooster Quarterly, Wooster Alumni News, Bulletin of the College of Wooster, The College of Wooster Bulletin, Wooster Alumni Bulletin,* and the current *Wooster.*) Alumni magazines at all colleges have changed in style over the decades. Many years ago they were essentially reports of campus events; more recently they have concentrated on features and social and cultural issues. Wooster's magazine was especially important for providing news over the early years of this history; I read every issue of every alumni magazine from the inauguration of Howard Lowry to the dedication of the Scot Center. The alumni magazine served as an extremely valuable summary source and makes the information readily available to interested parties; in many cases, the same material, in more detail and less easily accessed, is available from other sources, notably minutes of Board of Trustees meetings. (I must call attention here to the minutes written by Deb Hilty during the years 1976–2001, when she was secretary of the College and secretary of the Board of Trustees. She made the minutes, which could be boring details, not just technically informative but occasionally even interesting.)

I read through every *Index* (the College yearbook) from 1944 to 2012 and every issue of the *Voice* (the student newspaper) from 1944 to 2012. And I undertook a considerable sampling of the *Daily Record,* the city of Wooster's (and its region's) chronicler. I also referred to the minutes of the Board of Trustees and its Executive Committee (earlier called the Administrative Committee)—again, not every word but nearly every page. The same goes for minutes of some faculty meetings. The annual official College catalogs were a frequent reference point. The 2010 alumni directory was invaluable for such vital matters as the spelling of names and periods of service for faculty and administrators. I've listed the names of everyone interviewed in "A Note about Personal Sources."

1. A VISIONARY ARRIVES

Prexy Wishart's victory over William Jennings Bryan is described by Gordon Tait, "Evolution: Wishart, Wooster, and William Jennings Bryan." *Journal of Presbyterian History* 62, no. 4 (Winter 1984) 306–21.

Much of the description of the Compton family is from interviews with John Compton, Arthur Holly Compton's son and Wooster trustee.

The description of Arthur Compton's World War II experiments comes from John Compton interviews and from the autobiography of James Bryant Conant, *My Several Lives: Memoirs of a Social Inventor* (New York: Harper & Row, 1970), 290.

The description of the process that led to the appointment of Howard Lowry as president is from James Blackwood's biography, *Howard Lowry: A Life in Education* (Wooster, Ohio: The College of Wooster, 1975), 152–54. Much of the material concerning Lowry's life and career comes from this book as well.

For Lowry as an instructor and his work in New York see Lucy Lillian Notestein, *Wooster of the Middle West,* vol. 2, *1911–1944* (Kent, Ohio: Kent State University Press, 1971), 329–30.

Much of the detail about the navy V-5 program at Wooster during World War II is from the Independent Study paper by Margaret Anne Pett, "Cadets on Campus: The Military Training Programs on The College of Wooster Campus during World War II " (supervised by Madonna Hettinger), 1999–2000.

Details on the social life at Wooster during World War II, especially among the girls, come primarily from a series of letters, notes, and memorabilia provided largely by Vivian Douglas Smith, class of 1947, and a number of her classmates.

The 1944–45 student handbook contains official social rules for students in Lowry's first year.

The 1944–45 catalog lists Lowry's first faculty and administrative appointments.

Lowry's inaugural address appears verbatim in the alumni magazine, November 1944, 30.

Lowry's full-scale introduction of Independent Study appears in a pamphlet titled "Wooster: Adventure in Education," published December 1, 1945. Two other versions of this pamphlet, slightly revised, appeared in 1948 and 1951.

2. THE VETS ARRIVE—AND I.S., TOO!

The Land Ordinance of 1785 can be found in *Documents of American History,* ed. Henry Steele Commager, 8th ed. (New York: Appleton-Century-Crofts, 1968), 123–24. The Morrill Act appears in the same edition, 412–13.

The GI Bill of Rights is discussed in Lawrence A. Cremin, *American Education: The Metropolitan Experience 1876–1980,* (New York: Harper & Row, 1980), 250, and, generally, in Clark Kerr, *The Uses of the University* (Cambridge, Mass.: Harvard University Press, 1963).

The data, and comment, on enrollment in 1945–46 are from the alumni magazine, October 1945; for 1946–47, alumni magazine, October 1946.

For descriptions of veterans' housing and the conditions under which they lived, see alumni magazine, October 1946; 1948 *Index;* 1949 *Index.*

Details of erecting veterans housing, city residents' help, move-in conditions come from the *Daily Record,* July 19, August 2, 8, October 23, December 6, 31, 1946.

Firsthand descriptions of postwar conditions are taken from the Al Van Wie interview.

The letters from "Senior Counselors" to freshmen girls dated in summer months 1943 came from girls in class of 1944 and were sent to freshmen in class of 1947; those dated summer of 1946 came from girls in class of 1947 (now seniors) to girls in class of 1950. Vivian Douglas Smith collection.

Information on the first Homecoming queen comes from *Voice,* October 4, 11, 25, 1946; and an informal interview with Olivia dePastina Bernabei, class of 1947, in Wooster during her sixty-fifth class reunion, June 2012.

The history of the College band is found in the alumni magazine, Winter 1983. Newest band information comes from e-mail exchange with Nancy Ditmer, band director, November 5, 2013. See also "Marching with the 'Finest Small College Band in the Land' at the College of Wooster in Ohio," Offenburger.com, October 22, 2008.

The story of the writing of the fight song, "Hail to the Black and Gold," its music and lyrics, is found in the 1948 *Index.* See also alumni magazine, November 1947.

The "Post-War Plan of the College" was published in the 1945–46 catalog.

The 1946–47 catalog names new faculty and administrators.

Faculty approval of I.S. is detailed in the minutes of the faculty meeting, April 16, 1945.

Reflections from Bill Kieffer, Win Logan, and Dave Moldstad on the faculty evaluation of I.S., as gathered from I.S. workshop for new faculty, are collected in "Howard Lowry's Educational Audacity," alumni magazine, Summer 1993.

For Clayton Ellsworth on faculty leave program, see alumni magazine, March 1948. See also "On Leave," alumni magazine, Spring 1982.

On early I.S. projects, see the alumni magazine, June 1948.

3. NOT AS QUIET AS IT SEEMED

Since I attended the College in the 1950s, some of this material—notably popular music and some performances and lectures—comes from personal recollection.

College expenses are listed in the 1950–51 catalog. Data on living expenses comes from "The Year 1950," *The People's History,* http://www.thepeoplehistory.com/.

Lowry's response to House Committee on Un-American Activities was printed in the *Daily Record,* June 20, 1949.

The student rules were published in 1952–53 and 1959–60 student handbooks.

The story of post-concert behavior by members of the Buddy Morrow band and Lowry's response to it, was written in an e-mail message to the author from Don Hartsough, 1954–55 president of the Student Senate.

Membership numbers in sections and clubs were counted from their photographs in the *Index* for sample years of 1953 and 1959. The reference to the 1970 *Index* illustrates changing fashion among students.

E. Blake Moore Jr., class of 1955, wrote the description of competitive touch football among sections in a letter to the author.

Information about the career of Viola Startzman Robertson, MD—and the work she did as medical director of the College—comes primarily from interviews with Dr. Startzman but was supplemented by interviews with Bev Asbury and Ken and Louise Plusquellec.

Much of the story of Robert Peters's career at Wooster comes from the text of Hayden Schilling's lecture to the Century Club of Wooster, November 15, 2011. Dean Taeusch's explanation to the Board of Trustees of the Peters period comes from the Wooster Board of Trustees' minutes of June 1953.

Information about the dedication of Wooster Inn is taken from the alumni magazine, December 1959. John Sell's report on losses at the Inn and plan to create management company that would lease operations to Ken Bogucki is taken from the minutes of Executive Committee of Board of Trustees, January 20, 2009. The story of how the Inn moved from being a money-losing adjunct of the College to holding its current privately operated status comes from an interview with Bogucki, general manager of the Inn. See also "A Little of Our History," a pamphlet provided to guests at the Inn. See also "A Recipe for Success," alumni magazine, Fall 2006.

The beginning of the Faculty Club is described in the alumni magazine, February 1954. Later history comes from the Faculty Club file in Special Collections.

"The Shack" was frequently referred to in yearbooks of the 1940s and 1950s, usually with pictures and occasionally with comparisons to the Student Union. Other details of its history come from the alumni magazine, April 1977.

4. CELEBRATION AND DISMAY

Much of the detail on early fund-raising, especially the Centennial Campaign, comes from interviews with Buck Smith.

Details of Lowry's administrative reorganization are taken from Doug Drushal's unpublished memoir of his father, Garber Drushal, "A Scot by Affection," which Doug Drushal provided the author.

Details about the trees on campus and their dying from disease are found in the alumni magazine, October 1968. Further status of trees on campus is described in the alumni magazine, Fall 2009. See also the well-illustrated map of trees on campus, from a Spring 2005 brochure, "Gift and Memorial Trees," available from the College News Bureau.

Information on the debate over the alma mater, "Love Song," and the proposed new alma mater, "The Elms Are in Their Beauty," is from the alumni magazine, November 1960.

For Rhodes Scholar information, see the alumni magazine, January 1964, July 1979.

Information on Wooster's archaeological digs at Pella in Jordan is taken from an interview with Bob Smith. See also alumni magazine, May 1966, January 1968.

Some detail on Lowry's condition during his waning years comes from interviews with Gordon Tait.

Details of Lowry's final addresses and final days come from interviews with Buck Smith. See also Blackwood, *Howard Lowry*, 313–15. Complete copies of his two final speeches, "The Sorcerer's Apprentice," baccalaureate in Wooster, June 4, 1967, and "On the Relevant," commencement at Ohio Wesleyan University in Delaware, June 11, 1967, are available in Special Collections.

5. SCIENTIA ET RELIGIO EX UNO FONTE

Details on the Presbyterian Scholars' questioning of religion at the College come from the *Voice*, December 9, 1960, supplemented by interviews with Gordon Tait.

Gordon Tait's memoir, "Personal Reflections on the History of Religion at The College of Wooster," available in Special Collections, was an important source for this chapter. See also Tait's "Change," a lecture to the class of 1962, Alumni Weekend 2007, and his lecture to the class of 1960, Alumni Weekend 2010; these are also in Special Collections.

The early history of the College, especially its religious history, is taken from Lucy Lillian Notestein, *Wooster of the Middle West*, vol. 1, *1866–1910* (1937; repr., Kent, Ohio: Kent State University Press, 1971), 1–3.

Information on the nursery school is compiled from its history, in Special Collections, and a January 26, 2014, e-mail to the author from Carol Stewart.

Details on the decision by the Presbyterian Church U.S.A. to release control of its affiliated colleges, and actions by the Board of Trustees in response, are contained in board minutes, April 12, June 6, 1969. The board approved the final amended articles of incorporation for the College as an independent entity on April 11, 1970. See also "The Church and Related Colleges or Universities," in minutes of the General Assembly of the United Presbyterian Church, USA, 1973, pt. 1, 581–83 and "The Church's Mission in Higher Education" in minutes of the General Assembly of the United Presbyterian Church, USA, 1981, pt. 1, 378–84.

The Memorandum of Understanding between The Synod of the Covenant and The College of Wooster is taken from Board of Trustees' minutes, October 27, 2006 (slightly revised in 2011).

For details of the special report of the Committee on Religious Dimension, see the Board of Trustees' minutes, May 31, 1968. Further information about this committee of the board over later years comes from interviews with its chairmen, John Compton and Gene Bay.

Details of changes from the "Department of Religion" to the "Department of Religious Studies" come largely from interviews with Bob Smith and Gordon Tait.

Details on courses in religious studies are taken from the 2011–12 catalog.

Information regarding Bev Asbury's career and tenure at Wooster comes from Asbury interviews. See also Asbury's "The Christian Stance: Inner Guidelines," sermon given at Westminster Presbyterian Church, Wooster, September 20, 1964.

Details of Ray Swartzback's career and tenure at Wooster come from an interview with his daughter, Linda Swartzback Pratt, and from copies of his sermons and post-Wooster lectures, which Pratt provided to the author. The quoted material is from Lecture 1, "Bring on the Lions," 15. For Swartzback's first pastorate, see Janette T. Harrington, "The Church That Nobody Wanted," *Presbyterian Life*, May 1, 1954, 7–9.

Details of Board of Trustees' memberships are taken from various board meetings (as membership rules were amended). Membership of the board is noted in each year's catalog. Honorary degrees awarded to Presbyterian ministers are noted in various catalogs.

Details on the creation and implementation of the Henry Jefferson Copeland Campus Chaplain position come from interviews with Copeland and Linda Morgan-Clement.

Details on Morgan-Clement's career and tenure at Wooster come from an interview with her.

6. "QUITE ASTOUNDING WOMEN"

The opening passage of this chapter comes from an interview with Yvonne Williams.

The roster of women faculty and their educational credentials at the beginning of Lowry's presidency is taken from the 1944–45 catalog.

Aileen Dunham gave her view of a woman professor's personal life in an interview with Beth Irwin Lewis, and further details come from a message to classmates from Priscilla Courtelyou Little, class of 1956, on the occasion of their fifty-fifth reunion.

The story of Fran Guille's book was printed in the *Daily Record,* May 10, 1968, and the events concerning the Truffaut film and her New York recognition were published in the alumni magazine, December 1975. Other details were drawn from files provided to the author by her longtime assistant, Carol McDaid, and the personal experience of the author, who attended the New York events.

Information about Vivian Holliday's personal and career experiences comes from interviews with her.

Details of women who retired in the 1960s or joined the faculty then are taken from catalogs of the period.

Beth Irwin Lewis described the Women's Table information in an interview; her words were supplemented by interviews with Holliday and Joanne Frey.

Details of the increasing role of women beginning in the 1970s come from interviews with Frey, Carolyn Durham, Jenna Hayward, and Holliday, and from catalogs of the period.

Details on the growth of women's studies (and its subsequent names) come from interviews with Durham, Nancy Grace, Susan Figge, Frye, and Madonna Hettinger. See also catalogs of the period and "Women's Studies," "Participating in a Radical Tradition: Women Faculty 1880–1960," and "Challenging Perceptions," all articles printed in the Winter 1992 alumni magazine.

7. THE JOURNEY TO DIVERSITY

The description of the 2003 reunion panel comes from an interview with Reggie Williams. Williams provided the author with a copy of his opening remarks. These are supplemented by informal conversations with Doug Hole, Jet Turner, and Reggie Minton.

The description of John Chittum's recruitment of Ted Williams and of the Williams family's early experiences in Wooster comes from interviews with Yvonne Williams.

The Mother's Day protest against the Williams family occurred May 14, 1961. It was not, however, reported in the *Daily Record* until a few weeks afterward. Two letters to the editor, one from President Lowry and the other from Ted and Yvonne Williams, were published side by side, June 1, 1961. An editorial calling for racial understanding was published June 6, 1961. Letters condemning the protest continued to be published through at least June 15, 1961.

Yvonne Williams provided the text of Henry Copeland's memorial tribute to Ted Williams, delivered December 3, 2005. See also program for "Celebration of the Life of Theodore R. Williams," available in Special Collections.

The Report of Faculty Committee on Negro Education is an attachment to the October 1967 Board of Trustees' minutes.

The description of Wooster faculty exchange with Miles College comes from interviews with Arn Lewis and Hayden Schilling. See also Will Hustwit, "A Brief History of the Wooster-Miles Exchange Program" (undated, provided to the author by Ron Hustwit).

Louisa Stroop Oliver detailed her Miles College experiences in an interview.

Sol Oliver told of experiences at Miles, his transfer to and experiences at Wooster, and his career in an interview.

Early efforts to establish black studies program at Wooster are described in interviews with Lewis, Schilling, and Paul Christianson. Further details on the program, officially established in 1973, come from an interview with Yvonne Williams. Some details on early days of program are printed in the Winter 1994 alumni magazine.

Information about the Black Students Manifesto in 1969 comes from a Ken McHargh interview.

The Board of Trustees' "Discussion on 'Racial Understanding'" comes from the board minutes of June 9, 1972.

Don Harward described the South African divestment issues in an interview.

Information about the student occupation of Galpin Hall comes from interviews with Henry Copeland, Ken Plusquellec, and Bill Snoddy, as well as an informal conversation with Sally Whitman. See also the *Daily Record,* April 20, 21, 1989; *Voice,* April 21, 1989.

The memo to "The Campus Community" from black student leaders was written April 25, 1989. See also Memo to Board of Trustees from President Copeland, April 27, 1989, Board of Trustees attachment.

On black student enrollment, see President Drushal's report to Board of Trustees, June 1970, and the Report of the Task Force on Diversity, 2006. Further information on black student enrollment and other minority and international enrollment comes from Office of Institutional Research (information collected for Integrated Postsecondary Education Information Data System [IPEDS], reported to National Center for Educational Statistics). Posse information comes from a memorandum to the author from Susan Lee, special assistant to the president for diversity affairs and campus climate.

Information about the faculty vote against black studies department, then establishment of black studies program, comes from the Winter 1994 alumni magazine

8. NEW AND RENEW

Information about renovation of older academic buildings, generally, is found in "Building on the Past," alumni magazine, Fall 1999.

Repurposing of original Frick Library is described in the Fall 1998 alumni magazine.

Details of remodeling of Ebert Art Center from Severance Gym come from the alumni magazine, Fall 1997.

On the first remodeling of Severance Chemistry, see the alumni magazine, December 1960; details of second remodeling come from the Fall 1999 issue. Ted Bogner and Sally Patton described, in interviews, dealing with potential cost overruns.

A story of the first remodeling of Kauke Hall was printed in the alumni magazine, Fall 1963; see also the Spring 2004 issue. Most details on second remodeling of Kauke Hall and other construction related to it come from interviews with Ted Bogner.

The remodeling of Taylor Hall was detailed in the Summer 1982 alumni magazine and Scovel Hall, the Summer 1985 issue. See also interviews with Ted Bogner.

Building of Wishart Hall was covered in the January 1967 alumni magazine and Freedlander Theatre the August 1975 issue.

Information about Merz Hall and Scheide Music Center comes from the alumni magazine, Winter 1988, and interviews with Stan Gault and Sally Patton.

The Beall Avenue "Streetscape" is detailed in memorandums to College community: April 20, 2005, August 14, September 18, 2008, February 2, 2010, in the Special Collections files. See also the alumni magazine, Winter 2010.

Remodelings of president's home are described in Drushal, "Scot by Affection," and were further elaborated on in an interview with Henry Copeland.

9. HOMES AWAY FROM HOME

Details on construction dates of residence halls were taken from the 2011–12 catalog.

Information about Lowry's distaste for the Wagner Hall roof and its modification comes from interviews with Buck Smith and Pete Bogner.

Funding of Armington, Bissman, Stevenson residence halls is detailed in the *Daily Record,* January 31, 1967. The Bogner company information comes from interviews with Ted Bogner, as does the history of local companies building College facilities.

The details of Lowry Center financing, including Lowry's embarrassment at having it named for him come from interviews with Buck Smith.

Luce Hall information is published in the alumni magazine, Winter 1991.

Details on various remodeling projects and off-campus housing are taken from the 2011–12 catalog.

Coed housing and the related visitation were issues over many years. Former dean of students Doris Coster wrote about Babcock Hall as a program center for both women and men in a memorandum to the author, March 11, 2011. Among the most significant stories, cited here, for example, are "Copeland Rejects SGA Visitation Proposal," *Voice,* June 2, 1978, and related stories, from the *Voice,* November 9, 1979, February 29, April 18, 1980. Coed housing was reported in the *Voice* over decades, from the late 1970s into the 2000s, in stories big and small, letters to the editor, editorials. Kurt Holmes, dean of students, described the culmination of the issue (which had become a nonissue by 2012), in a February 28, 2013, interview.

Details on Scot Center are given in the alumni magazine of Summer 2012; see also College press releases. In interviews, Laurie Stickelmaier and Ted Bogner spoke about construction and cost details, and, also in interviews, Grant Cornwell gave details on its planning.

10. EX LIBRIS

The early history of library comes from Notestein, *Wooster of the Middle* West, 1:85–86.

Information about library remodeling comes from an interview with Ted Bogner.

The November 1962 alumni magazine carried a story about the books being moved from Frick to Andrews Library. See also Memorandum from Librarian, "Books to be Carried Into the Andrews Library, September 18, 1962," Library files, Special Collections.

The creation of Gault Library is covered in the alumni magazine, Winter 1996, and interviews with Stan Gault provided further information.

Damon Hickey described Special Collections in an interview, as well as the history of changes in library services and various library organizations and consortiums. He also provided additional material on consortiums.

11. THE SCOTS TALE

A considerable amount of information for this chapter comes directly from the author of this book. While a Wooster student, I was also sports editor of the *Daily Record* for three years. For a number of years before that, I worked for the sports department of the *Daily Record,* and from my childhood attended College athletic events. My Independent Study project was a history of Wooster athletics, not coincidentally titled "The Scots Tale."

On World War II athletics, see Ed Arn, "Black and Gold, A History of Athletics, The College of Wooster, 1870–1945," an unpublished monograph, available in Special Collections.

On the creation of Scot nickname, see the alumni magazine, June 1948. In an interview, Al Van Wie explained the Shipe modification.

In an interview, Jack Lengyel discussed his experience.

Much of detail concerning Van Wie's experiences as basketball coach and athletic director comes from interviews with Van Wie.

Details on the golf team's national championship, including the members' subsequent careers, comes from a memorandum to author from Coach Bob Nye.

Baseball records can be found in the College news department.

Sailing club information is per the 1957 *Index*.

Information on women's athletics can be found in the alumni magazine, Spring 1989. John Finn, director of public information provided further details. On the number of high school girls and college women participating in organized sports before and after Title IX, see the *New York Times,* June 17, 2012.

Details on North Coast Athletic Conference come from interviews with Henry Copeland and Van Wie. See also *Voice,* September 24, 1982, February 25, 1983.

Details on early plans for the new gymnasium come from a series of letters to Arthur O. Angilly, the College architect based in New York, from Mose Hole, the athletic director, and President Lowry, February 26 through May 22, 1946, copies in Special Collections, Development file. Further details come from "A Proposal for Physical Education Facilities at The College of Wooster," prepared by R. B. Westkaemper, November 1963, copy in Special Collections, Development file. The story of "urgent need" for a new gymnasium was published in the *Voice,* December 11, 1964. Further details from proposal for the Essential Extra Campaign were found in "A Program for Life Beyond the Classroom," copy in Special Collections, Development file (material also in attachment to board minutes). Van Wie provided further details in a memorandum to the author.

12. A CHAPEL FOR ITS TIME

Lowry's view of prospective chapel is given in the minutes of Board of Trustees, December 1964.

On early negotiations for the new Chapel, see the correspondence in files of McGaw Chapel, Special Collections. See also board minutes from December 1967 (special meeting). Art Palmer wrote about the working committee in a memorandum to Lowry, April 27, 1966.

See Blackwood, *Howard Lowry,* 299 301, and the interview with Buck Smith for information on funds for new Chapel.

In an interview, Buck Smith described the June 1967 board meeting discussion between Cary Wagner and Lowry.

Description of weakness of old Chapel from Blackwood, *Howard Lowry,* 265, and interview with Ted Bogner.

Clare Adel Schreiber wrote about contrasts between Memorial Chapel and McGaw Chapel in "The Notion of Place," *Daily Record,* October 8, 1969 (the article was reprinted from alumni magazine, September–October 1969).

On the Victor Christ-Janer conception of new Chapel, see the *Daily Record,* June 13, 1970. Arn Lewis wrote about planning and execution of new Chapel, "Building on the Past," alumni magazine, Fall 1999.

In interviews, Peter Bogner and Ted Bogner discussed problems constructing the new Chapel.

On the Chapel dedication, see the alumni magazine, November–December 1971.

Details of the McGaws' weekend in Wooster come from interviews and correspondence with Beverly Kimble Siligmueller, Darcey Johnston DeRose, and Jim DeRose.

Stories of the student protest over Homecoming weekend and related events were printed in the *Voice,* October 29, 1971.

The text of Kimble's statement as Homecoming queen was printed in the *Voice,* October 29, 1971. Personal details concerning protest come from interviews with Beverly Kimble Siligmueller, Darcey Johnston DeRose, and Jim DeRose.

13. THE WORST OF TIMES . . . AND REVIVAL

Details of Lowry's death and funeral can be found in Blackwood, *Howard Lowry,* 316–17. See also the interview with Buck Smith.

On the designation of Drushal as acting president and steps toward selection of search committee, see the Board of Trustees' minutes, July 1967.

Details of the College borrowing process come from interviews with Doug Drushal and Lincoln Oviatt. See also Board of Trustees' minutes, October 1966, June, December 1967 (special meeting).

Details of final search committee meeting in Cleveland come from interviews with Paul Christianson, Arn Lewis, and Gordon Tait.

On Garber Drushal's early life and career, see Doug Drushal, "Scot by Affection."

Details of efforts to solve financial problems, including the Essential Extras Campaign, come primarily from interviews with Buck Smith. Doug Drushal provided supplementary information.

Discussion of changes in Board of Trustees' operations comes largely from Bill Pocock's report, "The Making of a Board, 1957–1986," printed in the alumni magazine, Fall 1989. (See also discussion of this report in chapter 15.)

Information about Hans Jenny, both his professional and personal lives, comes from interviews with Henry Copeland, Buck Smith, Bill Snoddy, and Doug Drushal. Jenny's views on college financing come from his report, "A Summing Up: In Which a Retiring V.P. Considers Problems and Proposes Solutions upon His Announced Retirement," published in the alumni magazine, Winter 1982.

Details on increasing enrollment come from interviews with Buck Smith and Henry Copeland, and Doug Drushal memoir.

Smoking rules are taken from several student handbooks: 1968–69, 1991–92, 2003–4.

Doris Coster provided information on the creation of Student Code of Conduct and Campus Council, in a memorandum to the author, March 11, 2011. See also 1969–70 student handbook and the alumni magazine, July 1969. The brief dissolution of Campus Council is reported in the *Voice,* October 14, 1982. (The author was present when leaders of Campus Council reported the dissolution to members of the Student-Trustee Relations Committee of the Board of Trustees.)

Curriculum changes beginning 1969–70 were reported in the *Daily Record,* May 4, 1969; see also 1969–70 catalog and the alumni magazine, July–August 1972.

14. THE WORLD INTRUDES

Norman Morrison's death and its aftermath at the College and elsewhere, including reprinted letters to the alumni magazine, are detailed in Karol Crosbie, "Reflections on Norman Morrison '56," alumni magazine, Fall 2000. Don Reiman, Morrison's friend and classmate, gave his tribute lecture, "Witnesses," at the College, June 7, 1981 (Twenty-fifth reunion of class of 1956). See also Paul Hendrickson, "Daughter of the Flames," by Paul Hendrickson, *Washington Post*, December 2, 1985, with subhead, "In 1965, Norman Morrison held his baby Emily and set himself on fire over the war in Vietnam. Today, the family remembers." See also the memoir of Morrison's widow, Anne Corpening Morrison Welsh, with Joyce Hollyday, *Held in the Light: Norman Morrison's Sacrifice for Peace and His Family's Journey of Healing* (Maryknoll, N.Y.: Orbis, 2008). See also Robert S. McNamara and Brian VanDeMark, *In Retrospect: The Tragedy and Lessons of Vietnam* (New York: Vintage, 1996).

On the antiwar protest by four Wooster students, their trial and sentencing, see the *Daily Record*, December 12, 1967. The Vigil upon their incarceration and harassment of those taking part in the vigil are covered in the *Daily Record*, December 13, 1967, and letters to the editor, pro and con, and editorial, *Daily Record*, December 16, 1967.

A copy of Garber Drushal's free speech statement of February 1, 1968, can be found in the antiwar files, Special Collections. See also Official College policy "in regard to students who violate civil law," *Voice*, January 12, 1968.

On the question-and-answer period in chapel by the four students arrested, see *Voice*, January 12, 1968. See also the article by the four students concerning conditions in Wayne County Jail, *Voice*, January 12, 1968. (This article by the students was reprinted in the *Daily Record*, with a response by Ed Eberhart, city solicitor [and College alumnus], explaining conditions generally in jail, and conceding that jail was not fireproof.)

Details on protests at the College during and after the Cambodian invasion and the killings at Kent State come from several sources. The *Voice*, May 8, 1970, described the Wooster march and the experiences of Wooster student reporters who were present during the Kent State events. Its May 15, 1970, issue reported actions at the College during the preceding week, and its issues of May 15 and 22, 1970, continued to report on related events at Wooster and on other campuses. Editor Estella Goodhart King prepared an extraordinary special issue of the alumni magazine, "The First Week in May," published in July 1968 and providing near-contemporaneous views and judgments from faculty and the president. Details relating to the protest meeting in Lowry Center on the night of May 5, 1970, come largely from interviews with Arn Lewis, Ron Hustwit, Henry Copeland, Doug Drushal, and Ken McHargh.

Details on "Participation '70," sponsored by the College, come from interviews with Alan Unger and Arn Lewis. See also an advertisement in the *New York Times*, Sunday, May 17, 1970, and a special issue of the *Voice*, June 9, 1970. The events of "Participation '70" received voluminous coverage in the *Daily Record* from June 28 through July 11, 1970.

15. THE WORD IS QUALITY

Details on Drushal's retirement come from Doug Drushal, "Scot by Affection."

Details on search committee for Drushal's successor are taken from Board of Trustees' minutes, October 1975.

In various interviews, Henry Copeland told of his career and response to the search, views on the presidency, and goals—as well as his views on Buck Smith, Hans Jenny, and Bill Snoddy.

Bill Snoddy's training and career information come from from interviews. Upon his retirement, Snoddy summarized financial changes at the College during his term in an article for the alumni magazine, "The Price of Change: Reflections of 40 Years of Wooster's Finances," Winter 1999.

In interviews, Copeland told about his hiring of Sally Patton. See also comment on Patton's term, memorandum to author from Mary Neagoy.

Quotations from Copeland's inauguration address, "A Place Apart," October 7, 1977, and his reflections on the response to it, in his convocation address, "The Heavenly City Revisited," September 15, 1982, appear in *An Improbable College and Other Convocation Addresses* (Wooster, Ohio: The College of Wooster, n.d.). See also his views on liberal arts education, given in response to a student interviewer, *Voice,* September 22, 1978.

Information about the beginning of business economics degree and departmental evaluations comes from interviews with Copeland and Bill Baird.

Executive Committee of Board of Trustees' discussion of "financial stress" comes from committee minutes, June 1994.

Don Harward discussed his background and career at Wooster in an interview; this was supplemented by interviews with Copeland and Hayden Schilling.

Discussion of changes in Board of Trustees comes from Pocock, "Making of a Board, 1957–1986," supplemented by interview with Copeland.

16. SEARCHING FOR A PRESIDENT

This chapter relies on information and judgments offered by those who participated directly in the search, either as members of the search committee or in other meaningful ways, but who in many cases gave their views on condition that they remained unattributed—partly for legal reasons, partly to avoid public criticism of friends and colleagues. The author also participated indirectly in the search.

Among those whose interviews were particularly important to the chapter were five faculty members on the search committee, Susan Figge, Madonna Hettinger, Ron Hustwit, Yvonne Williams, and Mark Wilson; three other faculty members, Gordon Collins, John Gates, and Jenna Hayward; two trustees on the search committee, John Compton and Jim Wilson; Stan Gault, chairman of the Board of Trustees; Henry Copeland, the retiring president, and Stan Hales, who became acting president.

Search committee appointment information is taken from Board of Trustees' minutes.

Susanne Woods's career information comes from from her personal Web site, www.susannewoods.com.

Anne Shaver information was taken from Denison University's 1994–95 faculty directory.

Board of Trustees' actions concerning the Woods withdrawal are taken from board minutes, June 29, 1995.

Courtney Leatherman, "Public Job, Private Life, Wooster's President-to-Be Bows Out Amid Talk of Relationship with a Woman," *Chronicle of Higher Education,* August 4, 1995.

17. THE LEGACY OF A HOMETOWN BOY

Details on Stan Gault's personal life and career come largely from interviews with him, supplemented by information provided by his staff.

Details about Wooster's major financial campaigns come largely from interviews with Sally Patton.

Development results come from official public reports of each campaign.

18. IN THE LONG RUN, WE'LL BE FINE

Much material in this chapter comes from interviews with Stan Hales; see also his convocation talk, "In Case of Emergency."

On search committee members, see Board of Trustees' minutes, October 1995.

Considerable information for this chapter comes from interviews with Jim Wilson, chairman of the Board of Trustees for the latter half of the Hales presidency. Additional details come from interviews with Stan Gault, chairman of the Board of Trustees at the start of the Hales presidency.

Sally Whitman provided information on Bettye Jo Mastrine.

Some information on Hales presidency comes from an interview with Susan Figge.

19. ALPHA AND OMEGA

Information about the ongoing development of the Freshman/First-Year Seminar (which had various names) comes from alumni magazines: April, December 1957, May 1964, March 1970, January 1975, Winter 1997.

Some information comes from files of and interviews with Vivian Holliday, who served as dean of the faculty for eight years.

Other information comes from interviews with Susan Figge and Yvonne Williams, both of whom served as dean of the faculty, and Don Harward, who served as vice president for academic affairs.

The most recent description of the first-year program comes from the 2011–12 catalog.

Each year for more then three decades, the alumni magazine has devoted most or all of its spring issue to reports of I.S. projects. Those cited here come from 2008, 2009, 2010, and 2011.

20. TEACHING AND RESEARCH, WELL REMEMBERED

Contributions and suggestions for mention in this chapter came from a number of people in discussions with the author. Gene Bay's message to the author illustrates the memories among many faculty members, both current and retired, many alumni, including the author. (One example: Carol Dix, an alumna, trustee, and hostess at that party, told the author the anecdote about Richard Gore at her party.) Much of the material comes from interviews conducted by the author.

A series of articles in the alumni magazine, during the editorship of Peter Havholm, focused on particular departments, their history and their then current roster: history, Spring 1987; chemistry, Spring 1992; economics, Winter 1993.

Information on application forms comes from personnel files, Special Collections.

Over the years, the alumni magazine regularly carried profiles of faculty upon their retirements. I cite here only a Fall 1980 question-and-answer session conducted by Lois McCall, with Bill Kieffer and Melcher Fobes, who both retired after the 1979–80 academic year.

See David L. Powell and John D. Reinheimer, "Brief History of the Chemistry Department at The College of Wooster," *Council on Undergraduate Research Newsletter* 6, no. 1 (January 1986).

See also Richard Gore, "The College of Wooster, Department of Music," 1952, Music department file, Special Collections.

21. THE FUTURE IS NOW

Much material on this presidential search comes from interviews with Jim Wilson, supplemented by information from an interview with Sol Oliver.

On the membership of the search committee, see Board of Trustees' minutes, February 2006.

Most information on Grant Cornwell's personal life and career comes from interviews with Cornwell. Particularly noted should be his views of how Wooster differed from St. Lawrence University; see, for example, the College Statute of Instruction. These interviews are also the principal source for details about Cornwell's actions as president.

Decisions on administrative change come from Cornwell interviews; these are officially recorded in College catalogs.

Details about the transition from Jim Wilson to David Gunning as chairman of the Board of Trustees, and Gunning's term, come largely from interviews with Wilson and Gunning.

Details about CoRE and APEX were taken from interviews with Cornwell and other administrators, personal tours, and official brochures.

Details about Wooster's efforts in technology over more than four decades come primarily from interviews with Bill Snoddy and Carl Zimmerman. See also Snoddy, "Price of Change." The report of the Battelle hook-up, including an interview with Zimmerman, was published in the *Daily Record,* January 11, 1969. Zimmerman also wrote a report on the hook-up that was published in the alumni magazine, May–June 1969. For details of the new system, see the *Daily Record,* December 8, 1970. See also historical reports that Snoddy and Zimmerman provided to author, available in the technology files in Special Collections.

Ellen Falduto supplied information on technology, current to 2012, on December 22–23, 2013.

Details on ten-year assessment of the College by the Higher Learning Commission of the North Central Association of Colleges and Schools come from the official report of the Commission, filed in the Office of the President and in Special Collections.

Sources Cited

The research for this book took many forms. Interviews and conversations, which gave the subjects the opportunity to reminisce as well as to provide important information, were particularly enjoyable for me, and I hope for them. These were lively interviews, nearly a hundred, with women and men who have been faculty, administrators, trustees, and other alumni of the College (in a few cases married to one of them or the child of one of them).

All of the interview transcripts will go to Special Collections. Here, two caveats: First, this project began as an oral history. The earliest interviews thus were recorded verbatim (with only a few abbreviations and explanations). When the book project itself was launched, I occasionally treated the interviews more as notes, and they will be seen as such, although I am confident they will be understandable. Second, on a few—surprisingly few—occasions, the interviewee asked me to turn off the recorder; or said that what she or he was about to say should not be a part of the transcript. So, I turned off the recorder, or I have edited out the particular comments. In every case, these comments helped me understand better what we were discussing and added to the utility of the book; in every case, these edits protected specific people and do not detract from the the history.

The dates given here mark formal interviews. In many cases, I had subsequent telephone, e-mail, or personal contact with the subjects, occasionally several times, for clarification and further information. All of the formal interviews were conducted in person, with one exception—I interviewed Don Harward by telephone. Titles in most cases are those in effect at the time of the interview, including those retired or holding emeritus status. A number of people interviewed, in particular Gordon Tait and Vivian Holliday, also provided written material from their copious personal files, most of which will also go to Special Collections. All other sources are listed in accompanying notes.

Beyond the formal interviews, the book benefits from many other personal contributions. I regret that I am unable to acknowledge every one of them in detail. But one must be noted: Vivian Douglas Smith, class of 1947. She and a dozen or so of her classmates conducted for more than a half-century a round-robin of handwritten letters. (The round-robin was recognized in a charming article on the front page of the Style section of the *Washington Post*, "In the Mail, the Class of '47's Lives Unfold," October 1, 2007, C1.) Smith rounded up her classmates to contribute, and these were enormously valuable for news of the early years. Named here as well are a number of other people—including, I am pleased to say, friends and contemporaries—who provided exceptional information and discussion. They are listed below as "Special Contributors." Further important information came from a group of "Other Contributors." In response to my request in *Wooster,* the current alumni magazine, dozens of alumni shared experiences, and they are listed as "Alumni Contributors." I no doubt have unintentionally omitted others, for which I apologize. Although much of that material did not find its way directly into the book, I read all of the letters and notes, which of course helped set the scenes. Their effort is most appreciated.

FORMAL INTERVIEWS

Bev Asbury—Former minister, Westminster Presbyterian Church, Wooster; Campus Chaplain, Emeritus, Vanderbilt University, March 28–29, 2010

Bill Baird—vice president of academic affairs, retired; Professor of Economics, Emeritus, February 24, 2010

Pete Bogner—president, retired, Bogner Construction Management Company, April 28, 2012

Ted Bogner—president, Bogner Construction Management Company, June 9, 2011, April 16, 2012

Ken Bogucki—Wooster Inn general manager, June 6, 2012

Paul Christenson—Mildred Foss Thompson Professor of English Language and Literature, Emeritus, September 20, 2010

Gordon Collins—Whitmore-Williams Professor of Psychology, Emeritus, February 23, 2012

John Compton—Professor of Philosophy, Emeritus; Vanderbilt University, trustee, Emeritus, April 6–7, 2010

Henry Copeland—President, Emeritus—October 14–15, 2009, September 16, 2011

Grant Cornwell—president—August 20, 24, October 9, 2012

Darcey Johnston DeRose—alumna; wife of trustee Jim DeRose, October 21, 2011

Jim DeRose—trustee, October 21, 2011

Doug Drushal—partner, Critchfield, Critchfield & Johnston; son of Garber Drushal, February 25, 2011

Carolyn Durham—Inez K. Gaylord Professor of French Language and Literature, February 27, 2012

Paul Edmiston—professor of chemistry, October 9, 2012

Bill Evans—Trustee, Emeritus; former chairman of Committee on Admissions, June 1, 2012

Susan Figge—Dean of the Faculty, Professor of German, Emerita, February 28, 2012

Joanne Frye—Professor of English and Women's Studies, Emerita, October 20, 2010

John Gates—Aileen Dunham Professor of History, Emeritus, August 27, 2011

Stan Gault—Chairman of Board of Trustees, Emeritus, August 3–5, 2009

David Gedalecia—Michael O. Fisher Professor of History, February 22, 2012

Nancy Grace—professor of English, February 22, 27, 2012

David Gunning—chairman of Board of Trustees, August 23, 2012

Stan Hales—President, Emeritus, August 1, 2009, September 22, 2010

Don Harward—former vice president for academic affairs; President of Bates College, Emeritus, June 18, 2012

Jenna Hayward—professor of English, June 7, 2011

Bill Hendrickson—alumnus, August 19, 2011

Sally Rhine Hendrickson—alumna, August 19, 2011

Madonna Hettinger—Lawrence Stanley Professor of Medieval History, February 24, 2012

Damon Hickey—Director of Libraries, Emeritus, February 23, 2011

Vivian Holliday—Aylesworth Professor of Classical Studies, Emeritus, Dean of the Faculty, February 24, 2010, March 2, 2011, August 21, 2012

Kurt Holmes—dean of students, February 28, 2013

John Hondros—Henry J. and Laura H. Copeland Professor of European History, Emeritus, February 25, 2012

Ron Hustwit—Frank Halliday Ferris Professor of Philosophy, August 25, 2011

Bill Kieffer—Professor of Chemistry, Emeritus, September 21, 2010

Frank Knorr—director of development, director of alumni relations, retired— August 27–28, 2011

Jack Lengyel—former football coach—October 22, 2011

Arn Lewis—Professor of Art, Emeritus—October 19, 2010

Beth Irwin Lewis—administrator, retired; Professor of History, Emeritus—October 21, 2010

Bill Longbrake—trustee, chairman of Committee on Finance, April 27, 2012, March 4, 2013

Ken McHargh—alumnus; U.S. Magistrate judge for Northern District of Ohio, May 1, 2012

Blake Moore—trustee—April 27, 2012

Steve Moore—basketball coach—August 22, 2012

Linda Morgan-Clement—Henry Jefferson Copeland Campus Chaplain and director of interfaith campus ministry, August 22, 2012

Louisa Stroup Oliver—alumna; wife of Sol Oliver, October 24, 2011

Sol Oliver—trustee; chief judge, U.S. District Court for Northern District of Ohio; husband of Louisa Stroup Oliver, October 24, 2011

Linc Oviatt—Of counsel, partner, retired, Critchfield, Critchfield & Johnston; former counsel to the College, June 8, 2011

Sally Patton—vice president for development, retired, October 18, 20, 2011

Ken Plusquellec—Dean of Students, Emeritus, August 3, 2009

Louise Plusquellec—alumna; wife of Ken Plusquellec, August 3, 2009

Linda Swartzback Pratt—daughter of Ray Swartzback, former minister, West-minster Presbyterian Church, April 25, 2012

Vi Startzman Robertson—medical director, retired, August 3–4, 2009

Hayden Schilling—Robert Critchfield Professor of English History, October 7–8, 2009

Clare Adel Schreiber—director, College Nursery School, retired; wife of Willy Schreiber, chairman of German department, October 20, 2010

Bob Smith—Fox Professor of Religion, Emeritus, September 21, 2010

Buck Smith—former vice president for development; president of Davis & Elkins College, March 17–18, 2012

Bill Snoddy—Vice President for Finance and Business, Emeritus, October 7, 2009

Larry Stewart—Mildred Foss Thompson Professor of English Language and Literature—October 27, 2011

Laurie Stickelmaier—vice president for finance and business, June 12, 2012

Gordon Tait—Mercer Professor of Religious Studies, Emeritus, February 25, 27, 2010

Alan Unger—alumnus; organizer of Participation '70, October 23, 2011

Al Van Wie—Athletic Director, Head Basketball and Tennis Coach, Emeritus, August 3, 6, 2009

Cynthia Weiler—alumna; wife of Blake Moore, May 3, 2012

Reggie Williams—trustee; president, retired, San Antonio Area Foundation, October 26, 2011

Yvonne Williams—Dean of the Faculty, Professor of Black Studies and Political Science, Emerita, August 1, 4, 2009

Jim Wilson—Chairman of Board of Trustees, Emeritus, October 8, 2009, February 25, 2010, June 2, 2011

Mark Wilson—Lewis M. and Marian Senter Nixon Professor of Natural Sciences and Geology, February 22, 2012

Josephine Wright—professor of music; Josephine Lincoln Morris Professor of Black Studies, April 16, 2013

Carl Zimmerman—Professor of Mathematics, Emeritus; director of academic computer services, retired, February 22, 2012

SPECIAL CONTRIBUTORS

Doris Coster—former dean of students, memorandum to the author

Scott Craig—author's high school and college classmate; son of Bill Craig, electronic and memorandum exchanges

David Lewellen—Alumnus and writer, research

E. Blake Moore Jr.—contemporary; father of trustee Blake Moore, electronic and memorandum exchanges

Vivian Douglas Smith—class of 1947

OTHER CONTRIBUTORS

Keith Beckett—director of physical education, athletics, and recreation
Olivia dePastina Bernabei—alumna
Jim Clarke—alumnus; trustee
Karol Crosbie—editor, *Wooster* (current name of alumni magazine)
Nancy Ditmer—professor of music
Ellen Falduto—chief information and planning officer
Dick Figge—Gingrich Professor of German, Emeritus
John Finn—director of public information
Scott Friedhoff—vice president for enrollment and college relations
John Gabriele—Raymond and Carolyn Dix Professor of Spanish
Mark Gooch—research librarian; coffee group
Don Hartsough—alumnus
Adriana Hoak—alumna
Doug Hole—alumnus
John Hopkins—associate vice president, college relations and marketing
Kathy Young Hothem—alumna; daughter of Racky Young
Chuck Hurst—Professor of Sociology, Emeritus; coffee group
Dick Jacobs—alumnus; classmate
Angela Johnston—secretary of the College, chief of staff to the president
Julia F. Jones—alumna
Hank Kreuzman—dean for curriculum and academic engagement
Beau Mastrine—director of campus grounds
Heidi McCormick—director of alumni relations and the Wooster Fund
Carol McDaid—assistant to Fran Guille
Reggie Minton—alumnus
Gary Newton—coffee group
Sandy Nichols—director of development
Anne Nurse—associate professor of sociology
Bob Nye—golf coach, retired
Gene Pollock—Hoge Professor of Economics, Emeritus; coffee group
Roger Ramseyer—instructor in education, retired; coffee group
Dick Reimer—Hoge Professor of Economics, Emeritus; coffee group
Sharon Rice—assistant director of alumni relations
Carol Pearson Schadelbauer—alumna; communications consultant
John Sell—James R. Wilson Professor of Business Economics
Beverly Kimble Siligmueller—alumna
Nancy Wilkin Sutherland—alumna; trustee
Jim Toedtman—alumnus
Jim (Jet) Turner—alumnus
Mary Karen Vellines—former vice president for enrollment
Sally Whitman—executive assistant for presidential events
Pat Young—alumna; daughter of Racky Young

ALUMNI CONTRIBUTORS

LizAnn Jacobs Atkins
Daren Batke
Jean Harrington Beck
Larry Caldwell
Paul D. Clarke
Mary Baker Dickerson
Linda Wells Ellsworth
Ted Fredley
Robert Glockler
Dick Graham
Renee Grogg
Diane L. Hamburger (trustee)
Ron Hamburger
Richard Harris
Brian Heater
Daniel Heischman
Bill Hewett
Dale Hoak
Nancy Holland
Bill Keene
Mikell Kloeters
Bob Mabbs
Lila Pittenger McCleary
Nancy Orahood Mellon
Steve Montgomery
Sally Neely
Joella Good Newberry
David Noble
Ellen Waters Pisor
Richard Poethig
Dick Quinby
Pat Miller Quinby
Muriel Rice Roberts
Dick Robertson
Leon Shmorhun
David Sterna
Stan Totten
Jack Visser
John Weymer

Index